MONEY, LANGUAGE, AND THOUGHT

MARC SHELL

Money, Language, and Thought

LITERARY AND PHILOSOPHIC ECONOMIES FROM THE MEDIEVAL TO THE MODERN ERA

THE JOHNS HOPKINS UNIVERSITY PRESS
BALTIMORE AND LONDON

Originally published by the University of California Press in 1982
Softshell Books edition, 1993

The Johns Hopkins University Press
2715 North Charles Street
Baltimore, Maryland 21218-4319
The Johns Hopkins Press Ltd., London

Library of Congress Cataloging-in-Publication Data

Shell, Marc.
  Money, language, and thought : literary and philosophic economies from
the medieval to the modern era / Marc Shell.
     p.   cm.
  Includes bibliographical references (p.) and index.
  ISBN 0-8018-4693-5 (pbk. : acid-free paper)
     1. Economics in literature.   2. Language and languages—Philosophy.
3. Money—Philosophy.   I. Title.
PN51.S3643   1993
302.2—dc20   93-16494

A catalog record for this book is available from the British Library.

To the memory of my father

Contents

List of Illustrations

Acknowledgments

FOR THEIR advice and encouragement, I am privileged to thank Kenneth Burke, Stanley Cavell, Paul de Man, Daniel Droixhe, Robert Fishman, Geoffrey Hartman, Peter Heller, Horst Hutter, Carol Jacobs, Martin Jay, Will Klings, J. Hillis Miller, Sylvia Osterbind, Ferruccio Rossi-Landi, Neil Schmitz, Judith Shklar, Jean Sommermeyer, George Steiner, Fred Turner, and Barry Weller.

For permission to reproduce the photographs, I am obliged to the American Antiquarian Society (Worcester, Mass.), the American Numismatic Society (New York), the Bibliothèque nationale (Paris), the Bodleian Library (Oxford), the British Museum (London), the Buffalo and Erie County Library (Buffalo, N.Y.), the George Arents Research Library (Syracuse, N.Y.), Hirmer Fotoarchiv (Munich), the Johns Hopkins University Library (Baltimore), the Library of Congress (Washington, D.C.), Ann Münchow (Aachen), the Museum des Deutschen Bundesbank (Frankfurt), Albert Pick (Hypobank, Munich), and the Staatliche Museen zu Berlin (Berlin, German Democratic Republic).

Money, Language, and Thought includes revised sections of essays first published in the *Canadian Review of Comparative Literature, Genre,* the *Kenyon Review, Modern Language Notes,* and *Philosophy and Social Criticism.*

I am most grateful to Susan Shell, who reminded me of work that remained—and still remains—to be completed.

Introduction

FROM ELECTRUM TO ELECTRICITY

BETWEEN the electrum money of ancient Lydia and the electric money of contemporary America there occurred a historically momentous change. The exchange value of the earliest coins derived wholly from the material substance (electrum) of the ingots of which the coins were made and not from the inscriptions stamped into these ingots. The eventual development of coins whose politically authorized inscriptions were inadequate to the weights and purities of the ingots into which the inscriptions were stamped precipitated awareness of quandaries about the relationship between face value (intellectual currency) and substantial value (material currency). This difference between inscription and thing grew greater with the introduction of paper moneys. Paper, the material substance on which the inscriptions were printed, was supposed to make no difference in exchange, and metal or electrum, the material substance to which the inscriptions referred, was connected with those inscriptions in increasingly abstract ways. With the advent of electronic fund-transfers the link between inscription and substance was broken. The matter of electric money does not matter.[1]

Ideology, which would define the relationship between thought and matter,[2] is necessarily concerned with this transformation from the ab-

1. Cf. D. W. Richardson, *Electric Money: Evolution of an Electronic Funds-Transfer System* (Cambridge, Mass., 1970); and Paul Mattick, "Die Zerstörung des Geldes," in Paul Mattick, Alfred Sohn-Rethel, and Hellmut G. Haasis, *Beiträge zur Kritik des Geldes* (Frankfurt, 1976), pp. 7–34.
2. According to Destutt de Tracy, who coined the term in 1769, *ideology* comprises reductive semantic analysis and the explanation of thought in terms of matter. See F. J. Picavet, *Les Idéologues* (Paris, 1891). See also chapter 5.

1

solute adequation between intellectual inscription and real substance to the complete disassociation of them. The philosophical and literary component of the story of that transformation begins with the culturally motivating discomfort of the Greeks at the institution of coinage, which, in the sixth and fifth centuries B.C., came to pervade Greek economic and intellectual life. For the Greeks coinage coincided with such political developments as tyranny and such aesthetic ones as tragedy. Some thinkers, moreover, came to recognize interactions between economic and intellectual exchange, or money and language. (*Sēmē* means "word" as well as "coin.") Heraclitus, for example, described the monetary exchange of commodities in a complex simile and series of metaphors whose logical exchanges of meaning define the unique form of simultaneous purchase and sale of wares that obtains in monetary transfer.[3] And Plato criticized the Sophists and pre-Socratics as merchants of the mind not only because they took money in exchange for useful or honeyed words but also because they were producers of a discourse whose internal exchanges of meaning were identical to the exchanges of commodities in monetary transactions. Plato feared the political tendency of their moneyed words, and represented their discourse in his dialogues as the audible symptom of an invisible invasion into language of a tyrannical form destructive of wisdom. Plato's critique extended to the ideal Form itself: Was not even Socratic dialectic, he wondered, pervaded by the monetary form of exchange? Was not dialectical division a kind of money changing, and dialectical hypothesizing a kind of hypothecation, or mortgaging? The upsetting confrontation of thought with its own internalization of economic form motivated thought to become the self-critical discourse of philosophy.

Judaea in the third century B.C. and the Arabian Peninsula in the sixth century A.D. experienced similar economic and intellectual quandaries with the introduction of coined money. The Jewish rabbis came to protest against the information of legal thought by new monetary forms. Making the proposition that "all wares acquire each other" the focus of a far-ranging debate about intellectual as well as material exchange, they elaborated conflicting interpretations of an *asimon*—a "current word" that is not yet legally minted or definitely meaningful.

3. "All things are an equal exchange for fire and fire for all things, as goods are for gold [*chrusos*] and gold for goods" (Heraclitus, Fragment 90, in H. Diels, *Fragmente der Vorsokratiker*, 5th ed. [Berlin, 1934]). For analysis of the uniquely monetary form of the linguistic exchanges in this fragment, see "Heraclitus and the Money Form," in my *The Economy of Literature* (Baltimore, 1978), pp. 49–62.

Similarly, Mohammed expressed the new economic exchange in the striking commercial content of the metaphors in the Koran, and he interiorized the new ways of exchanging commodities as modes of metaphorization, or of exchanging meanings.[4]

Christendom in the twelfth century was already much influenced by the Greek, Jewish, and Islamic attempts to confront the numismatic money of the mind. Christian thinkers had begun to deal with verbal troping as an economic process when revolutionary fiduciary forms and financial procedures began to develop. At first Europeans were as incredulous of these institutions as the Greeks had been fearful of coinage. Marco Polo's description of Kublai Khan's paper moneys, for example, was dismissed as a lie, and Philip II claimed to understand nothing about "immaterial money."[5] Despite, and perhaps because of, this telling resistance to the new modes of symbolization and production, the last eight hundred years is the story of the introduction and acceptance of capital institutions and intellectual processes that moved Christendom from the age of electrum coins towards the age of electric money.

For most Christian thinkers before the twelfth century, the new ways of exchange and production remained "external" objects for contemplation. They thought about monetary symbolization and generation as about any other theme or problem. Yet money, which refers to a system of tropes, is also an "internal" participant in the logical or semiological organization of language, which itself refers to a system of tropes.[6] Whether or not a writer mentioned money or was aware of its

4. For the rabbis, see *Baba Mezi'a*, trans. Salis Daiches and H. Freedman (1935), 44a; in *The Babylonian Talmud*, ed. I. Epstein (London, 1935–48). For the Koran, see Charles C. Torrey, *The Commercial Terms in the Koran* (Leyden, 1892).

5. For Marco Polo, see the descriptive notes in *The Book of Ser Marco Polo*, ed. and trans. Colonel Sir Henry Yule, rev. Henri Cordier, 2 vols. (London, 1903), 1:426–30. For Philip II of Spain, see his note to the financial report presented to him on Feb. 11, 1580, by Francesco de Garnica (in General Archives of Simancas, "Guerra Antigua," file 94, no. 43); and J.-G. da Silva, "Réalités économiques et prises de conscience: quelques témoignages sur le XVIe siècle," *Annales: Économies, Sociétés, Civilisations* 14 (1959): 737.

6. Economic and linguistic troping, symbolization, and production have been interrelated in a few recent works. To the titles discussed in *The Economy of Literature* (esp. pp. 1–10) might be added: Ferruccio Rossi-Landi, *Semiotica e ideologia: applicazioni della teoria del linguagio come lavoro e come mercato. Indagni sulla alienazione linguistica* (Milan, 1979); Klaus F. Riegel, *Foundations of Dialectical Psychology* (New York, 1979), esp. chapter 3, "Comparison Between Monetary and Linguistic Systems"; Kurt Heinzelman, *The Economics of the Imagination* (Amherst, 1980); and other titles, noted below.

potentially subversive role in his thinking, the new forms of metaphorization or exchanges of meaning that accompanied the new forms of economic symbolization and production were changing the meaning of meaning itself. This participation of economic form in literature and philosophy, even in the discourse about truth, is defined neither by what literature and philosophy talk about (sometimes money, sometimes not) nor by why they talk about it (sometimes for money, sometimes not) but rather by the tropic interaction between economic and linguistic symbolization and production. A formal money of the mind informs all discourse and is as unaffected by whether or not the thematic content of a particular work includes money as by whether or not the material content of the ink in which the work may be inscribed includes gold.

There has been no sustained critique of this interaction between thought and economics in the postclassical era. Yet some thinkers—the ones we shall study are among them—have recognized and tried to confront and to account self-critically for the money of the mind informing their own thought. Elucidating the money talk in their linguistic production, as I plan to do in this book, helps to locate the "language of wares" that speaks ventriloquistically, as it were, through the mouths of theologians, poets, and philosophers. In America, where I write, that language introduces itself in Edgar Allan Poe's disquieting short story about the gold bug at work within the industry of letters.

1 / The Gold Bug

INTRODUCTION TO
"THE INDUSTRY OF LETTERS"
IN AMERICA

It has always been one of the arts of [U.S.] federalism to address itself most strongly to human cupidity, as though sordid interest alone was the controlling influence which actuates mankind. During Jefferson's [Democratic Republican] administration foreign rapacity was defended [by the Federalists], and he was falsely charged with producing the commercial embarrassments which existed. And while the country was afterwards struggling in a sanguinary conflict with a powerful enemy, the leaders of this party [Harrison of the Federalists, for example], regardless of the liberty and independence of the Republic, sighed aloud, in lugubrious tones, for "the *golden* days of commercial prosperity." The same false charges are now made against the present administration of the general government [that of the Democratic Republican Van Buren], and the same tones are now loudly uttered with the variation only of a single word, occasioned by the modern whig [Federalist] discovery that gold is a "humbug," and "*paper*" is therefore substituted for "*golden.*"

SAMUEL YOUNG, "Oration Delivered
at the Democratic Republican Celebration
of the 64th Anniversary of the Independence
of the United States," July 4, 1840

Monetary and Aesthetic Theory

AMERICA was the historical birthplace of the widespread use of paper money in the Western world,[1] and a debate about coined and paper

1. I distinguish the popular, long-term use of paper money in America from its restricted use (by merchants and bankers in eleventh-century Italy, for example) and from its short-term use (by the French during the paper money experiment of 1720, for example). I also distinguish scriptural money, which is created by the process of bookkeeping, from fiduciary money, or banknotes (cf. Fernand Braudel, *Capitalism and Material Life, 1400–1800*, trans. Miriam Kochan [New York, 1975], pp. 357–72). At times from the fifteenth to eighteenth centuries, paper money circulated in such places as Granada, Naples, Sweden, Cologne, and Vienna (Horst Wagenführ, *Der goldene Kompass* [Stuttgart, 1959], pp. 73–76), but no widespread, long-lived use of paper money developed before the American one. On the almost continuous use of paper money in America (since before 1686), see Eric P. Newman, *The Early Paper Money of America* (Racine, Wis., 1967).

5

money dominated American political discourse from 1825 to 1875. The "paper money men" (as the advocates of paper money were called) were set against the "gold bugs" (as the advocates of gold, in opposition to paper money, were called).[2] Such books as William Cobbett's long paper *Paper Against Gold* made plenty of both gold and paper money.

The paper money debate was concerned with symbolization in general, and hence not only with money but also with aesthetics. Symbolization in this context concerns the relationship between the substantial thing and its sign. Solid gold (from which the ingots of gold coin were made) was associated with the substance of value. Whether one regarded paper as an appropriate symbol (as did "paper money men") or as an inappropriate and downright misleading one (as did "gold bugs"), that sign was "insubstantial" insofar as the paper counted for nothing as a commodity and was thus "insensible" in the economic system of exchange.

The paper of money was called an appearance or shadow. Figure 1, a cartoon entitled "A Shadow Is Not a Substance," depicts the relationship between substance and shadow—paper moneys were called "greenbacks"—which some thinkers believed to obtain not only in monetary but also in aesthetic representation. That this purported relationship between reality and appearance is both monetary and aesthetic helps to explain many poets' and economists' association of paper money with ghostliness.[3]

In America, comparisons were made between the way a mere shadow or piece of paper becomes credited as substantial money and the way an artistic appearance is taken for the real thing by a willing suspension of disbelief. Congress, it was said, could turn paper into gold by an "act of Congress" that made it money. Why could not an artist turn paper with a design or story on it into gold? Thus an American cartoon shows one paper bearing the design of a cow and the inscription, "This is a cow by the act of the artist," and another paper that reads "This is money by the act of Congress" (figure 2).

2. Thomas Love Peacock, *Paper Money Lyrics* (1837), uses the term *paper money men*. By "the end of the nineteenth century the term 'gold bug' was [also] applied in America to scheming capitalists like Jay Gould [cf. gold], who tried to corner the gold market, or to fanatical advocates of a gold standard over a silver standard" (Barton Levi St. Armand, "Poe's 'Sober Mystification': The Uses of Alchemy in 'The Gold-Bug,'" *Poe Studies* 4 [1971]: 7, n. 20).

3. In Goethe's *Faust*, for example, the banknote (*Geldschein*) as ghost (*Gespenst*) is a major topos, and in Karl Marx's works paper money is frequently associated with the shadow of Peter Schlemihl.

Understanding the relationship between substance and sign was complicated by the known existence and practical monetary validity of counterfeit notes (i.e., illegal copies of legitimate ghost moneys) and, more significant for understanding such movements as American symbolism, of phantom bank notes: "There were no real banks, no officers, or actual assets of any kind to make these notes by 'phantom' banks of any real value,—except the ability to 'pass' them on some unsuspecting person."[4] These papers—with their fictional designs, insignia, signatures, and even ciphers—passed for ghost money and hence for solid specie. Even the "bank note reporters" and "counterfeit detectors"—the critics in the fray—could be counterfeited or entirely fabricated by confidence men.[5] Ghosts, counterfeit ghosts, and phantoms passed all alike.

The fear that all literature was, like money, in this sense a merely passable "naught"—a mere cipher—troubled Melville, an expert on confidence, for whom the tropic center of symbolization is an "algebraic x" threatening language and money with devaluation and annihilation.[6] Credit, or belief, involves the very ground of aesthetic experience, and the same medium that seems to confer belief in fiduciary money (bank notes) and in scriptural money (created by the process of bookkeeping) also seems to confer it in literature. That medium is writing. The apparently diabolical "interplay of money and mere writing to a point where the two be[come] confused"[7] involves a general ideological development: the tendency of paper money to distort our "natural" understanding of the relationship between symbols and things. The sign of the monetary diabolus, which many Americans insisted was like the one that God impressed in Cain's forehead,[8] condemns

4. Royal Bank of Canada, *The Story of Canada's Currency*, 2nd ed. (Ottawa, 1966), p. 13.

5. See Ted N. Weissbuch, "A Note on the Confidence-Man's Counterfeit Detector," *Emerson Quarterly*, no. 19 (Second Quarter 1960), pp. 16–18; and William H. Dillistin, *Bank Note Reporters and Counterfeit Detectors*, Numismatic Notes and Monographs, no. 114, American Numismatic Society (New York, 1949).

6. See Charles Feidelson, *Symbolism and American Literature*, (Chicago, 1953), esp. p. 159.

7. Braudel, *Capitalism and Material Life*, pp. 357–58.

8. "You send these notes out into the world stamped with irredeemability. You put on them the mark of Cain, and, like Cain, they will go forth to be vagabonds and fugitives on the earth. . . ." Representative George Pendleton (Ohio) thus opposed the issuance of legal tender in January 29, 1862 (*Congressional Globe*, 37th Cong., 2nd sess. 1. 549 ff.; rpr. in P. A. Samuelson and H. E. Krooss, *Documentary History of Banking and Currency in the United States*, 4 vols. [New York, 1969], p. 1276).

men to misunderstand the world of symbols and things in which they live.

This debate in aesthetics and economics, with its large, political dimensions, seemed to require a new kind of study of money together with other kinds of symbols. Thus Clinton Roosevelt, a prominent member of the Locofocos, argued in his "Paradox of Political Economy" in 1859, when Van Buren (advocate for gold) had lost the presidency, that the American Association for the Advancement of Science should establish an "*ontological department* for the discussion and establishment of general principles of political economy."[9] (In Germany, such a discussion already existed in the shape of a far-ranging debate between the proponents of idealism and the proponents of realism. Thomas Nast brought this debate to American newspapers in such cartoons as "Ideal Money" [figure 3].)[10] Joseph G. Baldwin explored how paper money asserts the spiritual over the material, and Albert Brisbane, in his *Philosophy of Money*, tried to provide an ontology for the study of monetary signs.[11]

The Bug for Gold

At a time when alchemists were trying to transform tin into gold by means of alchemy and financiers were turning paper into gold by means of the newly widespread institution of paper money, Edgar Allan Poe was a poor author who could only wish to exchange his literary papers for money. Among these papers were those that compose "The

9. Clinton Roosevelt, "On the Paradox of Political Economy in the Coexistence of Excessive Production and Excessive Population," in *Proceedings of the American Association for the Advancement of Science*, 13th Meeting, August 1859 (Cambridge, 1860), pp. 344–52. See Joseph Dorfman, *The Economic Mind in American Civilization, 1606–1865* (New York, 1946), 2; 660–61.

10. For the German debate, see chapters 4 and 5. Thomas Nast was born in Germany (1840) and studied in America with German emigrés.

11. Joseph G. Baldwin, *The Flush Times of Alabama and Mississippi: A Series of Sketches* (New York, 1852), concerns "that halcyon period, ranging from the year of Grace, 1835, to 1837 . . . , that golden era, when shinplasters were the sole currency . . . and credit was a franchise" (p. 1). Baldwin's narrator tells the story of a man who "bought goods . . . like other men; but he got them under a state of poetic illusion, and paid for them in an imaginary way" (p. 4). "How well [he] asserted the Spiritual over the Material!" exclaims the storyteller (p. 5). (On Baldwin, see Neil Schmitz, "Tall Tale, Tall Talk: Pursuing the Lie in Jacksonian Literature," *American Literature* 48 (1977): 473–77.) For Albert Brisbane, see his *Philosophy of Money* (n.p. [U.S.], 1863?).

Gold-Bug" (1843), a popular tale that tells how a certain Legrand (an impoverished Southern aristocrat in many ways resembling Poe himself) used his intellect to decipher a paper and thus find gold.[12]

Money in the sense of treasure is one theme of "The Gold-Bug." "The intent of [Poe]," wrote one reviewer in 1845, "was evidently to write a popular tale: money, and the finding of money being chosen as the most popular thesis."[13] Poe knew the popularity of the topos. He wrote in 1841 that "a main source of the interest which [Samuel Warren's "Ten Thousand a Year"] possesses for the mass, is to be referred to as the pecuniary nature of its theme . . . it is an affair of pounds, shillings and pence";[14] and in "The Gold-Bug" the narrator and the treasure hunter Legrand discuss the many histories and stories about "money-diggers" (822, 833–34).[15] However, "The Gold-Bug" itself differs from most tales about money as treasure. For example, as Legrand points out, in "The Gold-Bug" the gold seekers become gold finders (834), which was not the usual topos in America. Moreover, although the ostensible theme of "The Gold-Bug" is the search for money in the sense of trea-

12. Poe derided attempts to get rich quick. His tale "Von Kempelen and His Discovery" mocks alchemy, for example, and, as Harry Levin argues (*The Power of Blackness: Hawthorne, Poe, Melville* [New York, 1964], esp. pp. 138–39), Poe "was to take a dim view of the California Gold Rush [of 1849] in the poem ["El Dorado"], and to argue that the success of alchemy would deflate the value of ore." Yet Poe regarded himself as a Virginia gentleman, and he was disappointed in his expectation of being heir to one of the wealthiest men in Richmond (Hervey Allen, *Israfel: The Life and Times of Edgar Allan Poe*, 2 vols. [New York, 1926], 1:116).

Alexis de Tocqueville indicted the literary milieu in which Poe worked in a chapter of his *Democracy in America* (1835–40) entitled "The Industry of Letters." In that industry Poe was not, as Charles Baudelaire noted, a "money-making author" (Charles Baudelaire, "Edgar Allan Poe: sa vie et ses ouvrages," in *Charles Baudelaire: oeuvres complètes*, ed. Yves Florenne [Paris, 1966], p. 8). Baudelaire complains that Poe's American biographers often criticized him for not having made more money, and he explains that Poe wrote "too much above the common intellectual level for him to be well paid" (p. 23).

13. Thomas Dunn English, *Aristidean* (October 1845); quoted by Thomas Olive Mabbott in his introduction to "The Gold-Bug," in Mabbott, ed., *Collected Works of Edgar Allan Poe*, 3 vols. (Cambridge, Mass., 1969–78), 3:799; hereafter referred to as *CW.*

14. Poe, review article, *Graham's* (November 1841).

15. Numbers in the text refer to pages of "The Gold-Bug" in *CW.* Mabbott follows the text of the J. Lorimer Graham copy of *Tales and Sketches.*

Washington Irving's "The Money-Diggers" is discussed by Robert J. Blanch, "The Background of Poe's 'Gold-Bug,'" *English Record* 16 (April 1966): 44–45. Seba Smith's "The Money Diggers," which was published in *Burton's Magazine* (7 [August 1840]: 81–91), is discussed by Killis Campbell, "Miscellaneous Notes on Poe," *Modern Language Notes* 28 (March 1913): 65–66.

sure, its actual thesis and mode of presentation suggest, as we shall see, a concern with money as currency and with paper money in particular as a unique sort of redeemable symbol. Thus the theme of treasure is internalized in the symbolic mode of the narration and in its symbols.

Poe did not enter directly into the political parties' debate about paper money, and it would be as misleading to say he was either a Federalist or a Democratic Republican where matters of gold and paper were concerned as to say that his work has no political tendency. To be sure, Poe associated with the *Democratic Review*, called Richard Adams Locke (who contributed to the *New Era*, which attacked paper money) "one of the few men of *unquestionable* genius whom the country possesses,"[16] and made pronouncements about wealth and cupidity;[17] and some of his tales—"King Pest," for example—can be interpreted as allegorical burlesques of Jackson's and Van Buren's monetary policy, much like *Quodlibet* (1840), the political satire by Poe's friend John Pendleton Kennedy.[18] Nevertheless, Poe was less concerned with partisan problems of monetary policy than with the implicit ideological relationship between aesthetic and monetary symbolization.

The Humbug: Entomological Specimen, Species of Madness, and Specie

In "The Gold-Bug" the gold bug seems at first to be an outlandish entomological specimen and an outrageous species of madness, but on closer consideration it presents itself as a unique kind of humbug. In 1840 Samuel Young called "humbug" the paper dollars that the banks were issuing for specie. "Humbug," as we shall see, is a good name for the gold bug in "The Gold-Bug" and for "The Gold-Bug" itself.

The bug that causes "gold fever" in "The Gold-Bug" has been classified by literary critics as though it were a specimen of beetle for ento-

16. See Arthur M. Schlesinger, Jr., *The Age of Jackson* (Boston, 1945), p. 232.

17. See Ernest Marchand, "Poe as Social Critic," *American Literature* 6 (March 1934–January 1935): 40.

18. The man with the bandaged leg in "King Pest" (1835) recalls Colonel Thomas Hart Benton, a senator who led President Jackson's fight for gold (Benton was called "Old Bullion," and gold coins were called "Benton mint drops") and against paper money (or "shinplasters"). (Cf. William Whipple, "Poe's Political Satire," *Texas Studies in English* 35 [1956]: 83, 86). See figures 4, 5, and 6. Kennedy's *Quodlibet*, an allegorical attack on the institution of paper money, is "one of [America's] few distinguished political satires" (Vernon L. Parrington, *Main Currents in American Thought* [New York, 1954], 2:53–54).

mological investigation.[19] It has been categorized in the same way that one would classify a tarantula, such as the one mentioned in the epigraph to "The Gold-Bug":

> What ho! what ho! this fellow is dancing mad!
> He hath been bitten by the Tarantula.
>
> *All in the Wrong*

Legrand, a great collector of "entomological specimens" (807), with, no doubt, a large "cabinet" (813), is himself at first an entomological classifier, and he gives the entomologists their first "wrong" lead.[20] The entomological critics collect and name different specimens of beetles from Sullivan Island (where "The Gold-Bug" takes place), and consider the relationship of the gold bug in Poe's story to the beetles discussed in Thomas Wyatt's *Synopsis of Natural History* (1839), which Poe helped to edit. They are like Legrand in his first catalogical researches in entomology, conchology (807, 808), botany, and even numismatics (the narrator calls coins and counters "specimens" [827] hitherto unseen by them). The specificity of description in Poe's style requires such knowledge as these classifying sciences offer. (Baudelaire pointed this out with reference to the catalogue of coins in the treasure trove.)[21] Yet this categorization into species is ultimately debunked in "The Gold-Bug": Legrand comes to regard such classification as one of several species of "sober mystification" (cf. 844). The self-dubbed "bug men" believe that "the whole bug is not a pure figment of the imagination,"[22] but we shall see that Poe's gold bug is ultimately associable with a "thing which is not."

The bug has also been classified as though it were a species of madness for psychological investigation. It has been categorized in the

19. See, for example, Carroll Laverty, "The Death's-Head on the Gold-Bug," *American Literature* 12 (March 1940):88–91; and Ellison A. Smyth, Jr., "Poe's Gold Bug from the Standpoint of an Entomologist," *Sewanee Review* 18 (January 1910): 67–72. Smyth, who spent weeks collecting beetles in the region where "The Gold-Bug" is supposed to take place, argues that the bug in the tale is one, or some combination, of the following: *Callichroma splendidum*, *Alaus oculatus*, *Euphoria fulgida*, and *Phanoeus carnifax* (dung beetle).

20. *All in the Wrong*, the source that Poe gives for his epigraph, is the wrong source. Frederick Reynold's *The Dramatist* (1789) is more likely, but equally irrelevant.

21. Baudelaire, "Edgar Allan Poe," p. 47. Baudelaire remarks that all of the coins were gold, but he forgets that before the chest itself was discovered the treasure hunters found "three or four loose pieces of gold and silver coin" (825). But perhaps Baudelaire was thinking only of the passage that concerns the treasure chest itself (827–28).

22. Smyth, "Poe's Gold Bug," pp. 71–72.

same way that one would classify the disease that the spider is said to cause—the dance of the tarantula. "The Gold-Bug" does present an interesting case study for psychoanalysts. They might, for example, classify the gold bug as a species of *Dukatenscheißer* ("dung beetle" or "shitter of ducats"), seeming to follow here the investigations of the bug men. They then might make the topical Freudian association of shiny metal with feces, or of lucre with filth.[23] *Bug* means "madman,"[24] and the psychoanalytic interpretation might tend to classify the particular species of madness from which Legrand, and presumably also Poe, suffers. By following such an analysis they might connect lucre with the imagination, which is a major aesthetic concern in "The Gold-Bug." But as Legrand has already beaten the entomological critics to the method of classifying insects, so he has beaten the psychological ones (including, perhaps, the narrator) to the method of classifying madnesses (including his own). He notes that "the mind struggles to establish a connexion—a sequence of cause and effect—and being unable to do so, suffers a species of temporary paralysis" (829). The tale itself constitutes, as we shall see, an implicit critique of the kind of classification and deciphering of evidence—Poe's text and Poe himself—in which both psychology and entomology engage.

Ultimately the gold bug is a tricky symbol that debunks ordinary classification of both physical and mental things. It is similar to the riddling bug in Poe's "The Sphinx," in which a bug that seemed to be enormous turns out to be inconsequentially small. It is like the "confidence man of merchandise" who is described in the *Literary World* (1849) as a "new species of the Jeremy Diddler."[25] The gold bug is a humbug. (See figure 6.) The first interpreter of "The Gold-Bug," a certain "D," seems to anticipate and admonish the entomological and psychological critics when he writes in "'The Gold-Bug'—a Decided Humbug" (1843) that "we have no hesitation in stating the fact, that *humbug* beyond all ques-

23. Marie Bonaparte, *The Life and Works of Edgar Allan Poe: A Psycho-Analytic Interpretation* (London, 1949), pp. 353–69, makes the conventional psychoanalytic argument. (Freud himself uses the term *Dukatenscheißer* in regard to another problem.) Bonaparte also draws attention to "the phallic significance of the golden insect" (p. 368), and notes that the "filth" here is also to be interpreted as "mother earth."

24. St. Armand, "Sober Mystification," p. 6.

25. *Literary World* (August 18, 1849), p. 133. Cf. Poe's "Diddling Considered as One of the Exact Sciences."

ontology: the logic of being and substance

tion is at last the 'Philosopher's stone,' in the discovery of which so many geniuses have heretofore been bewildered." [26]

This term *humbug* appears frequently in the controversy in 1843 about the monetary circumstances surrounding the publication of "The Gold-Bug" and the way that it was cashed in for gold. Poe first sent his story to *Graham's*, and was paid fifty-two dollars for it. He then withdrew his work in order to enter it in a contest with a prize of one hundred dollars that was being held by the *Dollar Newspaper*. "The Gold-Bug" won first prize. (The second prize was awarded to Robert Morris's "The Banker's Daughter.") Contemporary reviewers suspected fraud in the payment of one hundred dollars by the *Dollar Newspaper* for a tale about the search for dollars. "D" complained that "the publisher [of the *Dollar*] announce[d] with a grand flourish the literary tournament, and . . . induce[d] a number of really meritorious writers to enter the lists and compete for the nominal prize, which ha[d] all the appearance at first of a 'Gold-Bug,' but . . . certain[ly] eventuate[d] in a humbug." He accused the contest and the tale itself of being a "literary *humbug*." There was an ensuing public controversy in which "D" and a certain "Mr. P" (probably Poe) confronted each other in the matter of "the prize story." [27] The discussion of the external economics of "The Gold-Bug" (Poe's winning the contest) thus came to illuminate for some readers its internal economics (Legrand's using a gold bug designed on paper to find gold). [28] "The Gold-Bug" itself, like the "act of art" that is the design of a gold bug on paper which "The Gold-Bug" describes, is exchanged for and hence to be taken for gold.

But what is this humbug in "The Gold-Bug"? A humbug is a thing that is not. Ontology, or the logic of being and substance, may help

26. "D," in *Philadelphia Daily Forum* (June 27, 1843). See William Henry Gravely, Jr., "An Incipient Libel Suit Involving Poe," *Modern Language Notes* 60 (May 1945), pp. 309–10. Political cartoonists of the period connected both entomological and psychological investigation with the logic of monetary policy; see, for example, "N. Tom O'Logical [cf. entomological] Studies: The Great Tumble Bug of Missouri Bent-On Rolling His Ball," issued by H. R. Robinson in 1837 (American Antiquarian Society).

27. "Mr. P's" editorial appears in the *Public Ledger* (July 4, 1843), p. 2, col. 4.

28. Most tales are told with some reward in mind. The extreme example is Scheherazade, who tells the tales of *The Thousand and One Arabian Nights* because she wants to live. "The Gold-Bug" earned Poe (the author of "The Thousand-and-Second Tale of Scheherazade") a partial livelihood out of a narrative interpretation of the symbol of death (the death's head nailed to the branch), and was published in London as "No. 1" of a never-completed series entitled *The One Thousand and One Romances*.

locate the logical place of the gold bug in "The Gold-Bug." Poe's contemporaries, as we have suggested, called for a new study of the connections between ontology and political economy. Such a study would shed light on the connection in "The Gold-Bug" between species in the physical world (including entomological ones) and species in the internal world of the mind (including psychological ones), a connection that links nature with the psyche, or things with our ideas of them. It is no accident, as we shall see, that Legrand's search for natural specimens and his study of different psychological species turns into a search for metallic specie. The turn from species and specimens to specie is a crucial articulation in "The Gold-Bug," which Poe wrote when the main public forum for discussing the relationship between symbols and things was the ideological debate about how, if at all, paper money represents substantial things.

From Nothing to Something

We humans sometimes make mountains out of molehills. But only God and his opposite number can make something out of nothing. Maybe alchemists can make gold out of tin, but they cannot make tin out of what Poe's Jupiter calls "*no tin*" (808–9). For us the terrible dictum—that nothin' will come of nothin'—seems to hold true.[29] Except, that is, in the shadowy realms of aesthetics and monetary policy.

One interpreter of "The Gold-Bug" argues that from the alchemical point of view Legrand does not discover but actually generates, produces, or reproduces the gold in the hole. "It is actually Legrand's Romantic imagination that helps to accomplish the multiplication of the gold-bug into Captain Kidd's treasure."[30] Legrand himself notes that "there seemed to glimmer, faintly within the most remote and secret chambers of my intellect, a glow-worm-like conception of that truth which last night's adventure [unearthing the gold] brought so magnificent a demonstration" (829). This generative power of the intellect, which Legrand associates with a psychic entomoid—the intellectual glowworm that is the humbug of the tale—is closely linked with financial institutions that render treasure from paper.

29. In "Mellonta Tauta," Poe quotes Lucretius, *De rerum natura*: "Ex nihilo nihil fit."

30. St. Armand, "Sober Mystification," p. 5.

Since Aristotle, finance has been accused of making something out of nothing or out of nothing natural.[31] Aristotle was concerned with the way that money in general was made to breed by usury, but since the eighteenth century men have been more concerned with the subversive manner of representation and exchange in the institution of paper money in particular. (The South Sea Bubble of 1720, including the increase in popular pamphleteering and the beginning of widespread political cartooning to which the Bubble gave rise, first directed public discussion to paper money as "the devil in specie" and as a "nothing" pretending to be "something.")[32]

For Poe and his contemporaries, the immediate distinction between coin and paper money could be expressed in terms of the relationship between an ingot and an inscription on it when both together compose a coin. This relationship of sign or symbol (the inscription) to substance (the ingot) is the heart of the aesthetic version of the paper money debate. There are two related questions here. First, when the inscription disappears from the surface of a coin, is the remaining ingot still a coin? In his numismatic catalogue the narrator mentions "coins so worn that we [can] make nothing of their inscription" (827). This "nothing" that we can make of their inscriptions does not make the ingots into "things which are not." However much they may lose their status as coins, they are still substantial metal commodities. Second, when the ingot itself disappears, and all that remains is the inscription—the literature—is the numismatic inscription still substantially valid, as is symbolic paper money? Can the shadow that is paper money thus become as valuable as, or even more valuable than, the substance that is specie? The narrator in Nathaniel Hawthorne's "Seven

31. Aristotle, *Politics* 1258.
32. See the cartoons of John Law's paper money system and their accompanying inscriptions, described in *Catalogue of Prints and Drawings in the British Museum* (London, 1873), div. 1, vol. 2. "De Eklips der Zuider Zon . . ." ("The Eclipse of the Sun . . . ," no. 1654) refers to "de drommel in specie" ("the devil in specie"). "De Verwarde Actionisten torenbouw tot Babel" ("The Babel-Tower of the Confused Stock-Jobbers," no. 1672) has a cartoon of John Law with the inscription "Law, whose affairs have turned from something to nothing." "The Bubblers Medley" (no. 1611) complains that "Asses there, / Give Solid Gold, for empty Air" and that "all the riches that we boast / Consist in Scraps of Paper." Figure 7 shows "The Bubbler's Kingdom in the Aireal-World" (no. 1622), from which we are encouraged to learn that "the Gold is Melted and nothing but Bubbles it produces" and that one "catch[es] at all and hold[s] Nothing."

Vagabonds" (1842) suggests as much when he gives a beggar a five-dollar bill with the claim that "it is a bill of the Suffolk Bank . . . and better than the specie."[33]

SYMBOL AND THING AS CAUSE AND EFFECT

The design of the gold bug, like the bug itself, can be considered as a cause of and metonymic link with the treasure. It can also be considered, less grandly, as a symbolic counterpart to or index of Captain Kidd's cartograph. "Since fortune has thought fit to bestow [the bug] upon me," says Legrand, "I have only to use it properly and I shall arrive at the gold of which it is the index" (815). Legrand is like both Midas and Pygmalion in his reaction to the design of the bug: he seems to believe that he can turn his "graphic" art (828), of which he is tolerably proud, into the real thing. He would transform his design of a specimen into specie, thus treating the designed paper as a necessary cause of an effect—the unearthing of gold—that he seeks.

The distinction of accidental from necessary relationships, both those between signs and substance and those between one event and another, is a major theoretical problem in "The Gold-Bug," as in most detective stories, and Legrand eventually comes to address it. Is the connection between the design of the gold bug and the gold, for example, merely accidental? That is, are they linked in the same way as two meanings connected by punning (Captain Kidd with the kid in the hieroglyphic signature), by malapropism ("gold" with "ghoul"—both suggested by Jupiter's dialectal "goole"), and by homonymity (the design of the bug with the pirate's insignium —both called "death's heads")?[34] Are they linked, that is, in the same way as the coincidences in the plot—Legrand and the narrator call them links in a chain of

33. In Hawthorne's "Seven Vagabonds," the beggar cashes the bill, but only at a discount unfavorable to the narrator. In one sense paper money is and should be more valuable than specie. Thus Braudel (*Capitalism and Material Life*, p. 365) notes that as early as the eighteenth century in Amsterdam "the 'ideal' bank money, the *florin de banque*, was quoted higher than real money in circulation, because of the inadequacies of circulating currency."

34. Jupiter's reference to "bug mouff" recalls a third sound- and look-alike: the moth called "Death's Head Sphinx," which plays a role in Poe's "The Sphinx" and was depicted in contemporary journals (e.g., *Saturday Magazine*, August 25, 1832). In Poe's "Some Words with a Mummy," the scarabeus is mentioned as the "insignium" of Egyptian families.

happy accidents—such as the "fortuitous" entrance of the Newfoundland dog from the cold outdoors?[35] Or is the connection between signs and substance and between one event and another somehow natural or logically necessary rather than accidental? That is, are they linked in the same way as words with things in onomatopoeia (hum with the sound of humming)[36] or as an animal with its native territory (an eagle, for example, with the United States)?

In implicitly considering these questions, Poe integrates into his tale problems involving money and aesthetics. In "A Shadow Is Not a Substance" (figure 1), for example, the specie can be viewed as one cause of the shadow. The specie and the sun are two links in the chain of cause and effect that a detective might say produces the shadow. In "The Gold-Bug" the events in the plot and the eventual discovery of gold are not connected by this kind of necessity. To say that the design of the gold bug on the paper is a link in a chain of symbols or events that leads inevitably to the gold is, adopting the terms of the cartoon, to say that the shadow is the cause of the substance rather than vice versa. According to the "gold bugs," this is the ostensibly absurd position of the "paper money men," of whom Legrand seems to be one as he marches through the dark forest with the designed paper clutched in his hand.

And yet, however absurd, the bug and the original design of the bug do lead somehow to the insignium and signature on Captain Kidd's valuable paper and even, as the narrator remarks, to "a letter between the stamp and the signature," or, as Legrand himself says, to "the text for these contexts" (833).

SPECIES OF CRYPTOGRAPH

The text of Kidd's paper is a cryptic cartograph in alphabetic cipher. Those critics who attack Poe for the supposedly inaccurate ciphering

35. Legrand's penning the design of the new found specimen of beetle has the apparent effect of introducing to the room a Newfoundland dog (809). In the tale this dog plays a number of key roles. His "mouth/mouffe" (823) and "claws/cause" (825) recall those of the gold bug that bit Legrand with its mouth and so caused the bug for gold. And immediately upon the entrance of the Newfoundland dog (cf. the entrance of the poodle in Goethe's *Faust*) Legrand catches sight of a new found design (the death's head) that leads him to new found treasure under the land.

36. Legrand makes his bug hum when he swings it by the string (817, 844). Cf. "humbug."

and cryptography in Kidd's message miss the point of the story.[37] First, these critics do not seem to know that a common form of cipher writing in the United States was the literary genre of paper money inscriptions, into which so-called "errors" were often purposefully incorporated in order to trap counterfeiters more easily.[38] Second, the cryptological critics fall into the same interpretative trap as the entomological and psychoanalytical ones. Deciphering the secret writing of the parchment and hence connecting sign with substance, as Legrand goes about it, is identical in method to the cataloguing of species involved in these and similar "exact" sciences. "Be assured," says Legrand, "that the specimen before us appertains to the very simplest species of cryptograph" (839, cf. 835). Legrand's deciphering the cipher on the parchment stands as a warning to those who would similarly decipher the book (Hebrew *sēpher*) that is "The Gold-Bug," whose center is a real cipher (Arabic *siffre*, or "O"), quite mystified and mystifying.

The Goolah Bug:
Linguistic Goolah and Monetary Goole

The distinction between substance and shadow in monetary and aesthetic theory affects the understanding of symbolization in general and of linguistic representation in particular. With the advent of paper money certain analogies, such as "paper is to gold as word is to meaning," came to exemplify and to inform logically the discourse about language. For example, critics called for a return to gold not only in money but also in aesthetics and language. Thus Emerson wrote that "a man's power to connect his thought with its proper symbol, and so to utter it" is corrupted when "new imagery ceases to be created, and

---

37. See W. K. Wimsatt, Jr., "What Poe Knew about Cryptography," *PMLA* 58 (1943): 775–79; and J. Woodrow Hassell, Jr., "The Problem of Realism in 'The Gold-Bug,'" *American Literature* 25 (May 1953): 179–92. For criticism of similar "lacks of verisimilitude" in "The Gold-Bug," see the discussion of the tulip tree in Eric Stockton, "Poe's Use of Negro Dialect in 'The Gold-Bug,'" in *Studies in Languages and Linguistics in Honor of Charles C. Fries*, ed. A. H. Marckwardt, (Ann Arbor, 1964), pp. 249–70; and Albert H. Tolman, "Was Poe Accurate?" in *The Views about Hamlet and Other Essays* (Boston and New York, 1904). Theodor W. Adorno, in a comment on deciphering in "The Gold-Bug," goes beyond the problem of cryptographic accuracy (Adorno, *Über Walter Benjamin*, ed. Rolf Tiedemann [Frankfurt, 1970], pp. 151–52).

38. See Newman, *Early Paper Money*, p. 93.

old words are perverted to stand for things which are not; a paper currency is employed, when there is no bullion in the vaults."[39]

As Emerson suggests, paper money differs from coined money in an intellectually significant way.[40] While a coin may be both symbol (as inscription or type) and commodity (as metallic ingot), paper is virtually all symbolic. Thus Wittgenstein chooses to compare meaningless sounds with scraps of paper rather than with unminted ingots; or, to put it the other way, he compares meaningful words with valuable paper money rather than with coins.[41] In "The Gold-Bug," what in the intellect or in the imagination of Legrand creates gold is like what turns paper into a valuable commodity. For the same reason as Wittgenstein, Marx distinguishes the disassociation of symbol from commodity that seems to occur in the minting of metal ingots into coin, from the less apparent and ideologically more subversive disassociation of symbol from commodity that occurs in printing money. As Marx argues, credit money (the extreme form of paper money) divorces the name entirely from what it is supposed to represent and so seems to allow an idealist transcendence, or conceptual annihilation, of commodities.[42] In the institution of paper money, sign and substance—paper and gold—are clearly disassociated, much as word is disassociated from meaning in punning.

39. Ralph Waldo Emerson, "Nature," in *The Collected Works of Ralph Waldo Emerson*, ed. A. R. Ferguson (Cambridge, Mass., 1971), 1:20. Cf. Washington Irving's description of inflation in France during John Law's paper money experiment of 1720: "Promissory notes, interchanged between scheming individuals, are liberally discounted at the banks, which became so many mints to coin words into cash; and as the supply of words is inexhaustible, it may readily be supposed what a vast amount of promissory capital is soon in circulation" (Irving, "The Great Mississippi Bubble: 'A Time of Unexampled Prosperity'" [1840] in Irving, *The Crayon Papers* [New York, (1883)], p. 38).

40. See Chapter 4, section on "Paper Money and Language."

41. "One might say: in all cases one means by thought what is living in the sentence. That without which it is dead, a mere sound sequence or sequence of written shapes. . . . Or what if we spoke of a something that distinguishes paper money from mere printed slips of paper and [that] gives [paper money] its meaning, its life" (Ludwig Wittgenstein, *Zettel*, ed. G. E. M. Anscombe and H. von Wright [Berkeley and Los Angeles, 1970], sec. 143).

42. For example: Karl Marx, *Das Kapital*, in Karl Marx and Friedrich Engels, *Werke*, ed. Institut für Marxismus-Leninismus beim ZK der SED (Berlin, 1956–68), 23:138–43 (translated as Marx, *Capital*, trans. S. Moore and E. Aveling [New York, 1967], 1:124–29); and Marx, *Zur Kritik der Politischen Ökonomie, Werke*, 13:94–95 (translated as *A Contribution to the Critique of Political Economy*, trans. S. W. Ryazanskaya [New York, 1970], pp. 115–16).

In "The Gold-Bug" the malapropian and punning speech of Jupiter, the manumitted black slave, is as important to our deciphering the meaning of the tale as his scythe was to Legrand's getting at the gold. "It would have been impossible to force our way but for the scythe and Jupiter" (817). Jupiter's dialect, which students of linguistics call "Goolah," is in this sense the real "goole" in "The Gold-Bug."[43]

Goolah was a linguistic dialect spoken by blacks living on the sea islands and tidewater coastal strip bordering South Carolina. There are instances in "The Gold-Bug" where Poe seems to depart from Goolah, and there is unnecessary eye dialect in the tale: not only the sound (ear dialect), but also the spelling is incorrect according to standard white American usage.[44] (Jupiter's "syphon" [812], for example, is eye dialect for "ciph'n," which is ear dialect or malapropism for "deciphering.") Jupiter's apparent inconsistencies ("no tin"/"noffin"/"notin"), however, tend to elucidate the central thesis of the tale, which concerns not so much money qua treasure, as paper money qua sign lacking a necessary relation to its referent. In "The Gold-Bug," Jupiter's language depends for its interpretational effectiveness on accidental connections between signs and referents, or words and meanings. (Many of Poe's contemporaries argued that in Goolah the "original" meanings of words had become completely obliterated. A Virginian journalist, for example, wrote in 1838 that "the etymology of [several] terms is quite untraceable as that of any terms in the Goolah . . . dialect."[45] Poe's tale entertains the hypothesis that a similar loss or absence of meaning is an essential aspect of all discourse.)

Jupiter's dialect provides an interpretative access to the discontinuity in the symbolization and plot of "The Gold-Bug." For example, the bug, which is described by Legrand in entomological terms as having

43. Stockton, who observes ("Poe's Use of Negro Dialect," p. 255) that Jupiter's "goole" (which occurs nine times in the tale) is merely "an interesting survival of the conservative pronunciation of 'gold' as /guld/," neglects to consider the additional *e* that makes Jupiter's "goole" sound like "Goolah." Similarly, Jean Ricardou, who argues ("L'Or du scarabée," *Théorie d'ensemble* [Paris, 1968], p. 374) that "Jupiter . . . [est] en mauvais termes avec le langage," fails to see that Jupiter's language is the key to the "cipher" that is "The Gold-Bug."

44. On Goolah, or Gullah, see Lorenzo Turner, *Africanisms in Gullah Dialect* (Chicago, 1949). For Poe's departures from Goolah, see Ambrose Gonzales, *The Black Border: Gullah Stories of the Carolina Coast* (Columbia, S.C., 1922), esp. pp. 12–13. The dramatization of the tale in Silas S. Steele's *The Gold-Bug, or, The Pirate's Treasure* (1843) made the sound (hence the ear dialect) even more important.

45. *Southern Literary Messenger* (Richmond, Va., 1838), vol. 4, p. 641, col. 1.

"antennae," is redefined by Jupiter as rather having *"no* tin in him" (808–9).[46] Poe's making Jupiter say "no tin" has been attacked as "stupid" by several critics, who fail to note the literary and economic status of the pun.[47] What could the pun mean? First, there is "no tin in" the bug (which would be important for alchemical interpretation), so it is of "real gold" or "solid gold" (809, 815, 833). Second, there is "no thing in[side]" the bug, so it is hollow in the physical sense. Third, there is "nothing in" the bug, that is, nothing to it. If there were nothing to the bug, it would be a cipher, an insubstantial ghost that might, like paper money, indicate something substantial.

In "The Gold-Bug" Goolah connects by verbal punning other threads of the story. For example, Jupiter's version of "goole-bug" tends to illuminate the connections or disconnections between devil, gold, and God: the ghoulish devil is heard or seen in "goole";[48] and God, in "my golly" (824) and "Lor-gol-a-marcy" (820).

Goolah also serves to bring into focus aspects of the paper money men's quest to become rich by manipulation of paper money ghosts. Jupiter's "gose" (812), for example, can be interpreted in three ways: as "ghost," which refers to phantom, or ghoul, banknotes; as the "goose," or person gulled into accepting counterfeit phantom banknotes in the belief that they are good as gold; and as the design of a goose that appeared on American banknotes.[49]

In "The Gold-Bug" Poe thus shows interest in a generation of some-

46. *An* in Greek means "no" in English, so that *antennae* may be understood as "no tin in."

47. See, for example, Killis Campbell, *The Mind of Poe and Other Studies* (Cambridge, Mass., 1933), p. 113, n. 2, and p. 115.

48. In "The Gold-Bug" a parallel is made between aesthetic imagination, which seems able to transform a mere nothing into something, and "the agency of no human" (831), of the "ghoulish" devil. Satan—"sartain" (812, 820, 824)—confers the "debil's own lot of money" (831). The *ghūl* (the Arabic term indicating a grave-robbing ghoul) finds his gold.

49. In his translation of "The Gold-Bug"—"Le Scarabée d'or"—Baudelaire translated *gose* as *oix* ("goose"). Mabbott, in his notes to "The Gold-Bug," (CW, 845–46), calls this an error, but "goose" is as correct as "ghost." The last major conversation in Melville's *The Confidence-Man: His Masquerade* turns around a potential goose's attempt to match up the design of a goose in his Counterfeit Detector with the design of a goose on a banknote (or "ghost") that he is attempting to authenticate. "Stay, now, here's another sign. It says that, if the bill is good, it must have in one corner . . . a goose . . . I can't see this goose." . . . "I don't see it—dear me—I don't see the goose. Is it a real goose?" The confidence man responds: "A perfect goose; beautiful goose" (Herman Melville, *The Confidence-Man: His Masquerade*, ed. Hershel Parker [New York, 1971], p. 214, cf. p. 209). Cf. the "ghastliness" of Legrand.

thing from nothing that is at once economic and linguistic. He took his studies of the "omnipotence of money" and of usury—themes that he praised in *Tortesa the Usurer* (1839), which he called the greatest play by an American[50]—and transformed them, on the one hand, into a story about the generation of gold from a bug or from a design of a bug, and on the other hand, into a discourse whose exemplary means of generating meaning is Goolah punning.

Aristotle argues that of all forms of generation usury is the most unnatural, and theorists since the medieval era have argued that punning is its linguistic counterpart, since punning makes an unnatural, even a diabolical, supplement of meaning from a sound that is properly attached to only one (if any) meaning. Thus, in terms of the economics of symbolization in "The Gold-Bug," Goolah is the linguistic counterpart of the productive imagination of Legrand, a counterpart that is also its symptomatic externalization, since Jupiter's language is there for us to see and to hear.

Last Words

"Seekers after gold dig up much earth and find little."[51] Heraclitus warns that the search for gold, for meaning, is a kind of misdirected bugaboo. There is something cryptic and disconcerting about the conclusion to "The Gold-Bug." Legrand's cryptography is successful, but the unearthing of the secreted coffer reveals coffinless skeletons in the cryptlike hole. "What are we to make of the skeletons found in the hole?" the narrator asks Legrand (844). This is an unanswered question in a detective story that only seems to answer all questions. "Who shall tell?" are the last words in "The Gold-Bug."

"The Gold-Bug" is a tale in which an impoverished aristocrat, who "saunters along the bank in quest of entomological specimens" (807), discovers there a paper that renders forth golden specie, most of which

50. N. P. Willis, *Tortesa the Usurer* (New York, 1839), act 1, scene 1. Poe writes that Willis' play is "we think by far the best play from the pen of an American author" (*Burton's Gentleman's Magazine* [August 1839]).

51. Heraclitus, Fragment 22, in H. Diels, *Fragmente der Vorsokratiker*, 5th ed. (Berlin, 1934). In an edition of "The Gold-Bug" for sixth-grade students, Theda Gildemeister suggests that, "as an antidote to any gold-craving influences which the story might arouse, the children could . . . read 'The Golden Touch,' by Hawthorne" (E. A. Poe, *The Gold-Bug*, ed. Theda Gildemeister [New York, 1902], p. 111).

is exchanged at the bank for commercial papers.[52] What began at a bank also ends at one. It is not ashes to ashes and dust to dust, as for the ghostly men whose remains are skeletons, but rather paper to paper. The treasure itself returns to the bank where, so to speak, it originated. It is as though it were a thing that was naught at all.

52. Legrand wanders at a "beach" (807) in the J. Lorimer Graham copy of the last manuscript (with revisions about 1849); the original version printed in *The Dollar Newspaper* of 1843, however, has Legrand conducting his search for conchological and entomological species at a "bank." Perhaps Poe wished to play down the explicitness of the financial theme in the new edition.

2 / *The Blank Check*

ACCOUNTING FOR THE GRAIL

THE INFINITELY LARGE gift and the free gift (one given gratis, without intending to obligate the recipient to reciprocate and without making him feel obligated to do so) may well be impossible in everyday exchange.[1] Hypotheses of such gifts, however, serve much thought about exchange and production as boundaries that define the ordinary world of contractual obligation through their extraordinary opposition to, or difference from, that world. The hypothesis of the infinitely large gift, for example, appears as the cornucopia, and the hypothesis of the free gift, as Pauline grace.[2] Such topoi are still abundant in our own myth of the "affluent society,"[3] but they were even more important towards the end of the medieval era. At that time the first widespread vernacular literature told of a cornucopian grail,[4] an extraordinary gift both infinitely large and free, which was said to be able to lift men out of the ordinary world of exchange into a world in which freedom and

1. For the first position, see Ralph Waldo Emerson, "Gifts" (in *Essays*, Second Series [Boston, 1885], p. 156): "We do not quite forgive a giver." For the second, see Thomas Hobbes, *Leviathan*, ed. M. J. Oakeshott (Oxford, 1946), p. 87.

2. On grace in this context see especially Saint Bernard, *De gratia et libero arbitrio* 6. 16.

3. Modern theorists of affluence include the Marquis de Condorcet, William Godwin, Charles Reade, Edward Bellamy, James A. Patten, John Ruskin, and John Kenneth Galbraith.

4. On the grail as a cornucopia, see Alfred Nutt, *Studies of the Legend of the Holy Grail* (London, 1888), pp. 74ff.; Helaine Newstead, *Bran the Blessed in Arthurian Romance* (New York, 1939), pp. 86–120; R. S. Loomis, *The Grail* (Cardiff, 1963); R. S. Loomis, "The Origin of the Grail Legends" in *Arthurian Literature in the Middle Ages*, ed. R. S. Loomis (Oxford, 1959), pp. 274–94; D. D. R. Owen, *The Evolution of the Grail Legend* (Edinburgh, 1968); and Arthur C. L. Brown, *The Origin of the Grail Legend* (New York, 1966), esp. p. 367 on the Irish *criol*.

totality were possible. The Holy Grail was the free source of everything. The grail legends depict a wasteland to which the limitless
production of material and spiritual goods stands as a defining and
conceptually unique limit.

In the Pauline economy of truth God is said to dispense or disseminate truth to his steward.[5] This steward must then further disseminate
truth according to the ability of ordinary men to germinate it. Appropriate dissemination by the steward (*oikonomos*) and germination by
ordinary men are major problems both in the economy of Christianity
and in the economies of such apparently Christian writers as Chrétien
de Troyes. In the Prologue to Chrétien's *Account of the Grail* (ca. A.D.
1190) what is dispensed or disseminated alternates between the true
spiritual nourishment that the grail gives to some men and the contents of a unique book (*livre*) that a count gives to the poet, a book of
which the poet plans to deliver (*delivre*) a rhymed account (*conte*).[6]
The *Account* begins with a version of Jesus' parable of the sower:
"Whoever disseminates little, gathers little, and whoever wishes a fair
harvest scatters his seed in such place that it returns fruit to him a hun-
dredfold, for in land which is worth nothing seed dries and fails."[7]
Chrétien is a poet-sower who must consider the relationship of the fertility of his seed both to the relative spiritual sterility of his audience
and to the material sterility of the wasteland of which he would tell
them. Spiritual fertility varies from person to person, so that Chrétien
must speak on several levels at the same time. His account of the grail
thus involves an inevitable esotericism. "No one," writes the author of
the *Pseudo-Prologue*, "should speak or sing the secrets of the grail."[8]
All the grail tales claim the status of riddle.

5. For *oikonomia* in the New Testament, see *Theological Dictionary of the New Testament*, ed. Gerhard Friedrich, trans. and ed. Geoffrey W. Bromiley, 10 vols. (Grand
Rapids, Mich., 1964–76), s.v. "*oikonomos*" and "*oikonomia*." For the term "economy
of truth" see Cardinal Newman's study of the *disciplina arcani* (Newman, *The Arians
of the Fourth Century* [London, 1919], pp. 65–77) and Marc Shell, *The Economy of
Literature* (Baltimore, 1978), pp. 104–7. According to Paul, "we must be regarded as
Christ's underlings and as stewards [*oikonomoi*] of the secrets of God" (1 Cor. 4:1, cf. 1
Pet. 4:10).

6. References are keyed to *Der Percevalroman von Christian von Troyes*, ed. Alfons
Hilka (Halle, 1932); here, 61–68. For the translation see Chrétien de Troyes, *The
Story of The Grail*, trans. and ed. Robert White Linker (Chapel Hill, N.C., 1952).

7. *Percevalroman*, 1–6. For the proverb see J. de Morawski, ed. *Proverbes français,
antérieurs au XVe siècle* (Paris, 1925), no. 2074. Cf. Luke 8, Matt. 13.

8. *Pseudo-Prologue*, 4–5, in *Percevalroman*, 417.

Corresponding to this alethiological economy, whose ineffable center is truth (*alētheia*), there is in the grail tales a strictly linguistic economy, whose center is a marvelous word or its meaning. The word *grail* itself operates, in two complementary ways, as the center of this "linguistic economy of abundance."[9] First, the sound of *graal*, associated with that of *kor*, is heard to give rise to such key terms as "horn" (*cors*), "body" (*cors*), "court" (*cors*), "heart" (*cuer*), and *Corbenic*.[10] Clever etymology—or logic of verbal production—establishes the linguistic production of these words by pretending to work from them back to *graal*, their common primordial etymon. Second, the etymological process is reversed in such a way that the interpreter works from *graal* to older, historical etymons or contemporary cognates. Thus Hélinand says that *graal* comes from *gradatim*, because one puts food on it, as onto a dish; or from *gratus*, because it is pleasing to everyone. The grail, he explains, is a cornucopian dish that produces pleasing things. Similarly, Robert de Boron explains the grail as "the platter that serves to satisfaction (*à gré*)" and calls it "the grail that pleases [*agrée*]." The Didot *Perceval* makes the same etymological association: "We call it *Graal* because it is so pleasing [*agrée*] to worthy men." Finally *Merlin* calls the grail "grace" itself: "And these people call this vessel from which they have this grace [*grâsce*]—Grail [*Graal*]."[11] Like the apos-

9. On the cornucopian aspects of language in general, see Lewis Mumford, *The Myth of the Machine* (New York, 1967), esp. "The Linguistic Economy of Abundance," pp. 94–97.

10. On some of the interrelationships of these words and the sounds *graal* and *kor*, see Newstead, *Bran the Blessed*, pp. 86–120; R. S. Loomis, "The Origin of the Grail Legends," pp. 287–90; and Jean Marx, *La Légende arthurienne et le graal* (Paris, 1952), pp. 124–25. Even such works as the *Livre de Caradoc*, Robert Biket's *Lai du Cor*, and the "Joie de la Cort" episode in Chrétien's *Erec* have been connected to the resourceful *graal*.

11. Hélinand is quoted in *Patrologiae cursus completus* [Series Latina], ed. Jacques Paul Migne, 221 vols. (Paris, 1844–64), vol. 212, col. 814. For Robert de Boron, see his *Le Roman de l'Estoire dou Graal*, ed. William A. Nitze (Paris, 1927) and Albert Pauphilet, *Etudes sur la Queste del Saint Graal* (Paris, 1921), pp. 17 and 18, n. 2. For the Didot and *Merlin*, see Emma Jung and Marie Louise von Franz, *The Grail Legend*, trans. Andrea Dykes (New York, 1970), p. 118. Giulio Evola, *Das Mysterium des Grals* (München, 1955), pp. 87–88, discusses many similar sentences in other grail tales, including *Perceval li Gallois*, *Grand St. Graal*, *Queste*, and *Perlesvax*. Modern students of the etymology of *graal* include Leo Spitzer, "The Name of the Holy Grail," *American Journal of Philology* 65 (1944): 354–63 on *cratis* (a "wooden basket"); W. Nitze, "Spitzer's Grail Etymology," *American Journal of Philology* 66 (1945): 279–81 on *crater* (a "mixing bowl"); and Henry and Reneé Kahane, *The Krater and the Grail* (Urbana, Ill., 1965).

tle's inkhorn (*cornu*) in figure 8a, the word *graal* operates in the grail tales as a "cornucopia of words,"[12] just as the grail itself operates as a plentiful cornucopia of nourishing food.

Dearth and Plenitude

In the grail tales the royal courts of the world (*corts reals*), such as those of King Arthur and even of Chrétien's patron, the count, are centers of wastelands. They are sterile deserts in comparison with the fruitful grail, which alone confers spiritual as well as material legitimacy on a brotherhood or a state. (In the Prologue to the *Account*, *graal* is thus rhymed—both identified and opposed with—*corts real* [61–68].) Courtly men are driven to seek out (or hypothesize) the grail by the need to make sense of and to demarcate conceptually the boundaries of earthly exchange and production and, once these boundaries are established, by the impulse to satisfy or overcome material desires (hunger and sex).

At the beginning of Chrétien's *Account*, for example, the hero Perceval is presented as a typical hungry adolescent who seeks food from his mother, expects food at the tent he mistakenly believes to be a chapel, demands food from the God he believes to live in the tent-chapel, and finally receives earthly food. Only divine nourishment, however, can satisfy the desire of this questing man. Perceval learns about the kind of food God provides when a hermit tells him on Good Friday that the food he failed to ask about at the grail castle was "real." The king of that castle is nourished by the grail:

> With a single host, which is carried [*porte*] to him in this grail, the holy man sustains and comforts his life. So holy a thing is the grail, and he is so spiritual, that to his life nothing more is needed than the host which comes in the grail.[13]

In the part of the *Account* that he completed, Chrétien merely hints at the marvelous qualities of the grail. The continuers of his unfinished

---

12. The phrase is used by Johann G. von Herder and Jean Paul. See *Deutsches Wörterbuch*, ed. Jacob and Wilhelm Grimm (Leipzig, 1854–1960), s.v. "Füllhorn."

13. *Percevalroman*, 6422–28. This passage may have been added by an acute interpolator. See Brown, *Origin of the Grail Legend*, p. 121; and "Did Chrétien Identify the Grail with the Mass?" *Modern Language Notes* 41 (1926): 226.

text, however, added a cornucopian grail serving food and wine, in order to avoid making Chrétien, who in their opinion implies the conceptually necessary existence of such a grail, a liar.[14]

In Wolfram's *Parzival* (ca. A.D. 1215), too, the grail is a spiritual as well as a material cornucopia.[15] It is the talisman that provides all things to the knightly community: the *wunsch von paradîs* ("perfection of paradise").[16] The knightly brotherhood and even Sigune are served food by this "power of the grail" (471). But the material wealth that the grail provides has been purchased by the "living death" of the royal Frimutel (230). The *wunsch* is the wish for the grace that may finally redeem the sick king and kingdom, the wish that God ultimately invests in the antiknight Parzival (148, 250). The transformation of physical into spiritual gifts in *Parzival* is hinted in the description of the dove that brings a wafer from heaven on Good Friday and places on it a stone associated with the "perfection of paradise" (470, 496). Like the continuers of Chrétien's *Account*, Wolfram insists on the necessity of the existence of this grail. If the grail did not exist, he says, there would be no source of all the things that we know: we would not only be unable to eat food, we would also be unable to speak words without lying (238). The grail is a hypothesis that must exist, because it alone allows access to truth.

With the *Quest of the Holy Grail* (ca. A.D. 1225) cornucopian material and spiritual production by the grail is already the explicit theme. "Because the grail serves to satisfaction [*à gré*]," says the *Quest*, "it should be called the Holy Grail [*Graal*]." Food from the grail seems to the courtiers of the wasteland to be merely physical, but that is because

---

14. See Manessier, in *The Continuations of the Old French Perceval of Chrétien de Troyes* (Pseudo-Wauchier, Wauchier de Denain, and Manessier), ed. William Joseph Roach (Philadelphia, 1949); and Jean Marx, *Nouvelles recherches sur la littérature arthurienne* (Paris, 1965), pp. 107–8, 180, 239–59.

15. On the cornucopia in Wolfram see M. F. Richey, *Studies of Wolfram von Eschenbach* (Edinburgh, 1957), p. 147; Manfred Brauneck, *Wolfram von Eschenbach: Parzival* (Bamberg, 1967), pp. 45–52; and Otto Springer, "Wolfram's Parzival," in *Arthurian Literature in the Middle Ages*, ed. R. S. Lewis (Oxford, 1959), p. 231.

16. Quotations are keyed to Wolfram von Eschenbach, *Parzival*, ed. Ernst Martin (Halle, 1900–1903); here, stanza 235. For the translation see Wolfram von Eschenbach, *Parzival*, trans. Helen M. Mustard and Charles E. Passage (New York, 1961). Of *wunsch von paradîs*, Loomis (*The Grail*, p. 211) writes that it is "a phrase not easily translated but presumably suggested by the paradisal plenty of food and drink supplied by the talisman."

they "are so blinded and beguiled that [they] could not see it plain, rather is its true substance [*semblance*] hidden from [them]." [17] But not to see "the mysteries and hidden sweets of God" is not to be truly fed. Some impure men (Bors) realize that their earthly vision is inadequate to see the good in its spiritual form (167). Pure men (Galahad) can see the spirit, but what they see cannot be spoken about. The source of all things, like the answer to a perfect riddle, is unspeakable.

The *Quest* uses analogues to help explain the unlimited source that is the defining limit: the table on which Joseph was supposed to have reenacted Jesus' miracle of multiplying loaves and fishes (75), for example, and the manna that nourishes the repentant Lancelot in the same way that it nourished the Jewish wanderers in the desert. An inexhaustible fountain where the heart (*cuer*) of the repentant man finds sweetness, [18] "the grace of the Holy Vessel" (15) flows into the wasteland in which wander we hapless men.

By the end of the *Quest* we readers, nourished by the literary spring that is the *Quest*, come to understand a little of "the grace of the Holy Vessel." The trope of tropes, however, is a trope barely heard by the ears of ordinary men. In Acts, men learn to speak in tongues;[19] but in the *Quest*, as in Chrétien's *Account*, the appearance of the grail strikes men dumb. ("Sin cut off your language/tongue" is the hermit's explanation of why Perceval failed to ask the all-important question at the grail castle [6409].) The appearance of the grail in the *Quest*, like food, stops the mouths of those who see it. (Only its disappearance unstops their mouths and allows them to thank God in words.) The kind of men who do not have good food to go into their mouths do not have good words to come out of their mouths. Luckily for us, the narrator of the *Quest* believes himself so well nourished with the truth that he can use words to deliver the goods to his auditors.

Promise and Delivery

Chrétien's *Account of the Grail* is structured by several series of barter-exchanges of material items, each one of which elucidates the way from

17. Quotations are keyed to *La Queste del Saint Graal*, ed. Albert Pauphilet (Paris, 1967); here, p. 16. For the translation see *The Quest of the Holy Grail*, trans. P. M. Matarasso (Baltimore, 1969). Cf. Robert de Boron, line 725.

18. Cf. John 4:14.

19. Cf. Acts 1:1–4, 3:4. On the phrase "la grâce dou Saint Vessel," see Etienne

a limited economy to an unlimited one. The episodes in which Perceval confronts the Red Knight (834–1304) and in which he considers three drops of blood (4162–602), taken together, provide a good example.

In the first episode, called "The Red Knight," Perceval discovers a Red Knight gainsaying Arthur's fief by the traditional seizure of a cup from the court. Perceval believes that his mother promised him armor, and he demands that King Arthur give him the armor of the Red Knight.

> Give me the arms of [the Red Knight] whom I met outside the door [*porte*], who is carrying off [*porte*] your golden cup. (998–99)

The relationship between "arms" and "cup" is established by an often repeated linguistic commensuration (the pun/homonym on *porte*), which suggests an equal material exchange. He who regains the gainsaid cup will receive armor as recompense.[20]

Perceval "does not prize worth a chive" anything Arthur has to say about the theft of the cup and about the possible kinship of the Red Knight to Perceval (and to Arthur). Arthur's words are seeds that fall on infertile, or at least unwatered, land. Because he took the cup, the Red Knight loses his arms and life to Perceval. (In *Parzival*, too, the narrator hints that there is some kind of commensurability between the knight's armored life and the cup [161].) When he cannot easily remove the armor from the body of the dead knight, Perceval complains of King Arthur, whom he mistakenly believes to have given it to him. He asks Arthur's messenger to "give" him the armor at once and to carry (*portez*) the cup to the king. The cup is returned (*raporte*) by the gate (*la porte*) near which Perceval first espied the armor.

In the court Perceval's acquisition of the cup is described by the messenger as a kind of sale. To Arthur's question "Does the Red Knight like Perceval and prize him so much that he rendered the cup to him of his own will?" the messenger responds, "Rather the youth sold [*vandue*] it

---

Gilson, "La Mystique de la grâce dans la *Queste del saint Graal*," *Romania* 51 (1925): 321–47.

20. The exchange may be plotted thus:

OBJECTS EXCHANGED	WORDS ASSOCIATED WITH OBJECT
cope	*porte*, as "carry"
armes	*porte*, as "gate"

If *armes*:*porte*::*cope*:*porte*, and if *porte* = *porte* by homonym or pun, then *armes* = (or is exchangeable for) *cope* in the exchange relationship.

to him so dearly that he killed him." However, one of Arthur's court-iers, Keu, wickedly misled Perceval by telling him that Arthur gave (*donner*) Perceval the Red Knight's armor. *Don* means both "gift" and "promise"; Arthur conflates these two meanings, and arguing that "promising without giving" is villainy, he rebukes Keu for foul, un-charitable language. Soon after his uncharitable "gift" of armor to Per-ceval, Keu manifests in deed his lack of charity when he "gives a blow [*cop*]" to a maiden who speaks well of Perceval. This blow (*cop*) recalls the cup (*cope*) that played a role in the exchange of the Red Knight's armor for his life, and the *coup douloureux* from which the kingdom suffers. Perceval promises that he will repay Keu for this injury to the maiden, and the fool rejoices that Perceval will take revenge, which he associates with a commercial accounting: "The blow that he gave the maiden will be dearly sold and well paid for [*chier vandue*] and re-turned." As the *Account of the Grail* unfolds, the prediction of the fool comes true.

In the second passage, called "Three Drops of Blood on the Snow," some of the exchanges that began in "The Red Knight" are replayed with differences. Keu demands that the meditating Perceval come to the king: "You will come indeed, by my faith, or you will pay heavily for it." As the fool predicted, Perceval wounds the impolite Keu. When the polite Gawain is successful in his bid to communicate with Per-ceval, Keu accuses Gawain of selling words, as does a sophist, for coins. "Well do you know how to sell your words which are very fair and polished." By a trope that plays against the theme of merchantry, we are reminded of previous sales (1228, cf. 1265) and of Perceval's evaluations of words, which in this scene he has refused to speak. (When the charcoal burner told Perceval about Arthur's castle, Per-ceval did "not prize worth a penny" anything he heard [859–60, cf. 968–69].) The money metaphor in the *Account* reminds us that coins are useless in a wasteland, just as in a land of uncivilized or naive savages.

When Gawain has brought Perceval to Arthur, we learn that Per-ceval will now be measured against the "polite" and supposed "mer-chant" Gawain, and also that his new life as a worldly knight will be short-lived. Arthur senses divine destiny in the naive young man who distrusted King Arthur's own words (4566–75). This man will solve the economic problem of the wasteland by discovering the perfect gift, which only the divine King can give. That gift will rise, as in a perfect circle of simultaneous purchase and sale, above the taliations and retaliations that inform the earthly economy of the Knights of the Round Table.

An Exchange Contract

The purifier of a wasteland, like Jesus in the fallen world and Oedipus in plague-ridden Thebes, must be willing and able to give all. This will and ability to give develop rarely, if ever, in ordinary human beings. In the grail tales, however, certain exchanges seem to make such sacrifice possible. One such series of exchanges and contracts is associated with the motif of the broken sword.

The sword motif is a popular one in the grail tales. In Chrétien's *Account of the Grail*, for example, one sword is given to Perceval after he fails to ask the all-important question at the grail castle (a "blurred reminiscence of the common account in which a young man is presented with the fragments of a sword and is asked to unite them"), and another, the "Sword of the Strange Ring [*Renge*]," is the object of a crucial quest.[21] (The sexual aspect both of the "broken sword" or "wounded thigh" of the probably emasculated fisher king and of the "ring" that encloses the sword suggests the problem of sterility.)

Similarly, in the continuation by Pseudo-Wauchier the invalid king alludes to an unhappy blow (*coup*) from which the kingdom suffers and then tells Gawain that he will receive answers to his questions about "the sword broken in two" if he unites the two pieces. Gawain tries, but he cannot do it. Only Perceval, with the help of the blacksmith Trebuchet's sacrifice or exchange of his life, is able to re-solve, or solder together, the broken pieces of the sword.[22] The blacksmith's sacrifice solves both quest and question, and by some sort of retribution (life for *coup*), or balancing of the spiritual books, helps to redeem the wasteland.

21. This is the quest announced by the woman at Montesclaire. See R. S. Loomis, *Arthurian Tradition and Chrétien de Troyes* (New York, 1949), pp. 407, 414. Other swords include those of Gornemont and Gawain ("Escalibar," which is given to Perceval by Arthur).

22. In Manessier's continuation of the *Account of the Grail*, "the broken sword which Gauwain attempted to repair in the Grail Castle and which Perceval did repair becomes not only the instrument of Bran's death . . . but also the instrument of retribution upon his slayer" (Loomis, *Arthurian Tradition*, p. 413). This retribution,

In the *Quest of the Holy Grail* the sacrifice is carefully delineated. Here the sword is associated explicitly with swords mentioned in the Bible, and according to the "interpreters" who speak in the *Quest* itself, they represent writing or the Holy Word.[23] The written inscription on the scabbard of the sword in the boat announces that the sword is an agent of redemption, a kind of bill of exchange, and states the conditions under which the exchange can be made:

> The belt of the scabbard must not be unfastened save by a woman's hand, and she the daughter of a king and queen. She shall exchange [*fera eschange*] it for another, fashioned from that thing about her person that is most precious to her, which she shall put in this one's stead. (205–6)

Perceval's sister fulfills these conditions. Exhibiting a rare charity (*chierté*), she "changes" the ring (*renges*) of the sword for something dearer or better (*plus chiere*), her hair (226–27). Then she exchanges her life's blood. The tale has prepared us to expect this blood sacrifice: the inscription on the scabbard is written in letters red as blood (203, 206), the scabbard itself is named "Memory of Blood" (227), and when Perceval's sister meets the servants who seek to bleed maidens into a "blood dish," the servants' description of the maiden they seek coincides with the description inscribed on the scabbard (239).

In the *Quest*, then, the original sin (associated with Eve and Guinevere) is overcome by the spiritual union of Perceval's virgin sister with Galahad at the moment Galahad agrees to serve her. Lest we forget Perceval's sister and her sacrifices, the author reminds us of them at the end of the *Quest*. The boat in which Perceval, Galahad, and Bors laid the body of Perceval's sister floats up to greet them as they enter the holy city (275), a charitable City of God that rises above the cupidinous exchanges of the earthly cities of this world. The free sacrifice of a woman helps to resolder the broken sword of the realm. The sister helps to resolve the brother's question about and quest for the Holy Grail.

---

however, is another form of vengeance; it does not so much make up for past sins as add a new one to the books, to which new tribute must be paid. As Joël H. Grisward, "Le Motif de l'épée jetée au lac: *La Mort d'Artur et La Mort de Batradz*," *Romania* 90 (1969), esp. pp. 302, suggests, there is in many stories this identity of sword and person.

23. Cf. Rev. 1:10, Eph. 6:17, and Heb. 4:12.

Ideal and Real Estate

The grail tales were most popular during the historical transition from an ideology of royal largesse (in which one king visibly dispenses political rights and material goods in return for the obligation of his subjects) to two interrelated ideologies united by their difference from the ideology of largesse. These are the otherwise competing ideologies of charity (in which one man is said to dispense goods invisibly) and of democratic merchantry (in which two or more men exchange goods visibly).

FROM LARGESSE TO CHARITY

Largesse had been praised in the "olden times" (during which were composed the *chansons de geste*) when "material gift giving by a wealthy [royal ruler] had been part of the economy of an age of migration and conquest."[24] This chivalrous virtue of largesse, "the queen which illuminates all virtues," was associated with Charlemagne and with Alexander the Great, "the ideal type of feudal seigneur, who distributed . . . to his followers the lands and riches which he had won with their aid."[25] The period between the end of the Carolingian empire and the eleventh century, however, "was marked by . . . the gradual disappearance of the royal institutions which served to . . . provide a legal basis for the maintenance of social order."[26] By the twelfth and thirteenth centuries many feudal seigniors had lost their wealth, material gift giving had ceased to fulfill its political and economic function of ensuring obligation, and the feudal seignory was reworking the old ideology of chivalrous largesse to suit its new condition (and to decry the merchant class to which it was losing its wealth). Writers of this period emphasized that Alexander was a pagan. The large giver, they argued, cupidinously demands a countergift, or is assumed by the re-

---

24. Marian Whitney, "Queen of Medieval Virtues: *Largesse*," *Vassar Medieval Studies*, ed. Christabel Forsyth Fiske (New Haven, Conn., 1923), p. 185. See also Lester K. Little, *Religious Poverty and the Profit Economy* (London, 1978), esp. "From Gift Economy to Profit Economy."

25. Paul Meyer, *Alexandre le Grand dans la littérature française du moyen âge* (Paris, 1886; rpr. Geneva, 1970), 2:373.

26. Howard Bloch, "Wasteland and Round Table: The Historical Significance of Myths of Dearth and Plenty in Old French Romance," *New Literary History* 11 (Winter 1980): 270–71.

cipient to expect a countergift; largesse, as the new movement conceived it, is merely a species of cupidity.[27]

The commonplace of real royal largesse thus gave way to the topos of ideal charity. The tales about a freely flowing grail attempt to turn, or convert, their auditors from an economy of cupidity, such as that described by Guido del Duca in Dante's *Purgatory*, toward a free and infinite economy of grace, such as that described in *Purgatory* as one where there are no private possessions to separate individuals and where the enrichment of each charitably enriches all.[28]

Such a transition or conversion affects the economy of the poet. Poets sing for their supper; the *Account* has to provide Chrétien's listeners with spiritual nourishment in order to become Chrétien's own meal ticket. The poet seeks to beget in his listeners the truth of God, and to get from them a material reward; he wants to give spiritual charity ("God is charity," says the Prologue [47]) and to receive material charity. In order to earn a material return on the ideal "investment" that is his poem, Chrétien flatters his audience by implying that it is a fruitful and rich one (not a wasteland): his hearers are able to grow fruit from the seed of the truth that he dispenses, he says, and they are rich enough to pay him for his labor. Like Paul, who formulated the Christian theory of the apostle as a stewardly economist, Chrétien hopes that by distributing spiritual goods to others he will reap material goods.[29]

27. In the grail stories every action and relation partakes either of charity or of its opposite, cupidity. St. Augustine writes: "Charitatem voco motum animi ad fruendum Deo propter ipsum, et se atque proximo propter Deum; cupiditatem autem, motum animi ad fruendum se et proximo et quolibet corpore non propter Deum" (Augustine, *De doctrina Christiana* 3. 16 [10]). See D. W. Robertson, Jr., "The Doctrine of Charity in Medieval Literary Gardens: A Topical Approach through Symbolism and Allegory," *Speculum* 26 (1951): 24–49. Medieval doctrines of charity concern corporeal and spiritual alms (or corporeal and spiritual acts of mercy). St. Thomas writes (second part of *Summa Theologiae*, Question 32) that acts of charity can be alms given to the needy out of compassion or for the sake of God.

We might note that, even in acts of charity, expectation of reward is not always lacking. Georg Ratzinger (*Geschichte der kirchlichen Armenpflege* [Freiburg, 1884]), G. G. W. Uhlhorn (*Die christliche Liebestätigkeit in der alten Kirche* [Stuttgart, 1882–90]), Leon Lallemand (*Histoire de la charité* [Paris, 1902–12]), and W. Leise (*Geschichte der Caritas* [Freiburg, 1922]), agree that most medieval almsgiving seems to lack "genuine" altruism. Cf. the discussion of the *Decretals* of Gregory IX by Brian Tierney, *Medieval Poor Law: A Sketch of Canonical Theory and Its Application in England* (Berkeley, 1959), p. 141.

28. Dante, *Purgatorio* 14:82–86 and 15:46–82.

29. Paul suggests that he and his fellow apostles are distributors of the "liberal gift"

(Chrétien writes that Phelipes' material charity does or should differ from Alexander's largesse according to the tenets of the proverb "Let not thy left hand know the good that thy right hand doeth." The invisible heart [*cuer*], not the visible hand, is the touchstone by which giving is to be measured: "God sees all secrets and knows all the secret places in hearts [*cuers*] and bowels [*corailles*]."[30] Since the heart is invisible to all but God, charitable giving is a counterpart to esoteric writing and cannot confer on the giver the kind of public power or guilt-ridden obligation that largesse was once thought to have conferred.)

In the Christian economy, one facet of the truth to be revealed is charity. In *Purgatory*, for example, Virgil says that the questioning Dante will understand the paradisiacal economy only when he understands charitable giving.[31] Charity in much medieval literary theory is the divine truth that is revealed by interpretation of the surface meaning (*sensum*) of written works.[32] When Chrétien tells his book-distributing patron that "God is charity" (47), however, he reminds his larger audience, with some irony, that DEUS CHARITAS EST is the inscription on the face of a coin[33] like the tax penny Jesus suggested might be rendered to Caesar,[34] like the coins that the author of the *Account of the Grail* hopes the count will transfer to the poet.

FROM HOARD TO GRAIL

The connection between quests for the Holy Grail and for the Nibelung's Hoard fascinated Richard Wagner. In Wagner's operas this connection is suggested by similarities between Alberich, who in the *Rhinegold* forswears spiritual love in order to gain access to the Rhine-

---

or "relief of the saint" (2 Cor. 8–11), but at the same time Paul tries to convince the Corinthians to be as materially generous to him and to others as were the Macedonians (the countrymen of the *large* Alexander!). "There should be no reluctance, no sense of compulsion; God loves a cheerful giver" (9:6–7), he reads into the parable of the sower. Although Paul suggests that he distributes to men the "gift of God beyond words," then, he asks for material gifts, if not for himself, at least for others (8:10–24). It is not Paul but rather John (2 John 4:16) who spoke the words that Chrétien (47–50) attributes to Paul.

30. For *corailles* instead of *antrailles*, see *Percevalroman*, note on 36.

31. Dante, *Purgatorio* 14:76–78.

32. On charity and interpretation, see D. W. Robertson, Jr., "Some Medieval Literary Terminology with Special Reference to Chrétien de Troyes," *Studies in Philology* 48 (1951): 691.

33. For the motto see Stuart Mosher, "Coin Mottoes and Their Translation," *Numismatist*, May 1948, p. 329.

34. Matt. 22:17–21. Cf. Luke 20:21–25 and Mark 12:14–17.

gold, and Klingsor, who in *Parsifal* forswears bodily love (castrates himself) in order to gain access to the grail. These operas are Wagner's most famous treatments of the Nibelung's Hoard and the grail, but an early prose work (which does not deal with the renunciation of love), *The Wibelungen: World History as Revealed in Saga*, lays the mythological groundwork for a more acute social theory, which Wagner never followed through.[35]

In the *Wibelungen*, Wagner argues that the medieval topos of the Nibelung's Hoard combines ideal and real historical qualities. The gradual disappearance of the myth of the Nibelung's Hoard, says Wagner, corresponds to the appearance of the ideal topos of the Holy Grail, on the one hand, and to the real foundation of capitalist economy, on the other. He further argues that the myth of the Nibelung's Hoard is a German version of the primordial myth of the sun god. In this version the sun god, who captures the cornucopian sun for men, is replaced by a hero who captures the Nibelung's Hoard—the source of immeasurable power (*unermessliche Macht*), the cynosure (*Inbegriff*) of all earthly rule. Wagner found the cornucopian qualities of the hoard already described in the medieval *Nibelungenlied*: "Even if one had paid all the people in the world with it, it would not have lost a mark in value! . . . In among the rest lay the rarest gem of all, a tiny wand of gold, and if any found its secret he could have been lord of all mankind!"[36] The powers conferred by this hoard include the ability to dispense material things to every man and hence to rule all men. (The latter power is a consequence of the former insofar as dispensation leads to gratitude or obligation.) The topos of the grail, as Wagner discovered, is an ideal response to the waning of real feudal powers.

Wagner considers the historical relationship between the ideal right and the real power of the Frankish kings by studying how Chlogio, the first Frankish royal authority (fifth century A.D.) came to hold the real power and the ideal right to rule. Chlogio captured a treasure hoard from the Roman "Caesar" and became the German "kaiser." This treasure included a war chest containing both real matter (*realen Stoff*)

---

35. Richard Wagner, *Die Wibelungen: Weltgeschichte aus der Sage* [1848], in Wagner, *Gesammelte Schriften und Dichtungen*, 4th ed., 12 vols. (Leipzig, 1907), vol. 2. References are keyed to sections. Translations are adapted from Wagner, *The Wibelungen: World History as Told in Saga*, in *Richard Wagner's Prose Works*, trans. W. A. Ellis, 8 vols. (London, 1892–99), 7:257–98.

36. *Das Nibelungenlied*, nach der Ausgabe von Karl Bartsch, ed. Helmut de Boor (Wiesbaden, 1965), Âventiure 19:1123–24; translated as *The Nibelungenlied*, trans. A. T. Hatto (Baltimore, 1965), p. 147.

and insignia of power (*Machtzeichen*) with ideal import (*ideale Be-deutung*) (5). George Bernard Shaw and other critics have argued that the Nibelung's Hoard in Wagner's thought is merely money in its real, material aspect.[37] However, the hoard and money should be allied only insofar as money, like the hoard, is an ideal sign as well as a real thing. Not in the material power that money seems to be, but rather in the numismatic knot of material ingot with sign is the power of the hoard to be explained: the ruler's ring (*Herscherreif*) of the Nibelungen includes both the "metal bowels of the earth" and the true sign (*Wahrzeichen*) on it, both the real ("substructural") and the ideal ("super-structural") means of justifying it (6).[38]

The union of real and ideal, or physical and spiritual, occurred a second time in history, in the person of the Frankish King Charlemagne, during whose reign as the first Holy Roman Emperor (A.D. 800–814) the secular ruler and the religious ruler were reunited "as body and spirit of mankind" (9). Thereafter the union of material and ideal gradually dissolved: "the real embodiment [*reale Verkörperung*] of the hoard . . . fell to pieces" (10). Wagner argues that "as the landed property of the king was diminished, so the authority of the king was invested with a more and more spiritual meaning." "As the worldly order of the kingship lost in real estate [*reale Besitz*], it approached a more ideal development" (10). By the time of Frederick Barbarossa, who ruled during the period just preceding the writing of the grail tales (his reign ended in A.D. 1190), the kaiserhood had become little more than a pure idea (*reine Idee*). Frederick tried to bring the material aspect of the empire into line with the ideal aspect by enforcing the old claim (*Ansprach zur Geltung*) of the kaiserhood that, just as the sun is the source of all light, so the emperor is the source of all rightful possession. Frederick fought for the principle that:

> there can exist no right to any sort of possession or enjoyment, in all this world, that does not emanate from the king and need his hallowing by his feoffment or sanction: all property or usufruct

37. George Bernard Shaw, "The Perfect Wagnerite," in *Selected Prose*, ed. Diarmuid Russel (London, 1953); cf. Robert Donington, *Wagner's 'Ring' and Its Symbols* (London, 1963). Shaw notes that Fafnir, who might have become a "capitalist" after winning the treasure, remains a mere "hoarder."

38. The jewel ring in the story of the Nibelungen is a signet ring. A signet ring is composed of valuable metal and a seal, and the coin that it mints with its impress is likewise composed of a "real" thing (the metal ingot) and an "ideal" one (the politically authoritative seal).

not bestowed or sanctioned by the king is lawless in itself, and counts as robbery; for the kaiser enfiefs and sanctions for the good, possession, or enjoyment of all, whereas the unit's self-seized gain is a theft from all. (11)

But the kaiser was unable to overcome the developing urban merchant classes of northern Italy, who needed economic and legalistic freedom. Frederick Barbarossa, "the last emperor," eventually ceded independence to the commercial republics; having thus given up the hoard, he set out on a crusade for Asia, where he had heard that a divine priest-king governed through the nurture of the Holy Grail (12).

> The legend of the Holy Grail . . . makes its entry into the world at this time when the kaiserhood attained its more ideal direction and the Nibelung's Hoard accordingly was losing more and more in material wealth, to yield to a higher spiritual [*geistliche*] content. The Holy Grail . . . ranks [*gelten*] as the ideal [*ideele*] representative or follower of the Nibelung's Hoard (12).

The ideal aspect of the hoard thus "evaporated" into the realm of poetry, but its "sediment" remained on earth in the form of real property (*reale Besitz*). This material "residue," says Wagner, was the actual (*tatsächlichen*) property (13) of a new merchant class. For this class the grail legends had an ideal meaning at once commercial and religious. The free bourgeoisie of northern Italy took up the quest for the Holy Grail through ideal fiduciary forms. With the waning of the Middle Ages the bourgeois became a creditor, and, like Shylock in Venice, he turned from religion to finance and jurisprudence.

Checking Out the Eucharist

> When we really know the history of gold . . .
> as a medium of exchange . . . during the
> Middle Ages, a flood of light will be shed upon
> many hidden trends and connections which at
> present elude our understanding.
> MARC BLOCH[39]

Since the ancients, theorists of money and language have considered money to be a combination of inscription (sign) with inscribed thing, a combination or knot that recalls Wagner's description of the

39. Marc Bloch, "The Problem of Gold in the Middle Ages," *Land and Work in Medieval Europe*, trans. J. E. Anderson (Berkeley, 1967), p. 186.

Nibelung's Hoard as both ideal and real. The time of the grail legends was one of transition from economic realism to economic nominalism, in which the signifying *intellectus* was given greater emphasis than the material *res*.[40] With the nominalist theorists the intellectual idea (money) was separated conceptually from the real thing (ingot), the *intellectus* from the substantial *res*. "It was in the thirteenth century," writes Marc Bloch, "that the intrinsic value of money was separated from money of account."[41] As understood in the new theories, money is, as some modern scholars aver,[42] a kind of "floating signifier," but it is a signifier that does not so much "herald the future widespread development of paper money" as express the hope for a kind of disembodied Word or a blank check.

That the grail should be both symbol and thing, both representation and product, is, in this context, the most disturbing aspect of the grail tales. The quandary seems at first to be a theological one, but it is also ideological. The grail tales seem to inveigh against financial merchantry, but, as we shall see, they are active participants in the popular expression of it.

The problem arises when, following the lead of the tales themselves, we ask whether the grail is a member of the group of all ordinary worldly things (like a horn, or *cors*) or a thing not of this world (perhaps like Christ's body, or *corpus Christi*). If the grail is a member of the group of all worldly things, then it is homogeneous with its products and produces itself. (A horn of plenty may produce a horn.) If, on the other hand, the grail is a thing not of this world, then it is heterogeneous with its products and has the same relation to them as God has to the material wafer and wine into which and from which He is mysteriously metamorphosed during the Eucharist.[43] The grail tales raise

40. On this movement see Marc Bloch, *Esquisse d'une histoire monétaire de l'Europe* (Paris, 1954).

41. Marc Bloch, "Économie nature ou économie argent," *Annales d'histoire sociale* 5 (1933): 7–16. On "money of account" see C. Cipolla, *Money, Prices and Civilization in the Mediterranean World from the Fifth to the Seventeenth Centuries* (Princeton, 1956).

42. Howard Bloch, "Money, Metaphor, and the Mediation of Social Difference in Old French Romance," manuscript.

43. An influential etymology derives *Holy Grail* (*Saint Graal*) from the "real/royal blood" (*sang real*) of Jesus. On the Eucharist in the grail tales, and on the grail as graceful chalice, see E. Antichkopf, "Le Saint Graal et les rites eucharistiques," *Romania* 55 (1929): 175–94.

this problem of the genus of the grail and then skirt it by rhetorical conflation of the container with the contained, of the *cors* with the *corpus Christi*. (In one grail tale a man says, "For my thoughts are completed since I see the thing [the grail] in which all things are," but he fails to say whether one of the things he sees in the container is the container itself.)[44] The tales present the grail as being a thing both of this world and not of this world, or as being a thing both homogeneous and heterogeneous with all things. The grail, which is the source of all things, is the source of itself; to put it another way, one of the contents of the container that is the grail is the container itself.

But how can anything be both the symbol of all things and the source of them? The etymonic Word in the Gospel of Saint John suggests an answer, for in some Christian theology the problem of symbolization and production is expressed in terms of the relationship between God the Father and God the Son, who is sent to earth or made flesh. (Unlike the Jewish son of Abraham, who is saved by the appearance of a horn [*cor*], the Christian son is sacrificed as the redeemer of mankind.)[45] The problem implicit in the relation between *cors* and *corpus Christi* is thus not particular to the Middle Ages. The theological expression of the general quandary about homogeneity and heterogeneity, however, seems to have changed during the twelfth and thirteenth centuries. During this period, widespread debates about the Eucharist focused on the doctrine according to which a material thing becomes a source of spiritual as well as (or instead of) corporeal nourishment. (In the Greek hermetic tradition that influenced Wolfram, it is said that "the word is drunk, the food of truth," and that "the knowledge of divine essence is eating and drinking from the Word of God.")[46] The association of food and drink with the Word of God dominated the

44. *Estoire du Saint Graal* (Lancelot Grail Cycle), in *Le Saint Graal, ou Josef d'Arimathie: première branche des romans de la Table Ronde* (Robert de Boron), ed. E. Hucher (Le Mans, 1874–78), 2:306.

45. Thus the Christian horn of salvation (*keras sōtērias*, Luke 1:69) is a version of the horn that sprouts for David (P. 132:17). Compare "On that day I will cause a horn to spring forth to the house of Israel, and I will open your lips among them" (Ezek. 29:21). The horns of a ram caught in a thicket save the Son (Isaac) of the Father (Abraham) (Gen. 22:13).

46. Clement of Alexandria (Titus Flavius Clemens). Cf. Hermes Trismegistus, who concludes his *Asclepius* with "Our souls have had, if I may say so, their full share of food in the course of this discussion of things divine." Quoted by H. and R. Kahane, *Krater*, pp. 19–20.

41

debate about transsubstantiation (*metabolē*) even after the Fourth Lateran Council decreed in 1215 that "the body and blood of Jesus . . . are truly contained in the sacrament of the altar under the species of bread and wine, the bread and wine respectively being transsubstantiated into body and blood by divine power, so that in order to the perfecting of the mystery of unity we may ourselves receive from his [body, or *cors*] what he himself receives from ours."[47] Such a position helps to explain the confusion surrounding the scene at the grail castle in which, some say, the hungry Perceval secs a *cors* (host)—perhaps *corpus Christi*—within a *cor* (dishlike horn).

The monetary as well as the eucharistic expression of problems of homogeneity/heterogeneity in production was also changing during this period. The begetting of money (minting) and the getting of things by means of money (exchange) were among the most important medieval analogues for explaining the doctrine of the Trinity. Peter Abelard, for example, presents a nominalistic doctrine of the Trinity through a complex image involving sealing or minting. In associating the Father, Son, and Holy Ghost with one another, Abelard distinguishes among the metal of a seal, the impression on the seal (*sigillabile*), and its productive use as a seal (*sigillans*).[48] More important for understanding the economics of the Eucharist are the relationship of Eucharist to charity (*eucharistia* means "thanksgiving") and the controversial argument, proposed by Bernard Laum in *Holy Money* at about the time T. S. Eliot published *The Waste Land*, that money is inextricably linked with food-communion rituals like the eucharistic ones suggested in the grail tales.[49] "The first form of money," argues Laum, "was shared food, which for many centuries preceded the evolution of coinage. Coinage . . . had the same significance as the Grail—that of a sacred relic symbolizing a holy meal among a loyal fellowship."[50] In the medieval Church, tokens called *méreaux* were given to clergymen

47. William Edward Collins, *Encyclopaedia Britannica*, 11th ed., s.v. "Eucharist."

48. Peter Abelard, *Theologia*, in *Patrologiae cursus completus* [Series Latina], 178:97–102.

49. See Bernard Laum, *Heiliges Geld* (Tübingen, 1924), and T. S. Eliot, *The Waste Land* (1922). For English expositions of Laum's views on anthropology, see Paul Einzig, *Primitive Money* (London, 1949), and William H. Desmonde, *Magic, Myth, and Money* (New York, 1962).

50. Desmonde, *Magic, Myth, and Money*, pp. 21–22.

for participation in the mass; these tokens, which could be passed on to laymen and exchanged for ordinary food, were often visually indistinguishable from coins.[51] (See figure 9.)

Theories of metallic money tend to share with discussions of the Eucharist the problem of homogeneity and heterogeneity, or confusion of representation with production. It is unclear whether metallic money is a member of the group of commodities (a group that includes coins *qua* metal) or another kind of thing (a symbol). Nominalist theorists noted that coined money is not only a commodity (ingot) but also a symbol (inscription); money, like the Verbal Eucharist, seems to constitute a common or architectonic denominator for all things. This simultaneous homogeneity and heterogeneity in the relationship between money and commodity, or between inscription and thing, raises the same metonymic problem of genus that makes mysterious the grail, the Eucharist, and the Word. Indeed, if money were available in cornucopian quantities in a place where its purchasing power was not limited (a polar opposite to a wasteland), it would both be an exchange for all (other) things, hence the means of getting (purchasing) them, and seem, like a eucharistic meal ticket, to be the source of their begetting (production). GRATIA DEI OMNE DONUM ("Every gift is by the grace of God") is one of many numismatic inscriptions about such a purportedly subversive confusion of grace (*charis*) with money, of mercy with merchantry.[52]

The grail presents unique relationships, both between food and words and between shared food and money, that recall the topos of the money-speaking being (the Grimms' donkey, for example, or La Fontaine's dog). These beings do not speak words that eventually get the Word; instead, they beget by expectoration limitless numbers of gold coins or ingots. "Talk . . . all in gold," says Jonson's Subtle. "When a

---

51. The difficulty of distinguishing between *méreaux* (or *jetons de présence*), ordinary jettons, and coins has made it difficult for numismatists to date precisely the introduction of *méreaux*. The earliest extant discussion of *méreaux* in France dates from 1375. See A. Blanchet, *Manuel de numismatique française*, III (*medailles, jetons, méreaux*) (Paris, 1930). For the confusion of communion and monetary tokens, see the *méreau* inscribed "MO" ("Moneta") mentioned by G. F. Hill, in *Encyclopaedia of Religion and Ethics*, ed. James Hastings (New York, 1924), s.v. "Token," 12:358.

52. Stuart Mosher, "Coin Mottoes and Their Translation" (continued), *The Numismatist*, July 1948, p. 471.

man calls the cooler *psygeus*, what are we to do?" asks Athenaeus. "Why, pay him with a word of your own, as if you were exchanging money," as if every man were a mint of words and hence the center of an economy of abundance.[53]

Many early coins, tokens of an economy of scarcity, show types of grail-like cornucopiae (see figure 11). But the grail itself is more precisely a type of the topos of the resourceful, infinitely exchangeable, and inexhaustible purse, for which the Greek Midas before, and the medieval Fortunatus after, the twelfth century wished.[54] The topos of such a purse arises from an age unacquainted (or just beginning to become acquainted) with checks and credit, with mere "sign or . . . symbol" money, an age of which it can almost be said that "the gift of boundless wealth could [not] be made another way."[55] The grail is a literary species of the blank check, the Arabic *sakh*, introduced to Europe by Jewish merchants before the fall of Jerusalem to the Crusaders in 1099.[56] The authors of the earliest grail tales lived in trading centers, such as Troyes, where gathered Knights Templar and Jewish merchants. The Templars were financiers as well as crusaders, and their patron saint, Bernard, was associated with the Knights of the Round Table and with the argument that charity is the principal agent of redemptive conversion.[57] It is argued that Chrétien of Troyes and Kyot,

53. "Tischen deck dich, Goldesel und Knüppel aus dem Sack," in *Kinder- und Hausmärchen, gesammelt durch die Brüder [Jacob und Wilhelm] Grimm* (Munich, 1963), no. 36, in which a donkey spits gold pieces or coins (*Goldstücke*) (p. 221); La Fontaine, "Le Petit Chien qui secoue de l'argent et des pierreries," *Contes et Nouvelles* 3:13, in La Fontaine, *Oeuvres complètes* (Paris, 1954), vol. 1; Ben Jonson, *The Alchemist*, 4. 1. 24–30; and Athenaeus, *Deipnosophistae*, trans. C. B. Gulick, 7 vols. (Cambridge, Mass., and London, 1955–61), 497c. For jewels or gold from the mouth, see also Marian Roalfe Cox, *Cinderella: Three Hundred and Forty-five Variants* (London, 1893), esp. pp. 313, 508–10; and figure 10.

54. On the topos of the inexhaustible purse, see the brothers Grimm, *Teutonic Mythology*, trans. James Steven Stallybrass, 4 vols. (London, 1882–88), esp. pp. 871 and 976.

55. Charles H. Herford, *Studies in the Literary Relations of England and Germany* (Cambridge, 1886), p. 208.

56. On the *sakh*, see Fernand Braudel, *The Mediterranean World in the Age of Philip II*, 2 vols. (New York, 1976) 2:816–17.

57. On merchantry in Wolfram and Chrétien, see Otto Springer, "Wolfram's Parzival," pp. 238–39. Helen Mustard and Charles Passage, *Parzival*, p. xlv, argue that Wolfram's knights are the historical Knights Templar. On Saint Bernard, see Urban T. Holmes and Sister M. Amelia Klenke, *Chrétien, Troyes and the Grail* (Chapel Hill,

who Wolfram says told the original grail story, were Jewish converts. [58]

The "intellectual" bill of exchange and other early forms of "unreal," or "disembodied," wealth were ideally expressed in the vernacular literature as a powerful new mode of literary symbolization. An agent of transformation (transsubstantiation) that promised infinite delivery, the grail was a boundless gift, an all free for all, which marked the boundaries of wealth, a concept at once an intellectual help for financial wizards beginning to dabble in credit economics and a spiritual salve for the dying aristocracy. (See figure 12, in which the check [*sakh*] that is the grail appears to supercede the checkerboard [*scaccarium*] of the exchequer.)[59] The grail was the sign of an age not only of impoverished aristocrats who, like the sinner/fisher king, seemed to await redemption, but also of a new merchant class, which greeted graceful mercy and money (*merces*) as its special emblems. "Soon after its birth," writes Wagner's contemporary Karl Marx, "modern society pulled Plutus by the hair of his head from the bowels of the earth and greeted gold as its Holy Grail."[60] If not to all Christians, at least to the old knight and the new merchant, the grail seemed to "answer for all things."[61]

In the sense that they tend to reinterpret or translate previous Christian and pagan traditions, the vernacular grail tales unmask or protest against the order of things. The resourceful and abundant center of a wasteland suffering from material scarcity, the grail is a plenum of verbal meaning and a producer of material things, and it stands in the same relation to the words and actions it combines as does a cornucopia to the things it produces. It is a free and infinitely large gift, a blank check, which solves or resolves the quest and the question of the

---

N.C., 1959), p. 63. On charity as an agent of conversion, see Saint Bernard, sermon 79.

58. See Urban T. Holmes, "A New Interpretation of Chrétien's *Conte del Graal*" (*Studies in Philology* 44 [1947]: 453–76) and Raphael Levy, "The Quest for Biographical Evidence in *Perceval*" (*Medievalia et Humanistica*, fasc. 6 [1950]: 76–83).

59. See the treatise *Dialogus de Scaccario* (ca. A.D. 1179) by Richard, bishop of London and treasurer of England; printed in Thomas Madox, *History and Antiquities of the Exchequer* (London, 1711). Cf. figures 40 and 41.

60. Karl Marx, *Das Kapital*, in *Werke*, ed. Institut für Marxismus-Leninismus beim ZK der SED (Berlin, 1956–68), 23:146–47; translated as *Capital*, trans. S. Moore and E. Aveling (New York, 1967), 1:132–33.

61. Eccles. 10:19.

wasteland. A telling symptom of the societies from which the tales arose and which, in some measure, they decry, the hypothesis of the grail is part of the language of commodities that an unfree and finite economy speaks ventriloquistically through the mouths of theologians, economists, and poets.

3 / The Wether and the Ewe

VERBAL USURY IN
THE MERCHANT OF VENICE

SOON AFTER the vernacular grail tales first appeared in Europe, new financial institutions began to challenge the theories of production and representation by which the tales were informed. Fiduciary means disturbingly similar to the Christian cornucopia that is the grail affected more and more the livelihood and thinking of impoverished aristocrats and merchants. The topos of the *roi-pecheur* (sinner/fisher king) was displaced by the Venetian "merchant prince." This "royal merchant,"[1] both landed aristocrat and moneyed trader, sought the golden fleece with marine fleets supported by interest loans and insurance.[2] The divine store generated gratis from the Holy Grail was replaced conceptually by the natural store of alien shores, whose wealth had to be husbanded or exploited by expensive means. The problems of divine economy and of the difference between producer and product came to be considered in terms of nature and the tension between natural and unnatural representation and exchange.

1. William Shakespeare, *The Merchant of Venice*, ed. Brents Stirling (Baltimore, 1973), 3. 2. 239. References are to act, scene, and line. The English "royal merchant" made his appearance in economic history much later than the merchant prince of Venice. Samuel Johnson (Johnson, ed., *Plays of Shakespeare* [London, 1765]) notes that "this epithet ["merchant prince"] was, in our poet's time, more striking and more readily understood, because [Sir Thomas] Gresham was then commonly dignified with the title of the *royal merchant*."

2. E. D. Pettet, *"The Merchant of Venice* and the Problem of Usury," *Essays and Studies by Members of the English Association* 31 (1945): 19, notes that "by the time Shakespeare was writing his plays the feudal aristocracy had come to feel the full pinch of the century's momentous economic developments" and that "there was only one way out—the usurer." In Christopher Marlowe's *Doctor Faustus* (1604), America is the "golden fleece" (*Doctor Faustus*, ed. Sylvan Barnet, [New York, 1969], 1. 1. 124–25).

Generation, or production, is the principal topic of Shakespeare's *The Merchant of Venice*. In this play the quest for material and spiritual riches—for money and love—involves two related conceptual difficulties: the similarity between natural sexual generation and monetary generation, and the apparent commensurability (even identity) of men and money. The revelation of these difficulties depends for its dramatic expression on a series of bonds in which individuals and properties are exchanged for each other. The play generates a grand political and economic critique of human production that, in a few hours, runs through the whole gamut of familial and political associations.

Use, Ewes, and Iewes

Antonio is an unfortunate "royal merchant" whose purse is exhausted and whose personal part in this comedy is sad. This *roi-pecheur* claims that neither money nor love saddens him. Yet the only person he loves, Bassanio, owes him "in money and in love" (1. 1. 131) and is "plot[ting] to get clear of all the debts [he] owes." Bassanio would free himself from Antonio, whose present lack of funds diminishes Bassanio's once "noble rate" of living. He would attach himself to one more "worthy" than Antonio.[3] Antonio offers to aid Bassanio with "[his] purse, [his] person" (138), but, as Bassanio already knows, these are insufficient. All that Antonio can do is borrow a purse for his friend by hazarding a vital part of his person.

Need to supplement oneself or one's own thus leads to borrowing and to tension between two ideas about moneylending. The first idea (that of the Greeks) focuses on breeding and the relationship of monetary generation to animal generation. The second idea (that of the Hebrews) focuses on the classification of groups of human beings and the laws concerning bonds that divide and join them together. These ideas are elucidated in the interview between Antonio, who says that his custom is neither to give nor to take unfair "advantage" or "excess," and Shylock, whose means of livelihood is usury.

"Few [persons]," writes Francis Bacon, "have spoken of usury use-

---

3. Throughout the play, *worth* refers both to monetary, or commercial, and to human value. See, for example, 1. 1. 35, 36, 61, and 118. Compare the similar ambiguity of *sure*, *good*, and *credit*.

fully."[4] Shakespeare's Shylock is one of them. Shylock is not a miser of words (which is what Mark Van Doren calls him), but rather (as Sigurd Burckhardt suggests) a user of words.[5] To my knowledge, no one since the medieval era has devoted attention to the category of verbal usury in jurisprudence, rhetoric, and philosophy. (The phrase "verbal usury" has been consistently overlooked even by compilers of dictionaries.) Yet "verbal usury" is an important technical term in the Jewish Talmud, in the Christian church fathers, and in the Islamic Traditions. There it refers to the generation of an illegal—the church fathers say unnatural—supplement to verbal meaning by use of such methods as punning and flattering.[6]

Shylock uses Antonio's words "I do never use it" (1. 3. 66) to generate by a pun an argument that would enlarge any debate about "use" to include consideration of the human genealogy of "Iewes" (as Shakespeare spelled *Jews*)[7] and also the animal generation of "ewes." Thus he supplements the principal meaning of "use." The genealogy, as we shall see, defines divisions between the Jewish and other peoples, and the generation of ewes serves to locate monetary generation in relation

4. Francis Bacon, "Of Usury," essay no. 41 in *Essays or Counsels, Civil and Moral,* in *The Works of Francis Bacon,* ed. J. Spedding, R. L. Ellis, and D. D. Heath, 15 vols. (Boston, 1860–64), 12:218. Hereafter this edition of Bacon will be referred to as *Works.*

5. Mark Van Doren (*"The Merchant of Venice:* An Interpretation," *Shakespeare* [New York, 1939]) argues that Shylock "is always repeating phrases, half to himself, as misers do—hoarding them if they are good." Cf. Sigurd Burckhardt (*Shakesperean Meanings* [Princeton, 1968], pp. 214–15).

6. For the Talmud, see *Baba Mezi'a* 75a–75b: "R. Simeon said: There is a form of verbal interest" (*Baba Mezi'a,* trans. Salis Daiches and H. Freedman [1935], Mishnah on p. 434 and Gemara on p. 435; in *The Babylonian Talmud,* ed. I. Epstein [London, 1935–48]). Thomas Patrick Hughes (*A Dictionary of Islam* [London, 1896], s.v. "Usury") notes that "in the Traditions, Muhammad is related to have said:—'Cursed be the taker of usury, the giver of usury, the writer of usury, and the witness of usury, for they are all equal' (*Sahīhu Muslim, Bābu 'r-Riba'*)." For the Christian church fathers, see note 50.

7. William Shakespeare, *The Merchant of Venice: A New Variorum Edition,* ed. H. H. Furness, 12th ed. (Philadelphia, 1916). *Jew* is derived from the Hebrew *Yehuda* and *Yudah,* the son of *Yakov* (Jacob), to whom Shylock refers in his speech about "ewes" and "use." Cf. the similarity between the sounds *ieu* in *adieu* and *Ju* in *Jude* in *Love's Labour's Lost,* ed. Richard David (London, 1968), 5. 2. 620. For the position that the Christian Portia, if not the Jew Shylock, pronounces *Jew* with the modern sound of *j,* see Kökeritz's phonetic transcription of Portia's "quality of mercy" speech (Helge Kökeritz, *Shakespeare's Pronunciation* [New Haven, Conn., 1953], pp. 354–55).

to animal generation. As the Jew uses moneys (which Bacon calls "[the tokens current and accepted] for values") to supplement principals, so he uses puns to exceed the principal meanings of words (which Bacon calls "the tokens current and accepted for conceits").[8]

Shylock argues from Genesis that, as Jacob's management of the sexual generation of lambs by Laban's "ewes" is natural, so too is the generation of "use" by money.[9] He compares "[sexual] generation" with monetary generation or usury. "Ewes" and "rams," he implies, are like monetary principals, and "lambs" are like monetary "interest" or "use" (1. 3. 74–86). Antonio tries to argue against Shylock's position by suggesting that "gold and silver" differ from "ewes and rams" (91). Yet Shylock did not argue that metals are generative (as did many alchemists),[10] but rather that, as Saint Bernardino of Siena says, "money as capital has a creative power [quandam seminalem rationem]."[11] Antonio thus misses the point of the Jew's analogy. Antonio does not use even the traditional Aristotelian and Thomist argument against the analogy between reproduction and monetary use;[12] he does not argue

8. Francis Bacon, The Advancement of Learning, 6.1 (Works, 9:110); cf. De augmentis scientiarum, 6.1 (Works, 2:409–27).

9. Cf. Gen. 30:32–42.

10. As reported by Ibn Khaldûn (The Maqaddimah, An Introduction to History [1377], 3 vols., trans. Franz Rosenthal [Princeton, 1967]), At-Tughra'i compares "the alchemical process ["the generation and creation of gold and silver"] with the individual similar instances noticed in nature, such as the (spontaneous) generation of scorpions, bees and snakes" (3:277). Ibn Khaldûn, who aimed to refute all alchemy, notes that "the alchemical treatment is . . . [properly] called a 'sterile treatment'" (3:279), as Antonio suggests that money is sterile and cannot breed; but Ibn Khaldûn, unlike Antonio, is careful to distinguish gold and silver from money, even when considering the scarcity of the precious metals and the role of these metals as "the standard of value by which the profits and capital accumulation of human beings are measured" (3:277).

11. Bernardino (1380–1444), quoted in Alfred von Martin, Sociology of the Renaissance, introd. Wallace K. Ferguson (New York, 1963), p. 49.

12. Aristotle objects to the identification of monetary offspring with natural offspring. He argues, for example, that "currency came into existence merely as a means of exchange; usury tries to make it increase [as though it were an end in itself]. This is the reason why usury is called by the word we commonly use [tokos]; for as the offspring resembles its parent, so the interest bred by money is like the principal which breeds it, and [as a son is styled by his father's name, so] it may be called 'currency the son of currency.' Hence we can understand why, of all modes of acquisition, usury is the most unnatural" (Aristotle, Politics, trans. H. Rackham [Cambridge, Mass., and London, 1967], 1258). For the identification of monetary offspring with natural offspring in Shakespeare, see Pompey's remark in Measure for Measure, ed. J. W. Lever (London, 1967), 3.2.5–7: "Twas never merry world since, of two usuries, the merriest [sexual] was put down, and the worser [monetary] allowed by order of law."

that, as Francis Bacon ironically puts it, "it is against nature for money to beget money,"[13] or, as Luther says, that "money is the sterile thing."[14] Shylock wants to discuss usury in these Greek and Christian terms, but he is thwarted because Antonio cannot or will not recognize any difference between a gold or silver coin and any other piece of gold or silver.

Antonio says that he wants Shylock to lend him money, not according to "nature," but according to Jewish law:

> . . . lend it not
> As to thy friends—for when did friendship take
> A breed of barren metal of his friend?—
> (1. 3. 128–30)

Antonio refers to the Jewish legal distinction between lending to a "brother" or fellow Jew and lending to an "other."[15] If Antonio were a Jew, suggests Antonio, Shylock would lend money to him gratis. (Tubal will lend money gratis to Shylock, who, like Antonio, does not himself have sufficient funds for Bassanio.) Antonio does not seem to understand that this Jewish distinction between brother and other is essentially connected with the problem of natural generation about which he insists that Shylock be silent. He does not see that the only way to determine who is a brother and who is an other is to determine the generation of every one. Such a determination was the aim of Shylock's interrupted genealogy of the Jews, which prefaced his tale about the generation of ewes. It was meant to distinguish between Jews and non-Jews.

---

13. Francis Bacon ("Of Usury," *Works*, 12:218) writes that "many have made witty invectives against usury. They say . . . that it is against nature for money to beget money and the like. . . ." Nicholas Oresme, "De monete" (in *The "De Moneta" of Nicholas Oresme and English Mint Documents*, ed. Charles Johnson [London, 1956], p. 25) writes that "it is monstrous and unnatural that an unfruitful thing should bear, that a thing specifically sterile, such as money, should bear fruit and multiply of itself."

14. "Pecunia est res sterilis" (Martin Luther, *Tischreden*, 6 vols. [Weimar, 1912–21], vol. 5, no. 5429).

15. "Thou shalt not lend upon usury to thy brother. . . . Unto a stranger thou mayest lend upon usury." (Deut. 23:19–20). Cf. Deut. 28:12 and Lev. 25:35–37. In the late sixteenth century Henry Smith wrote: "Of a stranger, saith God thou mayest take usury; but thou takest usury of thy brother; therefore this condemneth thee, BECAUSE THOU USETH THY BROTHER LIKE A STRANGER" ("The Examination of Usury: The First Sermon," in *The Works of Henry Smith*, 2 vols. [Edinburgh, 1866–67], 1:97–98). See Benjamin Nelson, *The Idea of Usury: From Tribal Brotherhood to Universal Otherhood*, 2nd ed. (Chicago, 1969).

When Jacob grazed his uncle Laban's sheep—
This Jacob from our holy Abram was,
As his wise mother wrought in his behalf,
The third possessor; ay, he was the third—
    (1. 3. 67–70)

Abraham fathered Isaac who fathered Jacob. Jews suppose that they are the descendants of Jacob. (Shylock often confuses himself with his forefather Jacob. The folio reads, "I, he was the third—"; and Jacob's first wife, Leah, was the namesake of Shylock's late wife. Leah was the sister of Rachel, for whose hand in marriage Jacob husbanded Laban's ewes.) The argument is complicated by the fact that the two successions—through Isaac and Jacob—to which Shylock refers were challenged. Ishmael, Isaac's older half-brother by Abraham and Hagar, was, according to some, robbed of his birthright. Muslims—the Prince of Morocco, the Turks, the Moorish woman pregnant by Launcelot, and Launcelot, who is called "Hagar's offspring" (2. 5. 42)— suppose that they are the descendants of Ishmael. Esau, by a similar argument, was robbed of his birthright by Jacob, his younger twin brother, who tricked him with a bit of clever merchantry. He exchanged food, which sustains an individual's life, for the possession of the lifeline of the Jewish tribe.[16]

Thus Shylock's discussion in terms of monetary use of the clever Jew's management of the sexual generation of ewes (his forefathers were shepherds as his brothers are moneylenders) is essentially connected with his discussion of the sexual generation of Iewes themselves. By speaking of the generation of Jews, Shylock is distinguishing precisely between others and brothers. Antonio fails to see the relationship between breeding and both the division of animals into species and the division of the human species into linguistic, racial, religious, and other groups.

For a Christian, such as we suppose Antonio to be, a brother is supposed to be any descendant of Adam and not, as for a Jew, a descendant of Jacob. For a Christian there is no need to know a man's individual genealogy to determine whether he is a brother. Yet the customs and

---

16. Compare this with the scene between Launcelot and old Gobbo (2. 2), which parodies the biblical scene in which Jacob dispossesses Esau by "stealing" his father's blessing. Also compare the byplay with Gobbo/Isaac's blindness and Launcelot/Esau-Jacob's hairiness (2. 2. 68–91).

the laws of the white, Christian Venetians and the practice of Belmont discriminate against others in more extreme ways than does Shylock's distinction between human brothers and others who are human. Shylock does treat Antonio as if he were from a group of human beings other than his own Jewish one, but Antonio treats Shylock as if he were from a species of animal other than the human one (a dog). Not to be a Jewish brother is to be less alien to a Jew than not to be a brother is to a Christian. Does Antonio treat Shylock as an animal because he believes that Shylock has some characteristics of the canine or of the "ewe-ish" species or that he lacks some characteristics of the human species?[17] Or is it because Antonio conflates special with tribal characteristics, and so believes that the difference between a human being and another animal is identical to the difference between a member of one's own tribe (a racial, religious, or familial group) and a member of another tribe? If the latter, then Antonio has transformed the Jewish distinction between human brothers (members of the Jewish tribe), from whom one cannot take interest, and human strangers (members of any other tribe), from whom one can take interest. He has changed it to a distinction between those beings whose religion is Christianity (a tribe that proselytizes and is theoretically "universal" or at least "humanist") and those whose religions are other than Christianity (in our play Judaism and Islam) and who are, on that account, nonhuman, though convertible to Christianity and to human being. Antonio may be one of those people who, if he should say "All men are my brothers," might well mean "Only my brothers are men, all others are animals," or even "Citizens of Italian states (Venice and Belmont) are human, but citizens of other states (Morocco, Turkey, and, if there were such a place, Jewdom) are animals."

If Shylock should wish to lend money to Antonio as if Antonio were a brother to all Jews (descended from Jacob) or as if Shylock were a

17. That Shylock has some characteristics of the canine species is suggested in terms of his sexual generation; Gratiano says that Shylock was produced by the "infusion" of the soul of a wolf "hanged for human slaughter" into the body of the "unhallowed dam" who was pregnant with the foetus Shylock (4. 1. 133–38). The infusion of the damned wolf into Shylock's dam is meant to explain Shylock's "wolfish" desires and perhaps also his failure to accept the Christian distinction between the naturalness of generation by dams (ewes) and the unnaturalness of generation by metal or money (use). That Shylock lacks some qualities of the human species is suggested by the Duke when he argues that one characteristic of human being is that any human— including even Tartars and Turks—would pity Antonio (4. 1. 17–33).

Christian brother to all men (descended from Adam), he would lend Antonio money without interest, but he might well exact, as Bacon reminds us that good Christians did, a monetary or corporeal penalty if the loan were not paid on time.[18] Perhaps a monetary penalty would be condemned as an unnatural offspring by a zealot like Antonio, who seems to condemn even marine insurance.[19] Only by taking no interest and substituting a corporeal penalty, then, could Shylock be or appear to be brotherly (gentile) to Antonio. This is what he does. To buy Antonio's friendship Shylock extends this kindness: he will lend him money and "take no doit / of usance" (1. 3. 136–37). He who spoke of the sexual "deed of kind" between animals (81) says that he will lend Antonio money as though he were a kind kinsman to him (138–39). Adapting the Christian method of securing loans, Shylock announces that he will take as a conditional surety an obligation to pay a corporeal penalty, a pound of flesh. The merchant Antonio, who assured his friend of funds, is very sure of the safe return of his uninsured commercial ventures, and Shylock allays the Christians' fears of danger by insisting that to a Jew "a pound of man's flesh taken from a man is not so estimable, profitable neither, / As flesh of muttons, beefs or goats"

18. John Comyns, A Digest of the Laws of England, 8 vols. (New York, 1824–26), 8:846. A pecuniary penalty was usually not considered interest because it was due only if the debt was not paid on time. Antonio would have done better to pay interest (in the Jewish manner) rather than to forfeit a pound of flesh (in an extreme version of the Christian manner). Of the Christian practice of disallowing interest but allowing securities, Francis Bacon writes: "As for mortgaging, or pawning, it will little mend the matter; for either men will not take the pawns without use, or if they do, they will look precisely for the forfeiture. I remember a cruel monied man in the country that would say, The devil take this usury, it keeps us from forfeitures of mortgages and Bonds" ("Of Usury," Works, 12:220).

19. It is odd that Antonio does not insure his ships. Marine insurance was common in Venice by the fifteenth century and in England by the sixteenth. Sir Nicholas Bacon suggests, in his address to Queen Elizabeth's first parliament (1559), that "the wise merchant in every adventure of danger give[s] part [of his purse] to have the rest assured." Perhaps Antonio leaves his ships uninsured because he is an unwise merchant who is too sure of their return or because the insurers he may have consulted are too unsure of their return (see 1. 3. 12–28). Perhaps his stated policy against lending or borrowing for profit extends to the institution of insurance, which some thinkers connect conceptually and historically with monetary interest. Demosthenes thus describes the historical origin of insurance: "Money was advanced on a ship or cargo, to be repaid with large interest if the voyage prosper, but not repaid at all if the ship be lost, the rate of interest being made high enough to pay not only for the use of the capital, but for the risk of losing it" (Encyclopaedia Britannica, 11th ed., s.v. "Insurance").

(161–63). The flesh of ewes is worth more (to one who is not a human cannibal or a man-eating dog) than flesh of man. By the terms of the contract, then, Shylock substitutes, for the use he would usually take, a conditional security on something supposedly worth less than even ewe's flesh.

Antonio would not speak of use—ewes and Iewes. But the discussion of usury and sexual generation that Antonio would not pursue is soon enacted in the related terms of a series of exchanges of a purse (three thousand ducats) for a part of a person (a pound of flesh) or for a whole person (since the part may be vital). The apparent commensurability between persons and purses that this enactment reveals turns out to be more typical of Christian law, which allows human beings to be purchased for money, than Jewish "iustice" and practice, which disallow it.

From Courtship to Court

The suitors to the person and purse of Portia believe that the trial by caskets is a hazardous gamble like most commercial ventures and loans. The inscriptions on the caskets would seem to support their opinion. Portia's father, however, established the trial to discover a real man for Portia, or at least a suitable one. The inner mettle of the suitors is supposed to be tested by how well each suitor surmises from the outsides of the three metallicly different caskets what the insides contain. Metals—including the silver and gold ones that Antonio said were useless—are supposed to have the useful role of distinguishing the right man for Portia to marry.

Most of Portia's suitors are said to be unmanly, and all are threatened with being unmanned. They are unmanly in that they are, in Portia's language, mere "beasts." Portia disqualifies them from Mankind on the basis of outward characteristics, such as type of clothing and complexion. She does not consider inward characteristics as measures of Man or of the men who court her: "If [the Prince of Morocco] have the condition of a saint and the complexion of a devil [black], I had rather he should shrive me than wive me" (1. 2. 120–22). Her tendency to banish persons from the human species or from the male sex is checked only in jest: "God made [Monsieur Le Bon, who is 'every man in no man'], and therefore let him pass for a man" (1. 2. 52–53). Yet we know that being divinely created does not mean that an animal is a man. God made females as well as males and animals as well as humans. Only knowledge of an animal's ontogeny and of its species' phylogeny can determine whether it is a man, a horse, a monkey, a dog, a ewe, or something else. Shylock claims to have access to such knowledge: for him, men are the animals descended from Adam (*Adam* means "man") and Jews are the men descended from Jacob.

Among the characteristics Portia heeds is language. Language is both a bond and a barrier between men. The ability to speak is a characteristic that binds men together into a species, but men speak different languages. Men who speak only one language are bound together by their language, but they are barred from speaking with men who speak any other. Because Portia has hardly "a poor pennyworth in the English" and her English suitor "hath neither Latin, French nor Italian" for example, the Englishman is to her only a counterfeit of a man: "He is a proper man's picture, but alas! who can converse with a dumb-show?" (64–68). The ability to speak language may distinguish men from the (other) animals, but inability to speak a particular language may make one man as dumb to another man as to any other animal.

The suitors that are, to Portia, not even men are threatened with being legitimately unmanned. Should a suitor choose the wrong casket, he must promise never to generate within the bonds of wedlock his own flesh and blood. (2. 1. 41–42). He will be made as barren as Antonio believes metal to be. His legitimate genealogical bloodline (if not the flesh and blood of his own body) will be cut. He will become, in this legal sense, a castrate.

A black man, outside of whom flows a white robe, is the first to choose. The Prince of Morocco seeks the picture of Portia inside one of the caskets. He must tell the substance from the superficies.

The outside of each casket is like that of a coin and also like that of an inscribed ring: all these items are composed of metal and of an inscription impressed into it. We have seen that failure to distinguish between coins (ducats) and the metals of which they are only partially composed (gold and silver) was associated with Antonio's dangerously hasty dismissal of Shylock's words about monetary generation. Here the "golden mind" (2. 7. 20) of Morocco considers each inscribed metal object before him in terms both of its inscription and of its metal. He chooses "the saying graved in gold" (36) and, on the basis of a numismatic analogy that confuses the impressed type on a coin (an angel) with what he hopes to find inside the casket (an "angel"), he chooses gold (55–59). The skull that he finds in the engraved gold casket comes from the grave. Morocco thus learns, from the written scroll that accompanies this "carrion Death," that he must now be as barren, legally speaking, as Antonio argued that gold was.

In this context, what is striking about the next suitor's method of choosing is that he considers each casket only in terms of its inscription. Arragon "assume[s] desert" (2. 9. 50) by coining himself with "the stamp of merit" (38) but without considering the metal of which the coinlike silver is made. Arragon is "sped," yet he is allowed to "take what wife [he] will to bed" (69). Unlike the black Muslim, the white Christian is allowed to try to generate kin in wedlock.

The third trial is that of Bassanio, he in whom outside appearance and inside reality are most unlike. He uses words, clothing, and gifts to dress up his suit.[20] Portia, who judges men by their glister or lackluster, has chosen for herself this being with a white complexion and with a desire for glistering gold, but she fears that the seeker of gold and silver may choose a casket made of one of the metals he seeks. Though bound to her father's will (which curbs her will) and to the properties that it promises, she planned nevertheless to mislead the young German (1. 2. 87–91) and now educates Bassanio to choose the lead casket.

To help Bassanio, Portia orders music to be played. This will have the effect of seasoning Bassanio, making him more royal and less merchantlike, more like

> . . . young Alcides, when he did redeem
> The virgin tribute paid by howling Troy
> To the sea monster.
> (3. 2. 55–57; compare 2. 1. 32–35)

Then follows a suggestive song about the generation ("breeding," "begetting," "engendering") of fancy, whose first lines end with words that rhyme with "lead" and whose last line "ring[s] fancy's knell" (3. 2.

---

20. Bassanio is even careful to instruct others in the use of words. For example, he fears that Gratiano is so "bold of voice" that he may cause Bassanio to be unsuccessful in Belmont (2. 2. 171–75; cf. 1. 1. 114–18). Although he allows Gratiano to "put on [his] boldest suit of mirth" in Venice, he tells Gratiano that in Belmont he should "put on sober habit," "talk with respect" and be "like one well studied in a sad ostent" (2. 2. 175–83). Cf. Antonio's impatience with Bassanio's angling use of words (1. 1. 153–60).

63–72). Bassanio, who still uses fanciful speech and dress, now learns to say that, or act as though, he dismisses them.

> So may the outward shows be least themselves;
> The world is still deceived with ornament.
> In law, what plea so tainted and corrupt
> But being seasoned with a gracious voice,
> Obscures the show of evil?
>   (3. 2. 73–77)

Bassanio thus criticizes deceivers who use ornament to their evil purpose, perhaps as Antonio believed that Shylock used scriptures. Bassanio does not seem to consider how he himself uses and has used words and gold to purchase "valor's excrement" (87). Nor does he consider that a seasoned voice may generate good as well as bad shows. Portia's song, for example, "seasoned" him to choose the lead casket in the courtship trial (cf. 5. 1. 107–8), and Balthasar-Portia's voice will obscure Shylock's case in the courtroom trial.

Bassanio, like the losing suitors, considers the problems of exchange about which the inscriptions on the caskets are written. Unlike them, however, he does not consider the inscriptions themselves. He pays heed, significantly, only to the metals (which is what Antonio did when he failed to distinguish between coin and precious metal). Bassanio calls gold a "hard food for Midas" (3. 2. 102)—who turned his daughter into gold—and silver a "pale and common drudge / 'Tween man and man" (103–4). As Karl Marx reminds us, silver is money, the intermediating "drudge" that pays Launcelot and that Bassanio has borrowed to finance his courtship,[21] and it is an ostentatious ornament like the silvery and beguiling tongue of "eloquence" (3. 2. 106).[22]

---

21. Karl Marx, *Ökonomisch-philosophische Manuskripte aus dem Jahre 1844*, in Karl Marx and Friedrich Engels, *Werke*, ed. Institut für Marxismus-Leninismus beim ZK der SED (Berlin, 1956–68), Ergänzungsband, pt. 1, pp. 562–67; translated as *Economic and Philosophical Manuscripts*, in Marx, *Early Writings*, trans. T. B. Bottomore (London, 1963), pp. 189–94.

Launcelot is the major go-between for religion and sex. He has left the Jew (Shylock) and gone over to the Christian (Bassanio), and has discussed with Jessica the possibility of her going over from Judaism to Christianity. He carries messages between Jews and Christians: a letter from Bassanio to Shylock that bids Shylock to supper; a letter from Jessica to Lorenzo that contains her instructions for elopement, theft, and disguise; and a message from Lorenzo to Jessica notifying her that Lorenzo will not fail her. For his going between Jessica and Lorenzo, he takes money each time. On Launcelot and the mixture of races, see note 55.

22. Cf. Burckhardt (*Shakespearean Meanings*, p. 209) and Sigmund Freud ("The

Inside the lead casket he chooses, Bassanio finds the portrait of Portia. But as he has learned to claim cunningly to set aside the "seeming truth which cunning puts on / To entrap the wisest" (3. 2. 100–101), so he knows not to be trapped into confusing this mere "counterfeit" of Portia with the genuinely valuable thing itself.[23] He would win the wealthy "lady of substance," and so presents Portia with his "title" to her: "I come by note"—he means the portrait—"to give and to receive" (140). The "note" is a kind of ticket to the person and purse of Portia that Bassanio, as master of etiquette, would "confirm, sign and ratify" with a kiss.

Portia promises Bassanio the "full sum of me" (157). She is a "fulsome ewe" (compare 1. 3. 82). Despite all the talk about lead, Portia is not bred so "dull" as lead (3. 2. 162). Like gold and silver ducats as the Iewe Shylock interprets them, she can generate riches.

But a fertile ewe, unlike a monetary principal, needs a potent ram to generate offspring. Herein lies an essential connection between the two major plots of the play. The marriage formula must be reciprocal. Bassanio cannot reciprocate, cannot give, because he is not his own man. Bassanio is about to win the ewe's "golden fleece" (3. 2. 241, compare 1. 1. 170), but Antonio's marine "fleets," his means of livelihood, which were to return gold for the Jew, are lost, and so too may be his life. The danger to Antonio—and the "paper" in which Antonio, who would not use money, encourages Bassanio to "use [his] pleasure" (3. 2. 320)[24]—compels Bassanio to admit that his courtship strategy depended not only on the gentleman's blood that circulates in his veins but also on Antonio's bond and the Jewish money that circulated to him. He is compelled to reveal to Portia that he is already engaged:

> . . . When I told you
> My state was nothing, I should then have told you
> That I was worse than nothing; for indeed

Theme of the Three Caskets," in *Collected Papers*, ed. J. Riviere and J. Strachey, 5 vols. (London, 1949–50), 4:244–56.

23. Bassanio's earlier description of Portia's hairs as the "golden fleece" (1. 1. 170) was meant to persuade Antonio to support his venture. Now Bassanio tries to ensure that he will not be misled by a similar artifice: "Here in her hairs / The painter plays the spider, and hath woven / A golden mesh t'entrap the hearts of men" (3. 2. 120–22).

24. For the sexual meanings of *use* see *Oxford English Dictionary*, s.v. "Use," sb., 3b, and v., 7c. *Use* is a standard term for sexual enjoyment in Shakespeare's *Sonnets*.

I have engaged myself to a dear friend,
Engaged my friend to his mere enemy
To feed my means
(3. 2. 258–63)

Thus Portia learns that Bassanio did not give and hazard all he has (as the inscription on the lead casket, so far ignored by the couple, demanded). He hazarded only the purse of Shylock and the person of Antonio.[25] Antonio, rather than Portia, is his "dearest friend" (292). Portia wanted to marry Bassanio right away (303), as her father required (2. 9. 5–6), but now she may fear that her interference in the trial by caskets resulted in her getting a suitor who is (as yet) unsuitable. She encourages him to leave before they marry.[26]

The commercial fate and love of Antonio have thus "interposed" between Portia and Bassanio. The problem of monetary "excess" (1. 3. 58) that Shylock and Antonio discussed in the bond scene has become the problem of "excess" or "surfeit" in the love between Bassanio and Portia (3. 2. 111–14, 157).[27] The courtship cannot be completed until the bond between Shylock and Antonio, which made the courtship possible, is nullified in court, until Bassanio's engagement to Antonio is somehow voided. The marriage bond cannot be concluded until the commercial bond is canceled. In the process of its cancellation the nature of the marriage bond and of human bondage in general will be relentlessly explored.

My Purse, My Person

Exchanges involving persons include (a) those in which a human life is traded for a human life, and (b) those in which a human life is bought

25. The associations of *purse* with *person* and of both terms with *use* occur in other works of Shakespeare. In *2 Henry IV*, for example, the Chief Justice accuses Falstaff: "You have . . . made her serve your uses both in purse and person" (*2 Henry IV*, ed. A. R. Humphreys [London, 1967], 2. 1. 112–15).

26. Bassanio "dispatch[es] all business and [is] gone" (3. 2. 322) without actually marrying Portia. English law recognized two kinds of spousals: *sponsalia per verba praesenti*, which was legally binding, and *sponsalia per verba de futuro*, which was not binding (Henry Swinburne, *A Treatise of Spousals* [London, 1686]). It is doubtful that an English court would rule that the events of 3. 2. constitute *sponsalia per verba praesenti*.

27. On "excess of love," see John Russell Brown, "Love's Wealth and the Judgement of *The Merchant of Venice*," in *Shakespeare and His Comedies* (London, 1962).

or sold for money. Definition of these exchanges and of their interrelations in *The Merchant of Venice* sheds light on the essential dilemma of this play about people and property.

LIFE FOR LIFE (BARTER)

The lex talionis for taking a life. No one in *The Merchant of Venice* takes anyone's life in the literal sense of killing him. Yet the Judaeo-Christian laws of taliation for murder—that one who takes the life of another must give his own life, and that nothing more should be taken from him or his—play a major role. Retaliation, which these laws both allow and limit, is a crucial problem in the attempt to define man and to comprehend interpersonal exchanges.

In his most famous defense of vengeance, Shylock suggests that desire for revenge is one characteristic of the human species (3. 1. 51–64). His remark, made to Christians, is out of character for a Jew, whose principal bond is not the natural one to the human species (descendants of Adam) but rather the tribal one to the laws of his Jewish forefathers (descendants of Jacob). In another defense of his revenge—or rather of his limited retaliation—Shylock depends on an interpretation of the Jewish law of retaliation. For the loss of his daughter—his own flesh and blood—he will take the flesh and blood of Antonio.

That Shylock's daughter is now as if dead to Shylock is a crucial "legal fiction" in the play. Once Shylock adopts it he cannot, according to the Hebraic lex talionis, accept anything other than a death for the loss of her. Nothing but a life can pay for a life. He cannot sell his revenge for money. His heavenly oath is to take life for life.

The fiction that Jessica is dead to Shylock is reinforced by the Jewish faith, which conflates conversion to another faith with death, and it arises from Jessica's divorce of and theft from her father. The divorce is important to the problems of law and sexual generation in the play. According to an interpretation of the Old Testament rule that one must honor one's parents, Jessica, if she is Shylock's "own flesh and blood" by Leah, must be "damned" for leaving the "dam" (3. 1. 26–30). To avoid damnation, therefore, Jessica must hope either that Leah and Shylock are not her natural progenitors or that the law commands one to honor those who are one's parents not in "blood" but in "manners" (2. 3. 11–19). The two possible hopes sum up an important difference between Judaism, which emphasizes the importance of bloodlines, and Christianity, which deemphasizes it. According to another Old

Testament rule—that the sins of the father are visited upon the children—Jessica is damned because Shylock is damnable (3. 5. 29–30) as one who takes *damna* or damages, which Antonio identifies with *interesse*. If she were a bastard, she would not be damned by Shylock's sins (compare 2. 3. 15), but her mother would have been an unholy dam. Thus Jessica is damned by either parent or both. Only complete deprecation of bloodlines—spiritual divorce—can free Jessica from the bonds or bounds of the Jewish tribe. Jessica accepts manners as the gauge of human being and marries a Christian. (From Shylock's perspective, of course, Jessica has been unmannerly: she has dressed in the suit of a bird-man and has sold Leah's ring for an ape of a man.)

Jessica's theft also helps to explain Shylock's fiction that she is dead. By her robbery Shylock suffered the monetary loss of his means of livelihood and the vitally personal loss of his life (his daughter, he says, is his flesh and blood). The cry that the Christians remember to report conflates these two kinds of losses:

> . . . my ducats and my daughter!
> A sealèd bag, two sealèd bags of ducats,
> Of double ducats. . . .
> And jewels—two stones, two rich and precious stones.
> . . . .
> She hath the stones upon her, and the ducats!
> (2. 8. 17–22; compare 2. 5. 18)

The two sealed bags and stones are the stores of Shylock's financial fertility and they are confused with his two testicles, the stores of male fertility. Shylock lost his *Geld* when Jessica "gild[ed herself] with . . . ducats" (2. 6. 49–50) and has also been "gelded."[28]

Losing his stones is serious. For Jews living under Christian law lending money was one of the only means of livelihood to maintain life. Moreover, according to Jewish law "he that is wounded in the stones . . . shall not enter the congregation of the Lord" (Deut. 23:1). Christian congregations, on the other hand, can include men who are castrated and men who are, like the celibate Antonio, comparable to

---

28. Cf. Ernest Jones' argument ("Anal-Erotic Character Traits," in *Papers on Psycho-Analysis* [Boston, 1961], esp. p. 430n) that with Shylock "Shakespeare clearly illustrates the equivalency and unconscious identity of the daughter and the ducats." For Jones, Shylock is an anal-erotic neurotic who associates his child and his money as products of defecation. I believe that Shylock associates them in the same way that he connects "life" with "livelihood."

castrated animals (4. 1. 114). The loss of his stones, of his sexual potency, makes Shylock more of a ewe than he can bear, and thus prepares him for an eventual turn from Judaism (from whose congregation he is henceforth excluded) to Christianity.

Shylock has lost his own flesh and blood. Hence his daughter is (as if) dead to him. For the "bad match" between himself and his daughter, Shylock will seek revenge or retaliation—the difference is only in "fiction"—in the "bad match" between Antonio and himself (3. 1. 38).

Marriage. The Judaeo-Christian lex talionis for murder benefits neither the murdered nor the murderer. He that takes (the life of another) and he that gives (his own life in return) are both losers. Yet there is a giving and taking of lives in which both parties are said to benefit immeasurably. This is marriage—another kind of barter of life for life. Marriage "blesseth him that gives and him that takes," much as mercy is supposed to do (4. 1. 182–85).

Marriage is a mutual and total alienation of person between a man and a woman. Its essential formula is Portia's response to Bassanio's demand that she ratify the promissory note (the portrait) that he presented to her: "Myself and what is mine to you and yours / Is now converted" (3. 2. 166–67). Earlier she had said:

> One half of me is yours, the other half yours—
> Mine own I would say; but if mine then yours,
> And so all yours!
> (3. 2. 16–18)

In the context of *The Merchant of Venice*—as in the context of English jurisprudence—marriage is a "legal fiction," an extreme form of trading one thing for another.[29] It is a fiction as essential to the movement of the play as Jessica's fictional death is to Shylock. Marriage is regarded as a unique solution to problems involved in the economy of persons. Yet the institutions with which marriage is associated suggest the problems that involve "bars between the owners and their rights" (3. 2. 19). First, marriage is a kind of suicide pact. (Antonio's deal with

---

29. Pierre de Tourtoulon (*Philosophy in the Development of Law*, trans. Martha McC. Read, pref. Morris R. Cohen, introd. Andrew A. Bruce [New York, 1922]) writes that "marriage is a fictitious purchase and sale," but notes that "very old fictions are no longer considered as such" (pp. 387–88). Cf. Lon L. Fuller, *Legal Fictions* (Stanford, Calif., 1967).

Shylock is another.) In marriage two individuals become one and so lose their original identities, their former lives. The dialectical formula that "both are two but each is one" here suggests the tension.[30] Second, marriage is a kind of slavery. By it, one belongs to another as by a contract in which one sells one's life. If slavery is wrong or rightfully impossible, then marriage of the kind that Portia foresees is similarly suspect. Third is a political problem involving social bondage. Losing one's will in the will of another is like losing one's individual will in the general will of the sovereign (in this play represented by the Duke). The bond of marriage can lead or accustom people to social bonds or contracts—a whole system of political economy—that allow not only the mutual alienation of two persons in the union of marriage but also the slavish alienation of the citizenry in sales in which men can be bought and sold. Republican Venice, as we shall now see, already suffers from slavish bondage in its political and legal institutions.

LIFE FOR MONEY

In bartering one human life for another the exchange seems equal. (A man is a man). Exchanges of persons in Venice, however, generally are not barter but assume a monetary form. For this kind of exchange we need to know not what a man is—not human being—but rather what a man is worth.

Wergeld. In the institution of wergeld (literally "man money"), one who takes the life of another gives not his own life but rather what the life he took was worth in monetary terms. Wergeld is not Jewish. In Jewish law there is no commensuration between human life and money. Though the lex talionis does allow commensuration between other things and money, it forbids any between human life and money. The rabbis interpret "eye for eye" as allowing and "life for life" as for-

30. In Shakespeare's "The Phoenix and the Turtle" (Shakespeare, *The Poems*, ed. F. T. Prince [London, 1960]), love accomplishes such a perfect marriage: "So they lov'd, as love in twain / Had the essence but in one: / Two distincts, division none; / Number there in love was slain. / . . . / Either was the other's mine. / Property was thus appalled / That the self was not the same: / Single nature's double name / Neither two nor one was called" (lines 25–40). The poem concerns a reciprocal alienation of person and purse (to both of which "mine" and "property" refer). Yet it is an "obsequy" (12) that "follows out" the mutual cancellation of the two individuals to a threnody in which we learn that "truth may seem but cannot be" and that the union can leave "no posterity." (Cf. Sonnet 36). See Plato, *Republic*, 524; *Theaetetus*, 185; *Hippias Major*, 300.

bidding monetary compensation.[31] In Jewish law the appropriate compensation for an eye is determined by using a legal fiction: one pretends that the injured party is a slave and then subtracts the market value of the slave after the injury from his value before the injury. The fiction that a free man is a slave to be bought and sold in an open market may seem abhorrent, but hypotheses such as this are logically necessary to every comparison of personal injury with compensatory purse that occurs in ancient and modern civil proceedings. Thus Jews may determine the monetary "worth" of "a Jewess' eye" (2. 5. 41), but only a foolish Christian like Launcelot would say that a human life has this kind of worth.

Christian jurisprudence, unlike Jewish, does make life and money commensurable. According to law codes in medieval Christendom, a murderer could pay for his crime with wergeld, or blood money. The symptomatic association—indeed, conceptual interchangeability—of person and purse, which such extreme cases as the one presented in *The Merchant of Venice* help to reveal, is typical of Christian feudal and capitalist states in general.[32] Though Shylock may be a kind of werewolf or wolf-man (4. 1. 133–38) who misinterprets the lex talionis, Venice itself allows the practice of wergeld, which, as presented in *The Merchant of Venice*, is both abhorrent and yet also, as we shall see, typical of and necessary to the political economy (the Duke) and the domestic economy (Portia).

Jailing, enslaving, and killing debtors. In Shakespeare's Venice money pays, not for someone's having taken the life of a man who is literally dead (no one is killed), but for the right to take the life of a

31. Exod. 21:23–24 reads, "Thou shalt give life for [*ta-chat*] life, eye for eye, tooth for tooth, hand for hand, foot for foot, burning for burning, wound for wound, stripe for stripe" (cf. Deut. 19:21). In legal language *ta-chat* can refer "to one thing's being given in the place of another by way of compensation" (David Daube, "Lex Talionis," *Studies in Biblical Law* [Cambridge, 1947], p. 103). The Talmud distinguishes between the compensation (*damna*) for taking a person's life and that for damaging part of his body. In the former case (homicide), no ransom is allowed; the penalty is death (cf. Num. 35:31, Lev. 24:17). Only in the latter case are person and purse considered commensurable for practical purposes.

32. In some medieval legal systems in Christendom "the life of every man below the King is assessed, according to his rank, at a certain value, and the wehrgeld may be received in atonement for his blood" (Henry Hart Milman, *History of Latin Christianity*, 8 vols. in 4 [New York, 1881], 1:538). According to one code, for example, "should anyone kill a bishop lawfully chosen, a tunic of lead [is] fitted to the person of the bishop, and the commutation for his murder [is] as much gold as that tunic

man still living. Purchases of living men depicted in this play include those that are associated with the institutions of debtor's prison, slavery, and execution for debt.

In Christian law not only a human eye but also human freedom and life itself can be put on the auction block. Loss of freedom by being put into prison was no important part of Jewish law (which originated with shepherd wanderers), but the institution of debtors' prison was one of the bulwarks of the civil law and political economy in Christian states (in which debtors' prisons originated from the jails to which ecclesiastical courts of equity sent defaulters on loans). Shakespeare depicts this institution when he shows Antonio being walked by his jailor as if he were a dog. He has lost the freedom of his person because he did not have money and none of his Christian brothers would give or lend him any.[33]

As a man's corporeal freedom could be lost for (lack of) money, so too, as a matter of legal course, could it be lost in slavery. Under Jewish law there is no absolute slavery for the same reason that there is no monetary compensation possible for murder. (A man's freedom cannot be bought but can only be rented for a period of not more than six years—the length of time that the suitor Jacob shepherded Laban's ewes, first to win Leah and then to win Rachel.) In Venice, however, a living human being can be bought and enslaved for the same reason that wergeld can make up for a murder.

It follows logically from the existence of debtors' prison and slavery that a man's very life can be sold for lack of money.[34] Indeed, in Roman law (from which the law of purchase and sale in most Christian states is

---

weighed (ibid; cf. Bavarian Law 11.1, in *Laws of the Alamans and Bavarians*, trans. John Rivers [Philadelphia, 1977], pp. 121–22). See also William Blackstone, *Commentaries on the Laws of England*, 4 vols. (Oxford, 1765–69; rpr. London, 1966), 4:188, 308–9, 406; Max Weber, *Ancient Judaism*, trans. and ed. Hans H. Gerth and Don Martindale (Glencoe, Ill., 1952), p. 62; and Georg Simmel, *The Philosophy of Money*, trans. Tom Bottomore and David Frisby (London, 1978), pp. 355–74.

33. Heinrich Heine (*Sämmtliche Werke* [Philadelphia, 1856], 5:324) remarks that Antonio's "brothers" in Venice do not lend him the ducats he needs.

34. In Alexander Silvayn's "Of a Jew, who would for his debt have a pound of the flesh of a Christian" (Declamation 95, in Silvayn, *The Orator*, trans. Lazarus Piot [London, 1596]), the Jew makes an argument that connects execution with slavery and prison: "It seemeth at the first sight, that it is a thing . . . strange [and] cruel, to bind a man to pay a pound of the flesh of his bodie, for want of money . . . but there are divers others that are more cruell, which because they are in use seeme nothing terrible at all: as to binde al the bodie unto a most lothsome prison, or unto an intollerable slaverie, where not only the whole body but also the senses and spirits are tormented."

derived) a man's life can actually be taken for (lack of) money. Roman law contains a critical provision for enslaving debtors who default and for executing them: "The debtor has until thirty days after judgement to pay his debt. If he does not then pay or give security, or sell himself, by entering into the *nexum*, his creditor can seize him, load him with chains and treat him as a slave. . . . Then, after sixty days more, if he still fails to pay, he is brought into the market place and either put to death or sold as a slave." Moreover, "where there were several creditors . . . the debtor might, at their election, be divided and his body partitioned between them" in pieces proportionate to each one's debt.[35] This rule from the Roman laws is harsh, but it is part of the original, though submerged, basis for English law[36] and also a logical extension of it. Shylock's case against Antonio does not contradict the institutions of Venice but merely reveals their more abhorrent aspects.

In the context of this gamut of exchanges involving purses and persons, neither the Duke nor Portia can without contradiction reject Shylock's case. The political economy (for which the Duke stands) and the domestic economy (whose crowning achievement, marriage, Portia hopes to attain) themselves depend upon and incorporate rules and practices like those on which Shylock's case relies.[37]

That the Duke—the representative of the state—does not rule against Shylock from the beginning of the trial indicates how much the

35. "Tertiis nundinis partis secanto" ("On the third market day [after the seizure of the defaulting debtor by his creditors] let them cut parts"). The Roman law is in the Twelve Tables (*Leges XII tabularum*, tab. 3.6, in Carl Georg Bruns, *Fontes iuris Romani antiqui* [Leipzig, 1893], p. 21). Aulus Gellius describes and comments upon this law (*The Attic Nights of Aulus Gellius*, trans. John C. Rolfe, 3 vols. [London, 1927–28], 20. 1. 45–54). Cf. L. Wenger, *Institutes of the Roman Law of Civil Procedure*, trans. O. H. Fish (New York, 1940), pp. 223–30; Max Weber, *Wirtschaft und Gesellschaft* (Tübingen, 1922), pp. 413–56; and Blackstone, *Commentaries*, 2:472–73. For the view that *secare* refers not to the cutting of the debtor's body but to "the piecemeal alienation of the debtor's property," see Max Radin, "*Secare partis*: The Early Roman Law of Execution against a Debtor," *American Journal of Philology* 43 (1922): 32, 43.

36. The submerged rights (under Elizabethan laws, such as Act 13 Edward I, c. 1) of a creditor to the body of his debtor are suggested in the language of the record of the case of William Shakespeare v. John Addenbrooke (1609), in which the process server writes, "I arrested . . . John, whose body I hold ready [*cujus corpus paratum habeo*]" (quoted by Tucker Brooke, *Shakespeare of Stratford* [New Haven, Conn., 1926], p. 58).

37. The Hegelian D. J. Snider writes (*System of Shakespeare's Dramas* [Saint Louis, 1877], 1:305) that "the general movement of [*The Merchant of Venice*] lies in the conflict between the Right of Property and the Existence of the Individual, and in the Mediation of this conflict through the Family [represented by Portia, the wife],

commerce of Venice is bound to contracts that are qualitatively similar to that of Shylock with Antonio. Freedom to contract, on which the commercial success of Venice is partly based, must be maintained at the potential cost of taking away the freedom of some men by imprisoning, enslaving, or killing them. This dilemma is readily understood. Antonio knows that "no lawful means can carry [him]" (4. 1. 9) because "the commodity that strangers have / With us in Venice, if it be denied, / Will much impeach the justice of the state . . ." (3. 3. 27–30). The alien Shylock actually threatens to "impeach the freedom of the state / If they deny him justice" (3. 2. 278–79). For (love of) the money that commercial freedom brings, the Duke cannot rule against Shylock.

Neither can Portia—the champion of marriage—rule against Shylock (4. 1. 175–77). The absolute ownership of another person through institutions like debtors' prison, slavery, and execution for debt may be abhorrent, but it is a necessary basis for the marriage Portia seeks. Marriage cannot avoid the alienation of persons that these institutions imply but can only work its way up through (in order, perhaps, to transcend) it. If Balthasar-Portia were to rule that the bond between Antonio and Shylock was illegitimate—arguing, for example, that all contracts seeking to take a human life have always been regarded as void, or that no man can rightfully contract to give to another his person under any circumstances or conditions[38]—she would, by the same argument, be ruling away the possibility of marriage, which involves an equally extreme alienation of person and is, for Shakespeare, the only real solution to the problems of property and person that *The Merchant of Venice* depicts. No more for Belmont's familial love than for Venice's political justice can Antonio be freed from deadly bondage to Shylock. The uncomforting but inescapable connections of the retaliation that Shylock seeks with both the marriage that Portia seeks and the commercial freedom that Venice seeks make Shylock's revenge on An-

---

which owes its origin in the present case to that same individual [Antonio] whom it rescues." I believe, however, that in this play the rights of property (the state) and the family (marriage) do not oppose each other in this way.

38. For the first position, see the argument that no one "can be bound by any solemn vow . . . / To do a murd'rous deed" (*2 Henry VI*, ed. A. S. Cairncross [London, 1969], 5. 1. 184–85); for the second, cf. the discussion of "despotical dominion" in Thomas Hobbes, *Leviathan* [1651], ed. Michael Oakeshott (Oxford, 1947), esp. p. 133.

tonio, or on Christians in general,[39] the most unsettling aspect of the play. Only a miracle or a revolution of family and state could avert disaster.

Cancellations

A solution to these conflicting problems of personal exchange seems to appear in the person of a "redeemer" who is at once both a *deus ex machina* (Balthasar in the court) and a disguised *dea in machina* (Portia in the courtship). Balthasar-Portia interrogates the phrase "a pound of flesh" (4. 1. 305), which names what Antonio hazarded, more closely than ever the suitors interpreted the inscriptions on the caskets. She subjects the smallest letter of the law, its iota, to minute scrutiny: "This bond doth give thee here no jot of blood" (304). If Shylock "shed / One drop of Christian blood" (307–8), she says, his property will be confiscated by the state of Venice.[40] Thus Shylock can purchase An-

39. As Shylock confuses himself with all Jews, so he confuses Antonio with all Christians. He speaks of the revenger as the first person singular ("I"), then as the third person singular ("Jew"), and finally as the second person plural ("us"/"we"; 3. 1. 51–62); similarly, he speaks of Antonio as an individual and then as a representative of all Christians. The confusion is symptomatic of how Shylock connects one of his own characteristics, the desire for revenge, with the human species, and how he conflates the characteristics of the individual Antonio with those of the whole group of Christians. The Christians do the same thing. Portia speaks of the crime of shedding Christian blood, when she means only that of Antonio (4. 1. 308), and Antonio speaks of the hardness of a Jewish heart, when he means only that of Shylock (4. 1. 78–80). See also the confusion of "I" and "We" in the Duke's first speeches in 4. 1.

40. Some spectators may say that Shylock has a right to shed blood as a means to take Antonio's flesh just as the purchaser of a plot of land, surrounded by the land of the seller, has a right of way to his land whether or not such a right is stipulated in the deed. In Richard Hengist Horne's adaptation of act 4, *Shylock in 1850: A Dramatic Reverie* (included in Shakespeare, *The Merchant of Venice*, ed. H. H. Furness [Philadelphia, 1888], pp. 400–403), Shylock thus argues against Portia's ruling that he can shed no jot of blood: "Flesh is made up of vessels, and they're filled / With blood alone,—nay, blood is liquid flesh"; "It is the very nature of all flesh / When cut to bleed."

In the context of *The Merchant of Venice*, there are defenses of Portia's ruling. For example, Portia outjews the Jew by interpreting the "letter" of Jewish dietary laws as well as that of the commercial bond. Jews cannot eat flesh from which every drop of blood has not been drained. (Compare this with the fusion of flesh and blood in the Christian Eucharist.) Portia's apparently picayune distinction between the flesh and blood of Antonio thus recalls Shylock's critical decision to break Jewish dietary laws (against eating pork and human flesh) by going to Bassanio's house to eat pork and to "feed upon / The prodigal Christian" (2. 5. 14–15). On Shylock's "cannibalism," see also the psychoanalytic argument of Robert Fliess, *Erogeneity and Libido* (New York, 1957), esp. pp. 80–88.

tonio, but only in exchange for his own property: Antonio's person sold for Shylock's purse.

Shylock is unwilling to pay the wergeld. He waives his right to the penalty on condition that he receive "the bond thrice" (316–17). Now we know that Shylock, despite earlier claims (85–87), can be bought off. Portia, however, wishes to reduce the ransom for Antonio to nothing (indeed to less than nothing) so that all of Bassanio (indeed more than all of him) can become hers. Shylock, she says, cannot have even the principal because he refused its tender "in open court." He can have nothing but the corporeal penalty, and that, as we have seen, only at a stiff price.

Fearing that Shylock may now withdraw the waiver of his right to the pound of flesh since his condition has not been met, Portia uses another literal interpretation of the phrase "a pound of flesh" to dissuade him from doing so. If he should take less or more than a pound, she says as "iusticer," Shylock will lose not only his property but also his life (his person as well as his purse). "Nor cut thou less nor more / But just a pound of flesh. If thou tak'st more / Or less than a just pound . . . / Thou diest, and all thy goods are confiscate" (323–30).[41] Now Shylock can take the life of Antonio, but only at the price of his own property and life.

Shylock must choose between this costly purchase and receiving nothing at all. His choice is a touchstone to his character and to *The Merchant of Venice* as a whole. If Shylock were a true revenger, willing to hazard all he has and is (as the inscription on the lead casket says), he would choose to kill Antonio. This would be the choice of a tragic hero, and it might sweep away Venice.[42] If, on the other hand, Shylock were a cowardly merchant of revenge (or, perhaps, a wary seer that the proposed terms are only bait to trap him), he would give up the forfei-

---

41. The Roman law states, "Si plus minusve secuerunt, se fraude esto" ("If [the creditors who exercise their right to cut up the body of a defaulting debtor] cut more or less, it shall be no crime" [tab. 3.6, in Bruns, *Fontes*, p. 21]). Portia goes against the grain of this original and theoretically rigorous form of Roman and Renaissance law. She gives Shylock more justice than he desires by arguing that Shylock, who asked for "an equal pound" (1. 3. 145), is entitled to "just" a pound. "Thou shalt have perfect and just weight, a perfect and just measure shalt thou have" (Deut. 25:15).

42. In Horne's version (*Shylock in 1850*), Shylock turns out to be not a comic merchant of revenge but rather one who hazards all he has: "Let ruin come!—so I can behold / That streaming breast, I care not if his blood / Swell to a second Galilean Sea, / And with its humming and abhorrent surge / Sweep away Venice!"

ture and ask to leave the court. This would be the choice of a comic scapegoat. As it happens, Shylock is so "merchant-like" as to "sell his revenge."[43] The bond thus seems to be canceled.

From this point on in the trial scene, the previous prosecutor becomes the defendant, and Venice, which he offended, is now enabled to persecute him. Balthasar-Portia uses a law that discriminates between citizens and aliens.

> If it be proved against an alien
> That by direct or indirect attempts
> He seeks the life of any citizen,
> The party 'gainst the which he doth contrive
> Shall seize one half his goods; the other half
> Comes to the privy coffer of the state;
> And the offender's life lies in the mercy
> Of the Duke. . . .
>
> (4. 1. 347–54)

The Venetian court thus turns directly to "the first and most obvious division of the people," as William Blackstone says, the division "into aliens and natural-born subjects."[44] The turn contradicts a universal humanist ethic like that proposed by Christianity ("All men are my brothers, none are 'aliens'"), and taking thus the life and property of Shylock would seem, would be, unmerciful. So the Duke grants what seems (at least) to be an unconditional pardon of the life of Shylock (366–67). He then returns to Shylock part of the half of his property

---

43. *2 Henry VI*, 4. 1. 41.

44. Blackstone, *Commentaries*, 1:354. What are the strictly legal reasons that neither Portia nor the Duke invoked this law earlier? Only some time after Portia's entrance is it shown either that Shylock intended actually to take the pound of flesh to which the bond seems to entitle him or that Antonio will die if Shylock should take it. Some time before her entrance the Duke expects Shylock to withdraw his claim (4. 1. 34), and Portia believes that Antonio can recover from his wound with the help of surgeons (254–55). (We do not learn that Antonio is to lose the flesh from "nearest the merchant's heart" until 231, and even such a loss would not rule out the possibility that Antonio may live, since the vital organ itself cannot be taken.)

Jacob Adler suggests that "[Shylock] wishes to humble and terrify Antonio in return for the insult and humiliation he has suffered at his hands. This is why he goes so far as to bring his knife and scales into the court. For Shylock, however, the desired climax was to refuse the pound of flesh with a gesture of divine compassion. When the verdict goes against him, he is crushed because he has been robbed of his opportunity, not because he lusts for Antonio's death" (quoted by Lulla Rosenfeld, in "The Yiddish Idol," *New York Times Magazine*, June 12, 1977, p. 42).

that the state had confiscated, but on one condition: that he humble himself (368–70). Thus the court would strain humility out of Shylock as it could not strain the quality of mercy.

The purse that Shylock would receive under these terms is not enough for his person. "You take my life," he says, "When you do take the means whereby I live" (374–75). Antonio earlier scoffed at Shylock's identification of a living being (ewe's offspring) with a means of livelihood (use), but now the Christian bankrupt better understands his own association—made in the first scene—of a person with a purse. In the last scene, indeed, he will say that Portia has given him both "life and living" (5. 1. 286). He offers Shylock even more money (*merces*). This offer has four restraining conditions.

The first condition tells the Jew's influence on the Christian. Antonio would be "content" to allow Shylock to have "one half of his goods" if Shylock lets Antonio have "the other half in use" (4. 1. 379–81). The sum total of Antonio's money will not be diminished by the new agreement, but his legal relationship to it will be. Antonio gives up his right to any aspect of Shylock's property but its "use." Employing language like that in the Statutes of Uses of Henry VII and Henry VIII, he forgoes his right to the principal and claims only the interest—the fruit, or usufruct—that Shylock's money, under Antonio's financial management, may breed.[45] He will keep the use from Shylock's money just as Jacob kept the lambs from Laban's ewes.

Certainly Antonio has begun to think of himself as a kind of usurer. Earlier in the trial, for example, he used the pun on *use* and *ewes* that he had learned from the Jew: "You may as well use question with the wolf / Why he hath made the ewe bleat for the lamb" (4. 1. 73–74). Antonio here said that he was a lamb, or prepubescent sheep, to be taken as "use" by Shylock, but he soon realizes that he is rather a wether, or gelded male sheep: "I am a tainted wether of the flock / Meetest for death" (114–15). A wether is sterile, as barren as Antonio believes metal to be and as Shylock became when he lost his stones.

---

45. "A use, in English law, [is] a confidence reposed in the tenant of land that he should dispose of the land according to the intention of the *cestui que use* ['he to whose use or benefit the trust was intended'], or him to whose use it was granted, and suffer him to take the profits" (Edward J. White, *Commentaries on the Law in Shakespeare* [St. Louis, 1911], p. 144, cf. p. 113). For "use," "usufruct," and "having in use," see Act 7 Henry VII, c. 2, para. 5; Act 27 Henry VIII, c. 10, pars. 1, 6, and 10. In his discussion of the English Statute of Uses, Francis Bacon considers the use of money as well as of land (Bacon, *Reading upon the Statute of Uses, Works*, 14:287–92).

Antonio is "the weakest kind of fruit" (115), as he says, because he is not fruit bearing, as was the money supplier Shylock.[46]

What the bankrupt Antonio will now have to use is exactly equal to what Shylock will have to use. Both users say "I am content" (380, 392) to this new deal, as if in some strange ceremony. Antonio and Shylock are matched as two gelded users of money. They are similar to two married persons as Portia describes them: one is, or has, half of what the other is, or has. The new bond between Antonio and Shylock thus prepares the way for the equal marriage still sought by Portia.[47]

Other conditions in Antonio's merciful offer to Shylock include Antonio's right "to render [the sum that Antonio will use] / Upon [Shylock's] death unto the gentleman / That lately stole his daughter," and Shylock's obligation to "record a gift," to will "all he dies possessed" to Lorenzo and Jessica. Finally the court would seem to turn Shylock, who has been treated as an other, or alien, into a (brother) Christian (381–88).

The Duke threatens to rescind his pardon of Shylock's life—it now

---

46. We punish the text to say that Antonio has to play a sad part because he has no private parts. For Antonio "the world" is "a stage where every man must play a part, / And mine a sad one" (1. 1. 77–79). Gratiano believes that Antonio can change his sad part (86–102), just as an actor changes character, but Salerio jokingly suggests that it is some permanent defect in Antonio's "nature" that makes him unable to laugh (50–56). We may well wonder whether Antonio's sadness is an alterable part, or a part of his unalterable nature. Cf. 5. 1. 144 on parts and gelding.

For Stanley Cavell (The Claim of Reason [Oxford, 1979], p. 480), the forfeit that is to be "cut off and taken / In which part of [Antonio's] body pleaseth [Shylock]" (1. 3. 146–47) suggests the foreskin that is cut during circumcision and also the testicles that are cut off during castration (which many people interpret to be the significance of circumcision or fear as its result). Cf. Theodor Reik, Fragments of a Great Confession (New York, 1949), esp. p. 336. Just as Shylock once intended to circumcise the bodily part of Antonio (and hence turn him into a Jewish brother), so Antonio now intends to circumcise the spiritual part of Shylock (and hence turn him into a Christian man). For Paul, a Christian is a Jew whose heart is circumcised: "For he is not a real Jew who is one outwardly, nor is true circumcision something external and physical. He is a Jew who is one inwardly, and real circumcision is a matter of the heart, spiritual and not literal" (Rom. 2:28–29).

47. W. H. Auden ("Brothers and Others," in The Dyer's Hand and Other Essays [New York, Random House], 1962) writes that "there is no reason to suppose that Shakespeare had read Dante, but he must have been familiar with the association of usury (which Shylock practiced) with sodomy of which Dante speaks in the Eleventh Canto of the Inferno . . . (ll. 50, 109–11). It can . . . hardly be an accident that Shylock the usurer has as his antagonist a man (Antonio) whose emotional life, though his conduct may be chaste, is concentrated upon a member of his own sex." My argument is that Antonio is more like a sterile wether than a sodomite.

becomes conditional—if Shylock does not agree to the terms of the agreement proposed by Antonio (389–90). Thus the life of Antonio, the threatened hypothec (conditional pledge or security) in the first Shylock-Antonio contract, is replaced by the life of Shylock in this second Shylock-Antonio contract. The legal court, if not the courtship, has found the sacrificial lamb it needed.[48]

That the Jew is strained to become a merciful Christian and that the Christian becomes a kind of usurer are two signs that the Venetian court cannot provide a satisfactory resolution to the ideological dilemmas of property and person that gave rise to the action of *The Merchant of Venice* in the first place.

Another sign connects the issues with which the court had to deal—the exchanges of life for life and of life for money—with the major issue of the courtship: how the Duke (for the state) and Antonio and Bassanio (for individual friendship) feel bound to compensate Balthasar-Portia, to whom Antonio is "much bound" (405) for his life. But how can one pay for a life?[49] Portia did have, as she says to those who would gratify her with money (406–10) or with food (399) for doing what she seems to them to have done gratis, what she herself calls a "mercenary" (416) motive: not to gain a purse of *merces* but to gain the person of Bassanio. Portia believed that both the merchant Antonio and herself were like Bassanio, so that saving Antonio was like saving herself (3. 4. 18–23). As Antonio helped Bassanio to purchase Portia, moreover, so Portia wanted to help Bassanio to purchase Antonio. For Portia, "redeeming" Antonio was also removing a present interposer (Antonio's bondage to Shylock) and a possible future interposition (Antonio's death) between Bassanio and herself. Thus Portia wanted to use the legal court to court Bassanio away from too great a sense of obligation to another.

---

48. Other endings to the duel between the Jew and the merchant are conceivable. The Reverend Dr. Kohler (*Jewish Advance*, December 13, 1878) notes that Shylock might easily have taken "that very knife that was to pay Antonio's forfeited bond" and "spilled his own blood."

49. The question pertains to redemption—the way that Portia saved Antonio—and to Venetian institutions like debtors' prison, slavery, and death for debt. It concerns not only problems of marriage but also Venetian politics and economics in general.

William Blackstone (*Commentaries*, 1:412) raises the problem: "Every sale implies a price, a *quid pro quo*, an equivalent given to the seller in lieu of what he transfers to the buyer: but what equivalent can be given for life, and liberty, both of which (in absolute slavery) are held to be in the master's disposal?"

That Antonio becomes, by the court's ruling, a monetary usurer brings to mind that he may already have been a usurer—a spiritual one. "Spiritual usury," say the church fathers, refers to hoping for gratitude, or some other kind of binding obligation, in return for giving a loan that is otherwise given gratis.[50] Perhaps Antonio's loan of his body for Bassanio's wealth not only bound, but was also made with the intention of binding, Bassanio to him.[51] Portia's fear that, for her purposes, too strong a bond has developed between Bassanio and his "dearest friend" (3. 2. 292) is justified many times in the play. During the trial, for example, Bassanio says to Antonio:

> . . . life itself, my wife, and all the world
> Are not with me esteemed above thy life.
> I would lose all, ay sacrifice them all
> Here to this devil, to deliver you.
> (4. 1. 282–85)

The bond between Bassanio and Antonio may make impossible the marriage union Portia seeks. She must discover whether Bassanio's sense of obligation to give "tribute" (420) to Balthasar-Portia for saving the life of Antonio is greater than his sense of obligation to Portia.

Portia gauges Bassanio's love for Antonio against his love for herself by asking for the ring that she gave to him after he chose the lead casket. Will Bassanio now choose Portia (who gave him the ring) or Balthasar, the savior of Antonio? Antonio convinces Bassanio to give Balthasar the ring: "Let him have the ring. / Let his deservings, and my love withal, / Be valued 'gainst your wife's commandèment" (447–49). Bassanio breaks Portia's binding commandment to keep the ring and gives

---

50. The *Glossa ordinaria* considers the "spiritual usury" that is approved by the parable of the talents (Matt. 25:14–30) (in *Patrologiae cursus completus* [Series Latina], ed. J. P. Migne, 221 vols. [Paris, 1844–64], vol. 113, col. 466, 478–79). Nelson (*Idea of Usury*, p. 65) notes that "Zwingli, like Luther and Melanchthon, seems loathe to concede that a strict prohibition of usury might be inferred from Scriptures. [Zwingli declares that] to deny the name of Christians to those who extend loans with a *hope* of profit is to torture the texts [especially Luke 6:34–35]". See Huldreich Zwingli, *Sämmtliche Werke*, unter Mitwirkung des Zwingli-Vereins in Zürich, ed. E. Egli, G. Finsler, W. Köhler, et al., 11 vols. (Berlin and Leipzig, 1905–35), 6:589.

51. See, for example, the words Antonio believes to be his last ones: "Tell [Portia] the process of Antonio's end, / Say how I love you, speak me fair in death; / And when the tale is told, bid her be judge / Whether Bassanio had not once a love" (4. 1. 272–75). Antonio leaves it unclear whether Portia is to judge whether Bassanio had this love "once upon a time" and has it no longer, or had "but one" love and none else.

it to Balthasar. The contract between Bassanio and Portia, like that between Antonio and Shylock, seems canceled.

Portia had warned Bassanio:

> I give [myself and mine] with this ring,
> Which when you part from, lose, or give away,
> Let it presage the ruin of your love
> And be my vantage to exclaim on you.
> (3. 2. 171–74)

Portia will make use of Bassanio's apparent breach of faith. She will
profit from the excesses and surfeits in money and love that qualify the
actions of the play. But will she somehow manage a real solution to the
dilemmas that we have seen at work in the courtroom scene?

Redemption?

The dilemmas involved in the merchant's bond and in the marriage
bond are partly exposed when Nerissa pretends to discover that the ring
she, like Portia, gave to her fiancé as a symbolic earnest of their marriage precontract is missing. Were Balthasar, the *deus ex machina* in
the court, and Portia, the *dea in machina* in the courtship, not the
same person, the tension in the play would be unresolvable. The transformation of the two Christian women disguised as men at the legal
bar back into women is thus necessary to the success of the marriage
union, as was the transformation of the Jewess disguised as a bird man
at the "festive bar" into a woman (Jessica). The manhood of woman,
who can "use . . . th'endeavor of a man" (3. 4. 48), is thus essential in
this play, but woman's manhood is also troubling in the context of
problems about usury, sexual generation, and the classification of animals into species and subspecies. For example, it is sometimes left unclear whether women, who do not plead *in propria persona* in court or
in courtship, are, like monkeys, members of another species than Man
or whether they are, like *castrati*, deformed or different—perhaps even
better—members of the species of Man, who are not only brotherly (as
descendants of Adam), but also otherly (since they are different from
males). The Jew Shylock, the black Morocco, and other aliens are already castrated one way or another, and now Gratiano seems to intuit
that the solution to the dilemmas facing them all is connected with
castrating the men to whom they gave their rings: "In faith I gave [the
ring] to the judge's clerk. / Would he were gelt that had it, for my part, /

Since you do take it, love, so much at heart" (5. 1. 143–45). He would unman the man whom we know to have been a woman.

The process of the last scene in *The Merchant of Venice* will indeed "mar the young clerk's pen" (237) by revealing the clerk (with a penis) to have been Nerissa, whose ring Gratiano, threatened with being cuckolded, finally learns that he must keep safe (306–7).

At this point, however, Gratiano tries to defend his giving the ring to the clerk by arguing that the ring was a mere "trifle." He claims that it was only

> . . . a hoop of gold, a paltry ring
> That she did give me, whose posy [inscription] was
> For all the world like cutler's poetry
> Upon a knife—'Love me, and leave me not.'
> (5. 1. 147–50)

The offended Nerissa's rejoinder is that neither the epigrammatic posy inscribed in a ring nor the metal of which the ring is made tells its true value. As in the episodes involving the suitors' interpretations of the inscribed caskets and coins, the gist is that one should attend to more than the statements impressed in and the exchange values of metals. The symptomatic derogation of Nerissa's gold ring by Gratiano further diminishes our trust in the ability of metals to test human metal and in Bassanio's choice of the lead casket. Will Bassanio, who gave Portia's ring to Balthasar, be able to pick up courting Portia where he left off?

Portia agrees to forgive Bassanio for "break[ing] an oath" (248) if he swears the only "oath of credit" she will accept, an oath "by [his] double self" (245). As it happens, Antonio offers to "second" Bassanio. In a striking spiritual recapitulation of the original bond between Antonio and Shylock, which seems to lift that bond from the level of bodies to that of souls, he says:

> I once did lend my body for his wealth,
> Which but for him that had your husband's ring
> Had quite miscarried. I dare be bound again,
> My soul upon the forfeit, that your lord
> Will never more break faith advisedly.
> (5. 1. 249–53)

If Antonio at the beginning of the play was a spiritual usurer who lent his body, he becomes at the end a user of money who lends his soul.

In exchange for Antonio's soul as "surety" (254) in this new bargain,

Portia gives the ring to Antonio. Antonio, who staked the beginning of the Bassanio-Portia courtship, now oversees its completion when he gives the ring to Bassanio.[52] He marries no woman (he does marry in one of Shakespeare's sources),[53] but he is the one who marries, or presides over the union of, Portia and Bassanio. Thus the tainted wether plays the role of holy hermit (5. 1. 32). The difficult fix is again "redeemed" by Antonio's personal surety.[54]

Finally, the problem of scarcity that drives men to hazardous and saddening ventures is solved by an abundant dispensation. Bassanio seemed to bring to Belmont from Venice a "horn full of good news"

52. The relationship of the exchanges of the ring(s) to the contracts in *The Merchant of Venice* is similar to the relationship of the exchanges of the ring to the wager in *Cymbeline*. Imogen gives Posthumus a diamond ring with the words "But keep it till you woo another wife" (*Cymbeline*, ed. R. Hosley [New York, 1968], 1. 1. 114). Posthumus (unlike Bassanio) seems to reciprocate in kind by giving Imogen an equally circular bracelet. After his voyage to Italy, Posthumus claims to distinguish between the gift and giver: "The one [the ring] may be sold or given, or if there were wealth enough for the purchase or merit for the gift. The other [Imogen] is not a thing for sale, and only the gift of the gods" (1. 4. 87–90). Nevertheless, Posthumus comes to measure the jewel that is Imogen against the diamond that she gave to him (1. 4. 154–61). He hazards (98) the ring that Iachimo cannot violate the *person* (corporeal chastity) of Imogen, and Iachimo wagers a *purse* of ten thousand ducats that he can. Like the conditions of the contract between Antonio and Shylock, the conditions of this match are set down by lawful counsel as a covenant (1. 4. 148–75). For the influence of the manaclelike ring on the plot of *Cymbeline*, which is brought full circle only when the ring is returned to its rightful owner, see *Cymbeline* 2. 3. 142–49, 2. 4. 49–61, and 5. 5. 181–86 and 414–17.

53. In the Adventures of Giannetto, in Giovanni Fiorentino's *Il Percorone* (Venice, 1565), Ansaldo (the counterpart to Shakespeare's Antonio) marries a servant of the wealthy lady. (See "Source of the Plot," in *Merchant of Venice*, ed. Furness, pp. 297–305.) In *The Merchant of Venice*, however, Antonio remains a wether. Like Morocco (who promised never to generate illegitimate offspring) and Shylock (who disowned his daughter), kind Antonio will have no descendant kin.

54. Some critics confuse Antonio with Jesus of Nazareth on the basis of notions about redemption of one life by another. Antonio's offering his own person as the surety on his friend's loan, however, may be an un-Christian and presumptuous imitation of Jesus' sacrifice on the cross. Martin Luther writes that "there is a common error, which has become a widespread custom, not only among merchants but throughout the world, by which one man becomes the surety for another" (Martin Luther, *Von Kaufshandlung und Wucher* [1524], in Luther, *Werke*, Kritische Gesamtausgabe, ed. J. K. F. Knaake, G. Kawerau, E. Thiele, and others [Weimar, 1883–], 25:298–305). Antonio seems to take the injunction that one should love one's neighbor as oneself to mean that he should value his neighbor's life not as his own but rather as more than his own. Antonio even values getting money for Bassinio more than the risk of losing his own life. Such "evaluation" was against Jewish teaching (e.g., that of Rabbi Akiba).

(47). His new servant Launcelot even imitates the sound of the post-horn (39–44). However, the real cornucopia in *The Merchant of Venice* is the "fulsome ewe" Portia, whose "full sum" displaces or seems to displace the partial sums of the Jews (Shylock and Tubal) and is asso-ciable with the quality of mercy that drops gratis from heaven. (Bas-sanio and Gratiano only *have* horns, like rams and like the cuckolds that Portia and Nerissa jestingly make them out to be.)

Portia manages two dispensations. She gives Antonio the news that his ships are "richly come to harbour" (5. 1. 277). (That Portia knew the contents of the sealed letter that brings this information suggests that these riches may come from her. "You shall not know" says she, "by what strange accident / I chanced on this letter.") And Portia's ser-vant announces that for Lorenzo and Jessica there will be plenty of "manna" (294)—not the food that drops as the gentle rain from heaven, but rather the money that Shylock was strained to promise them in his "special deed of gift" (292). Thus the Jew, whose conditional dispensa-tion of wealth to the Christian Antonio was the means by which the courtship of persons in *The Merchant of Venice* began, is connected even with this last apportionment of funds by Portia.

If the kind of generation for which Portia stands is to displace fully that represented by Shylock, it must include not only the dispensation or generation of money but also that of natural offspring. Significantly, however, Portia and Bassanio do not themselves mention children. And any hint of natural offspring to be generated by the Christians connects generation, as Shylock would and as Antonio would not, with usury or with miscegenation—miscegenation like the generation of an illegitimate child by Launcelot and the Moorish woman (3. 5. 35) and like that of the "parti-colored lambs" Shylock compared to in-terest (1. 3. 72–86).[55] For example, a connection with interest is made when Gratiano (Bassanio's foil) looks forward to "couching with the doctor's clerk" (5. 1. 305). A birth consequent from this act would pro-

55. Portia, who dehumanized and unmanned the Prince of Morocco, might con-sider the insemination of the Moorish woman by Launcelot to be interbreeding of ani-mal species rather than miscegenation of human races. (It may be argued that her unsuccessful white suitor, unlike her black one, is allowed to marry despite the fact that he chose the wrong casket [2. 9. 69].) Compare Jacob's management of the black and white ewes and rams (Gen. 30:38–42), and Iago's claim in *Othello* (ed. A. Ker-nan [New York, 1963], 1. 1. 85–86) that "an old black ram [the Moor Othello] / Is tupping your [Brabantio's] white ewe [Desdemona]."

duce not only a human offspring, but also a monetary offspring from Gratiano's and Nerissa's proposed wager with Bassanio and Portia:

> GRATIANO. We'll play with them [Bassanio and Portia] the first
> boy for a thousand ducats.
> NERISSA. What, and stake down?
> GRATIANO. No, we shall ne'er win at that sport, and stake down.
> (3. 2. 213–17)

The "stake" is the monetary deposit of the wager, a kind of monetary principal (the instrument used by the investor to generate monetary offspring), and also the penis (the instrument of the male progenitor of human offspring). The domestic economy that Portia, champion of marriage, seems to represent is one in which children (if they exist) will continue to be connected with ducats.

That Shylock's purse and his theory of purses are still behind, or still substantiate, the action of the persons in the last scene is a sign that Belmont, though a place (literally, *topos*) of marriage and abundance, is inextricably linked with commercial exchanges and scarcity. The path from Shylock's doctrine of "life for life" to the corresponding doctrine of Portia suggests that the end of the play does not transcend or fully overcome the dilemmas that gave rise to the action in the beginning.

The Merchant of Venice begins in a sad commercial republic and ends in a happier place. It may seem, therefore, that Venice stands in the same relation to Belmont as a commercial contract to a marriage contract, a torch or candle to a moon, or the music of the earth to the heavenly music of the spheres.[56] It may be that Belmont is "a substitute" that "shines brightly as a king," but it does so only "until a king be by" (5. 1. 94–95). And what if the king is not there? The apparent contradictions in the end of the play reinforce our impression of the absence of real royalty. The final dispensation only seems to lift the ventures of the Venetians' quest for love and money from the level of a human body (Antonio staked his in Venice) to the level of a human

---

56. Lorenzo tells Jessica that the earthly music we can hear is an imitation of the music of the spheres. It is an agent of conversion with the power to turn "the hot condition of the blood" to modesty (5. 1. 70–79). "For the time," it can change the nature of a thing (82). That Jessica is affected by music (69) may be a sign that she can be turned—not, perhaps, from woman to man (which would involve a change of sexual nature), but from Jewess to Christian. (The convert Shylock, we recall, disliked the festive music to the strains of which his daughter eloped.) Compare this with Portia's attempt to season Bassanio's suit by music.

soul (Antonio staked his in Belmont), or from merchantry to mercy. The action has demonstrated that souls are as interconnected with bodies as lives (persons) are connected with means of livelihood (purses). The beautiful marriage bond is not far removed from the ugly bond that made it possible in the first place.

Thus topical Belmont is not an Idea like that in Platonic dialectic. The play is generated as Platonic dialectic is,[57] and it divides or classifies the whole of generation into parts as Platonic dialectic does,[58] but the series of contractual hypotheses that generates the dramatic movement of this political play does not cartwheel to the heavens as does Platonic dialectic. That it does not do so lends the play its brilliantly critical aspect.

57. Plato's Socrates says that dialectic is a kind of hypothesization that gets wholly over mere things by working its way up through partial hypotheses, or by putting these hypotheses down (*Republic*). In his discourse, *hupothēsis* usually means "that which is placed under or substantiates," but it can also mean "the plot of a drama," which proceeds from hypothesis to hypothesis as do dialectical arguments. Plato's ironic Socrates might describe the dialectic of *The Merchant of Venice* in the following manner. The intrigue begins when a borrower conditionally deposits part of his human person with a lender in return for a purse. This hypothetical hypothec is the generative hypothesis from which the action begins; it is the prompter (*hupothētēs*) of the subsequent action of the plot (*hupothēsis*) of *The Merchant of Venice*. This first contract between Antonio and Shylock gives way to the marriage precontract between Bassanio and Portia, to a second contract between Antonio and Shylock, and finally to the marriage union of two persons. The plot of the whole play is generated, as is the trial scene it contains, from a series of such hypothetical, fictional, or trial beginnings and endings.

58. Plato's Stranger says that dialectic is a division (*diairēsis*) that breaks wholes down into parts and builds parts up into one whole (*Sophist* and *Statesman*). The ironic Stranger might describe the anatomy of the divisions in *The Merchant of Venice* as follows. Generation comprises sexual generation and asexual generation. Sexual generation comprises the generation of human beings and the generation of (other) animals. Asexual generation comprises linguistic generation and monetary generation. Linguistic generation comprises the generation of supplemental meaning from words and the generation of a plot from hypotheses (or first principles). Monetary generation comprises the generation of monetary interest from hypothecs (or principals).

```
                            GENERATION
        ┌───────────────────────┴───────────────────────┐
      SEXUAL                                          ASEXUAL
   ┌─────┴───────────┐                        ┌──────────┴──────────┐
 Human        "Other" Animals            Linguistic              Monetary
                                         ┌────┴────┐          ┌──────┴──────┐
                                       Words     Plot     Merchantry     Usury
```

There are significant problems in these divisions. For example, Shylock uses language to generate an argument that monetary generation (use) is not asexual but sexual. Conventional divisions of language, sex, race, and religion are conflated with divisions of species. That natural divisions into species turn on the possibility of interbreeding, moreover, underscores how much dialectical division turns on the understanding of generation.

The Merchant of Venice may be treated as a medieval duel (a kind of moot court of law, torture, or combat) in which the synthesis of the dual theses (the defense and the prosecution) is merely an illusion. Perhaps Shylock's early elimination from the stage tends to make us believe or want to believe in the dissolution of the differences between Jew and Christian or between moneylender and nobleman. But the drama is not a tragedy in which, as the dialectician Hegel puts it, two opposite forces are canceled (*aufgehoben*)—destroyed, incorporated, and transcended.[59] (The marriage bond is very like the revenge bond. Since the former is not canceled—it is rather the expected end—neither can the latter be canceled anywhere but in Portia's topical court and courtship.) The confrontation between Christian and Jew—"the difference of [their] spirit[s]" (4. 1. 366)—or between capitalist merchant and feudal royal aristocrat, and the subsequent conversions between the two groups (Shylock's to Christianity, for example, and the royal merchant Antonio's to Jewish usury) hints that such a dramatic movement is possible. But the end of the comedy does not depict the tragic destruction of an old order (one that would sweep Venice away) or the creation of a new domestic and political economy. No single bond is genuinely canceled and redeemed. The fate of Shylock, who sold his revenge, is not a tragic dispensation or reckoning (*moira*) but rather a comic apportionment managed by the comedist Portia.

Yet there are in this comedy suggestions of a tragedy to come. The marriage in Belmont seems to be a stopgap measure taken against the tendency for the tension between purse and person, which thoroughly informs all aspects of life in Venice, to work itself out by destroying the commercial republic. The marrying Christians reveal this tendency. They have already begun to shear the golden fleece from the ewe. Should this fleece, like uninsured marine fleets, prove to be less fruitful of spiritual and material wealth than the infinitely generative Holy

59. G. W. F. Hegel, *Phänomenologie des Geistes*, in Hegel, *Werke*, 20 vols. (Frankfurt, 1970), 3:327–42; translated as *Phenomenology of Mind*, trans. J. B. Baillie (New York, 1967), pp. 462–82. Snider (*System of Shakespeare's Dramas*, 1:307) argues that "the Collision which supplies the nerve of [*The Merchant of Venice*] may be stated, in a general form, to be between Christianity and Judaism . . . as realized in the practical life of men. . . ." Burckhardt (*Shakespearean Meanings*, pp. 144–46, 194) compares dialectical transcendence with political succession in Shakespeare's historical dramas; the same comparison might be made with the successions of the Jewish forefathers (1. 3. 67–70).

Grail, they will eventually have again to seek out the money of Tubal. (Tubal was the ultimate source of the three thousand ducats, and he is left almost untouched by the trials of the play.) The Jewish moneylender behind the scenes of the last act of the courtly world is not easily forgotten. The aristocratic court of the comedist Portia cannot long exist without a day of reckoning in the court of tragedy.

4 / *Language and Property*

THE ECONOMICS OF TRANSLATION
IN GOETHE'S *FAUST*

Gellt est verbum Diaboli, per quod omnia in mundo creat, sicut Deus per verum verbum creat.

MARTIN LUTHER[1]

IN GOETHE'S *Faust*, as in Shakespeare's *Merchant of Venice*, contracts in which one party leaves a conditional deposit with another provide the ground for the dramatic generation of the plot. In Part One, for example, Faust deposits his soul in order to transfer to himself special powers, and in Part Two the Emperor deposits his subterranean estate in an attempt to save the empire from ruin. Faust's contract with Mephistopheles elucidates his attempt to translate linguistically the "Word" of the Bible (*Grundtext*) into action, and the Emperor's contract elucidates an attempt to translate, by the medium of paper money, real estate (*Grundbesitz*) into gold. In *Faust*, as we shall see, translational contracts connect the intellectual possession of an idea, which concerns language, with the possession as property of a commodity like gold, which concerns economics. The way in which linguistic and economic translations are identified with and opposed to each other in *Faust* suggests an economy significant to the study of literature and of philosophical dialectic in general.

Translation

When he first appears on stage, Faust is intellectually and financially bankrupt (364, 374).[2] He would overcome this dual dilemma by min-

---

1. "Money is the word of the devil, through which he creates everything in the world, just as God creates through the true word" (Martin Luther, *Tischreden*, 6 vols. [Weimar, 1912–21], vol. 1, no. 391). See H. Barge, *Luther und der Frühkapitalismus* (Gütersloh, 1951).

2. Johann Wolfgang von Goethe, *Faust*, ed. Erich Trunz (1949), lines 364, 374; in Trunz, ed., *Goethes Werke*, 14 vols. (Hamburg, 1949–60), vol. 3. (Hereafter this edi-

84

ing the meaning of verbal and pictorial symbols. He seems to say: "In order to make mine the hidden treasures of the symbolic world and of myself, I must give myself over to magic." His first attempt to interpret or translate to himself the meaning of a sign (*Zeichen*; 427, 434) results in his learning that he is not a god (439). His second attempt results in his learning that he is not a superman (*Übermensch*; 490). Faust, who believed himself to be the image of God, is like (*gleichen*) only the spirit he can conceive (*begreifen*; 512). Who is this spirit?

Before Faust and we learn the answer to this question, Faust's search is interrupted, ironically, by his famulus, Wagner. Wagner has overheard Faust's monologues (as have we). He mistakenly believes that Faust was merely reciting an antique play (as *Faust* appears to some modern readers), and assures Faust that such recitation is profitable (524). Faust agrees with Wagner's apprehension that his words were playful, but only because they cannot yield active results (556). He wonders whether it is ever necessary to juggle words (553). Wagner believes that language is the means (*Mittel*) by which to translate (*übertragen*) to oneself the source (*Quelle*) that all men seek (562–63); Faust distrusts bibliolatrous researches because they obscure the meaning he seeks. For Faust one's own soul (*eigne Seele*) is the holy source. He pities Wagner for his fruitless philological search to acquire intellectual treasure (*Schatz*) and alludes to Heraclitus' fragment about those who seek to translate to themselves, or to mine, gold and cannot discover it (604–5, compare 6766–67).[3]

Throughout *Faust*, as we shall see, the general problem of acquisition is expressed in terms of translation. In this work of literature, as in German and the Indo-European languages in general, such words as *Übertragung* mean both "economic transference of property" and "linguistic transfer of meaning."[4] Translation in *Faust* thus includes

---

tion of Goethe's works will be referred to as Hamburg Edition.) The numbers in the text refer to lines. Most translations are mine; a few are adapted from the *Faust* translations by Philip Wayne (Harmondsworth, Middlesex, 1949), Walter Kaufman (New York, 1961), and Walter Arndt (New York, 1976).

3. Heraclitus, Fragment 22, in H. Diels, *Fragmente der Vorsokratiker*, 5th ed. (Berlin, 1934).

4. *Translatio* refers to intra- and interlinguistic translation and also to propertal transfer (*Encyclopedic Dictionary of Roman Law* [Philadelphia, 1953], s.v. "*translatio*"). Compare English *translation* and *tralation*; French *translation*; German *Übertragung* and *Übersetzung*; Italian *translatio, metafora, translatore*, and *transferimento*; and Spanish *traslatico, traslado*, and *traslación*. Similarly the non-Indo-European Hebrew *haavarah* means intralinguistic translation (metaphor) and transfer of property.

the inheritance of intellectual property from previous generations. On the one hand, Faust seems to have wanted to carry on the medical tradition bequeathed to him by his father. "What you have acquired from your father, earn it, if you would possess it" (682–83). On the other hand, Faust now knows the difficulties of appropriating knowledge, and he knows that his father did not practice true medicine. On Easter Day, when the people sing the praises of Faust the doctor's son (1007), for example, he insists that he served his father only as a steward who distributed a dangerous drug (*Gift*; 1053). He argues that the people should praise only the divine Father and/or Son, who made a pact with the people on the first Easter Day. Wagner is unable to understand Faust's dissatisfaction with himself. "Does not an honest man do enough if he conscientiously and diligently pursues the art that another has transferred (*übertragen*) to him?" (1057–59). Wagner cannot understand that Faust, in his dissatisfaction, is living up to the standards that God expects from him. In the Prologue to *Faust*, God the Father insists that Faust, who refuses merely to carry on the medical knowledge of his father, is not so much a *Doktor* (which is what Mephistopheles calls him [941]) as the knight of God (299).

Although the servant of God, Faust needs the devil, or at least a devilish agent. "Outside the gates" of the human city, Faust recognizes that he is a mere *Mensch* (940), but soon he wishes to become or to form an alliance with a sub- or nonhuman *Unmensch* (compare 3349). He wishes for a magic mantle that can carry (*tragen*) him to alien (*fremde*) lands (1123). Almost immediately there appears on stage an inhuman being, a poodle, that will soon become, by means of an act of linguistic translation, an agent of translation in general.

Wagner believes that when one opens up an ancient parchment the very heavens will descend on one (1108–9). Faust, however, does not share Wagner's reverence for the written word. He seeks to translate (*übertragen*) into his own medium the alien source that is the holy Original or sacred *Grundtext* (1220–23). Martin Luther, Protestant contemporary of the historical Faustus, translated the apostle John's sentence about the universal origin, "En archē ēn ho logos," as "Im Anfang war das Wort" ("In the beginning was the Word"; compare 1224).[5] Faust protests, however, that he cannot treasure the Word as

---

5. Cf. Goethe, "Übersetzungen" [Translations] (in *Noten und Abhandlungen zu besserem Verständnis des West-östlichen Divans*, Hamburg Edition, 2:255–58), in which Goethe considers Luther's translation of the Bible.

much as the *logos* (1226, compare 1216). (Perhaps, too, he holds that in the beginning there was something other than the *logos*.) He translates John's *logos* into his own terms as Act (*Tat*; 1237). "In mining the meaning from words," Faust seems to say, "I must change it in order to make it mine."

For Faust's active translation of the divine Word, most traditional scholars would excommunicate him from the university on such grounds as bad Greek and religious heresy. Here in Faust's study that translation makes for the transformation of the poodle into the devilish *Unmensch* (nonhuman being) Mephistopheles (1238–321). (I shall suggest later why the translation should precipitate the appearance of the infernal beast.) Faust's translation, or perhaps his inscription of it with a feather pen (*Feder*; 1231), thus prepares the way for (or is itself an architectonic part of) the motive spring (*Triebfeder*) of the tragedy: the deal that Mephistopheles strikes with Faust.

Unlike the other spirits with whom Faust communicated, Mephistopheles likes and is like Faust (1646). Faust and Mephistopheles conclude a pact (*Pakt*; 1414) or bond (*Bündnis*; 1741) apparently different from Jesus's bond (*Bünde*; 748) of the first Easter Day, the mere symbol of which frightens Mephistopheles (1300–2). Mephistopheles proposes that he serve Faust, in return for which Faust shall do the like (*das gleiche*) for him when they meet in the beyond (1658–59). Faust counterproposes a bet and states the terms: "If to the moment I should say, 'Abide, you are so fair,' put me in fetters on that day" (1699–1701). By this wager, which brings to earth the bet in heaven between God and Mephistopheles (compare 315–17), Faust makes a hypothec, or hypothetical deposit, of his soul in return for a still undefined power, and Mephistopheles gambles that he can give Faust the (Rousseauian) rest for which, it seems to Mephistopheles, Faust yearns.[6] Just as the plot of Shakespeare's *Merchant of Venice* begins with the bond in which Antonio lays down his body as a conditional security, so the motive spring of Goethe's *Faust* is this pact in which Faust risks losing his soul. The plot (*hupothēsis*) of *Faust* contains many such conditional deposits—hypothetical hypothecs—which seem to move the plot forward. Its moving force is the prompter (*hupothētēs*) Mephistopheles, who enables Faust to progress by a kind of spiritual or intellectual hypothesization.

6. See Jean-Jacques Rousseau, *Les Rêveries du promeneur solitaire*, fifth promenade, in *Oeuvres complètes* (Paris, 1959–), 1:1046.

Before he begins to serve Faust, Mephistopheles demands that their oral agreement be written down (1714–15). Faust mocks Mephistopheles' Wagnerian demand, and uses the language of the mint to criticize written documents. "A parchment, inscribed and sealed [*beschrieben und beprägt*], is a ghost [*Gespenst*] that we all shy away from" (1726–27). Faust puts no credence in written documents: "The word is already dead in the feather [*Feder*]" (1728). But Mephistopheles is insistent. Although he does not care what kind of paper is used, he demands that Faust sign (*unterzeichen*) in blood (1731–37). To humor the vampyric devil, Faust writes his signature in blood.[7] The signed pact is a "letter of hypothecation," which, like the bond between Shylock and Antonio in Shakespeare's *The Merchant of Venice*, grounds the subsequent action of the drama.[8] Mephistopheles, as we shall see, treats the writing that certifies the hypothetical hypothecation of Faust's soul as a credit note, brandishing it during the drama as a deed entitling him to Faust's soul (11613, compare 6576).

Having secured the deed, Mephistopheles begins to attempt to secure the soul. Playing on Faust's own conceit, that he is shrewder than other men (366), Mephistopheles tries to convince him to look at the world shrewdly enough to understand or receive the power that Mephistopheles claims he would transfer to him (1816–18). Faust, he says, could be as strong as six horses by appropriating their nonhuman legs to his proper human self:

7. The devil in "The Legend of Theophilus from the Nativity of Our Lady" (in *The Sources of the Faust Tradition*, ed. P. M. Palmer and R. P. Moore [New York, 1966], p. 76; cited hereafter as *Sources*) is one of the first Mephistopheles figures to insist that the contract be signed in blood (and, incidentally, that it be sealed or stamped with a ring). In Goethe's *Faust*, Mephistopheles is a kind of vampire, or *Fledermaus*, which seeks blood (5479, 9979, 7789, 7981, 8823, and stage direction at 5298). For the eighteenth-century understanding of the relationship between blood (the circulatory medium of the individual body, in which the soul is often said to reside) and money (the circulatory medium of the body politic), see John Law's arguments that "money is the blood of the State and must circulate" and that "credit is to business what the brain is to the human body" (quoted by Frederick C. Green, "John Law," in Green, *Eighteenth Century Studies* [New York, 1964], p. 7); A. R. J. Turgot, *Réflexions sur la formation et la distribution des richesses* (1766) (in *Oeuvres*, ed. E. Daire [Paris, 1844], 1:45); and François Quesnay, *Essai physique sur l'économie animale* (Paris, 1736) and *Tableau économique* (Paris, 1758).

8. Michael Greener (*A Dictionary of Commerce* [Middlesex, 1971], p. 170) defines "letter of hypothecation" in the following way. "Shippers may borrow from a bank, using the goods they are shipping as security. Until repaid, the banker has a lien on the goods, as they are listed in the bill of lading. The lien, which of course is not a possessory lien, is conveyed by a 'letter of hypothecation.'"

If I can purchase six stallions, are not their powers mine? I tear
along and I am a right proper man, as if I had twenty-four
legs. (1824–27)

That "twenty-four" modifies "legs" tells us something about what the
devil has to offer. Previous Faust stories spoke of twenty-four years during which Faust might enjoy his new powers, or of a sum of twenty-
four unit measures of money. Goethe's Faust, however, is not interested in receiving the traditional sum of money (1599, 1679).[9] It
is Goethe's innovation that in his *Faust* "twenty-four" modifies the
number of horses' legs—the superhuman and beastly horsepower—
that Mephistopheles promises to make Faust's own. (Similarly, "seven"
later modifies Mephistopheles' seven-league boots [stage direction between 10066 and 10067].)

Mephistopheles enjoins Faust to disdain reason and science and to
refuse to speculate about the "horsepower" that he offers (1830–33,
compare 1851–67).[10] Goethe's Faust does not speculate here about the
craft of the devil, whose full significance it requires the action of the
rest of *Faust* to unfold. Yet one young German reader, Karl Marx, who
was much taken with Mephistopheles, wrote for Faust a soliloquy that
purports to reveal the economic aspect of the devil's appropriative
power. Taking Hegel's hint that to refuse to speculate on the matter of
appropriation is to fall into the trap of the devil,[11] Marx's Faust argues
that the power Mephistopheles promises him is the ability of money to

9. For "twenty-four years," see *The Historie of the Damnable Life and Deserved
Death of Doctor John Faustus* [1592 and 1594], modernized and ed. William Rose
(London, 1925), chap. 54 and p. 76; "Description of a Faust Performance in Danzig in
1668. Found in the Diary of G. Schroder, Councilman of Danzig," in *Sources*, p. 245;
and *The Old German Puppet Play of Doctor Faust*, introd. T. C. H. Hedderwick (London, 1887), p. 10. For the offer of money, see *The History of Doctor Johann Faustus*
(1580), ed. J. Haile (Urbana, Ill., 1965), p. 36; and *Sources*, p. 284. In *The Old German Puppet Play*, Faust demands an infinite amount of money.
10. Among the powerful "horses" that Mephistopheles supplies are the magic
horses (*Faust*, "Trüber Tag. Feld," p. 138, line 37) that Faust and Mephistopheles ride
past the gallows where Gretchen is to be executed (4399–404). Cf. Chiron the centaur
in *Faust* Part Two, act 2.
11. Dialecticians are often attracted to or repelled by Mephistopheles' injunction
to Faust to disdain speculative reason (1830–33). For example, Karl Marx and Friedrich Engels, *Die großen Männer des Exils*, in Marx and Engels, *Werke*, ed. Institut für
Marxismus-Leninismus beim ZK der SED [Berlin, 1956–68], 8:236. (Hereafter this
edition of Marx and Engels will be referred to as MEW.) Equally controversial is the
monologue that Mephistopheles delivers between Faust's exit and the Student's entrance (1851–67); for Hegel's interpretation, see note 97.

purchase all things or qualities and hence to produce them for, or in, the purchaser.[12] Marx's way of allying the devil with money suggests important questions about production, or *poiēsis*, that we shall pursue, but it avoids problems of aesthetic and economic symbolization and reproduction considered in *Faust* itself. In *Faust* Part Two, as we shall see, the relationship between symbol and thing, which is presented in Part One primarily as the difference between word and concept, is represented as the tension between coined or paper money and commodity. The seemingly appropriative power of money, which Mephistopheles here offers to Faust, is actually a powerful logic of symbolization, a money of the mind, with which the devil, as Luther has him, plans to abuse unthinking men in order to damn them.

Just after Mephistopheles' famous statement about Faust's going over (*sich übergeben*; 1866) to the devil, Goethe shows how Mephistopheles is planning to damn Faust by showing how he damns his foil, the Student who interrupts Faust's conversation with Mephistopheles. Pretending to be Faust, Mephistopheles disorients the Student by confusing his understanding of the relation of words to things and concepts. His method is to disjoin words and things, to urge the Student to attend only to the written word (1952–53). He praises the "possessibility" of written knowledge, which, as the Student comes to believe, one can carry (*tragen*; 1967) about in black and white. The gate to the temple of certainty is to hold "fast" to the words of the master (1990–92). No need, it seems, to work to understand concepts. At first the Student is loath to accept Mephistopheles' advice, and argues that there must be a concept for each word (1993). But Mephistopheles argues that even where concepts fail the proper word can be found (1995–96).[13] The Student is duped by Mephistopheles' argument that one should credit or believe in (*glauben*; 1999) mere words and that nothing, not even an iota, can be robbed or misappropriated (*rauben*) from a word. A

12. In his essay of 1844 on the power of money, Marx quotes *Faust* (1820–27) and then presents his own Faustian monologue about the monetary qualities of the power of the devil. "As an individual I am *lame*, but money provides me with twenty-four legs. . . . I who can have, through the power of money, *everything* for which the human heart longs, do I not possess all human abilities?" (Karl Marx, *Ökonomisch-philosophische Manskripte aus dem Jahre 1844*, MEW, Ergänzungsband, pt. 1, pp. 564–65; translated as *Economic and Philosophical Manuscripts*, in Karl Marx, *Early Writings*, trans. T. B. Bottomore [London, 1963], p. 191).

13. Elsewhere, too, Mephistopheles uses words to subvert the minds of men (2313–15).

word, like an intellectual possession, is secure from robbery. (At the end of *Faust* there is some suggestion that Mephistopheles, who believes in the power of the note he has asked Faust to sign, himself believes that nothing can be taken from its written words.) Mephistopheles neglected to sign his agreement with Faust, and he is pleased to sign the notebook of Faust's foil, the Student who came to see Faust with money and fresh blood (2045, 1877). Slightly altering the words of Eve to the serpent, he makes his sign (*Zeichen*; 2046). When next we see this foil to Faust, he is an easily damned Baccalaureus (6790).

It is not so easy to damn Faust. In Part One Goethe begins to explain Faust's eventual salvation in terms of Faust's intuition of nameless concepts (*Begriffen*). Faust, for example, conceives (*greifen*) a feeling of love for which he knows no name or word (3059–66): he seems to believe in the ineffability of the divine symbol (1307). Mephistopheles tries to take advantage of Faust's intuition of the ineffable by arguing that Faust's feeling for Gretchen is mere animal desire, and Gretchen herself is displeased that Faust does not name the divine.[14] Throughout the drama, however, Faust continues to stand by the ineffability of feelings and concepts. Words, he argues, bring a false sense of certainty. Faust's refusal to be misled by crediting signs that have no meaning is a characteristic that enables him, though allied with a horsepowerful *Unmensch*, to become a true *Mensch*.

Wealth and Poetry

Faust Part Two begins with an empire that is in hock (*verpfändet*; 4874) just as Part One began with the bankruptcy of an individual who lacked money. In Part Two, as we shall see, the Emperor makes a social bond that recapitulates at the political level the bond Faust made with Mephistopheles.

Mephistopheles insinuates himself into the court of the econom-

14. Faust also has no name for the feeling for divinity (3451–56). Cf. Johann Gottlieb Fichte's discussion of Faust's doctrine that "Gefühl ist alles" ("Feeling is all" [3456]) in *Ueber den Grund Unseres Glaubens an eine götliche Weltregierung* (1798) (in Fichte, *Sämmtliche Werke*, ed. J. H. Fichte [Berlin, 1945; rpr. Berlin, 1965], vol. 5, esp. pp. 188–89). Gretchen notes that, although Faust's unwillingness or inability to name God is like that of her priest, it differs in a way that may be used by devilish forces (3467). Indeed, Faust, who wanted to learn the name of the devil (1328) and can or will not name God, often seems to value too highly the words of Gretchen herself (3079–80).

ically pressed empire and cleverly directs the courtiers' attention away from their thesaural problem, the lack of goods and specie to pay off their debts, to a fiduciary solution, a dependency on a new kind of credit. He argues that the Emperor can pay off his creditors (*Gläubiger*) merely by being believed. "How could credit be lacking [*mangelten*] where undenied majesty commands?" (4878–79). Mephistopheles insinuates that lack of money (*Geld*; 4890), not treasure, is the problem plaguing the empire. If men only believed in the empire, then the Emperor would not need to mine the land for gold. Mephistopheles pretends to be interested in mining, in bringing goods and specie that are deep under the ground up to the light of day (4892); he seems to be a social vampire that would bleed the veins of the mountains and discover "unminted and minted gold" (4894), both medium of exchange and commodity. In fact, however, his interest is only in the medium, and in using the effects of the mint on the minds of men.

Mephistopheles' stated plan is to employ man's natural and spiritual power (*Natur- und Geisteskraft*; 4896) to produce (perhaps to represent) subterranean treasure. The Chancellor argues correctly that this plan is inimical to feudalism and Christianity,[15] but Mephistopheles counters with a critical credo of his own: "What you do not mint, you mean, counts for nothing [*gelte nicht*]" (4922). And prompting, or speaking ventriloquistically through a dummylike astrologer, he argues that gold can be a cornucopia like the sun.[16] The Emperor cares more for satisfying his desires than for scrutinizing the actual source of the promised means to do so (cf. 4945–46). Believing that Mephistopheles intends to use the underground, rather than the crediting minds of gullible men, as his source of treasure, the convinced Emperor grants to Mephistopheles the shadowy obscurity of the underground. He hopes that whatever therein is valuable will come to the light of day (5034; a hope that, ironically, echoes God's statement in the "Prologue in Heaven" that a good man will eventually see the light).

15. On Goethe's interpretation of the fall of feudalism, see L. Goldmann, *Recherches dialectiques* (Paris, 1959), p. 227; and Georg Lukács, *Goethe and His Age* (London, 1968), p. 164.

16. The alchemical language in these scenes recalls Hans Sachs, "Geschicht Keyser Maximiliani loblicher gedechtnus mit dem alchemisten" (in *Hans Sachs*, ed. A. v. Keller and E. Goetze [Tübingen, 1886], pp. 422–26). On the ventriloquistic language of commodities (*Warensprache*), see Karl Marx, *Das Kapital*, MEW, 23:66–67, 97 (translated as *Capital*, trans. S. Moore and E. Aveling [New York, 1967], 1:52, 83) and Marx, "Auszüge aus James Mills Buch 'Elémens d'economie politique,'" MEW, Ergänzungsband, pt. 1, p. 461.

By whom or what will the promised gold be discovered? In Part Two Mephistopheles suggests that the members of the court might take up hoes in order to mine the treasures of the earth (5039), as he suggested in Part One that Faust might hoe in the fields in order to regain youth (2354). In Part Two the Emperor seems to accept this type of work as a means of raising a herd of golden calfs (5040–41). (Faust rejected the hoe as a suitable means [*Mittel*; 2360–64].) The desire of the Emperor for the things of which Mephistopheles has told him, however, becomes so great that it must be restrained. Mephistopheles therefore diverts the Emperor's attention to what will seem, like goods and specie, to satisfy his desire: the deceptive but credited productions of magical art. "The strange coalescing, abstraction, and anticipation of ownership of property, which constitutes the meaning of money," writes Georg Simmel, "is like aesthetic pleasure in permitting consciousness a free play, a portentous extension into an unresisting medium, and the incorporation of all possibilities without violation or deterioration by reality."[17] In *Faust* Part Two, as in Part One, the medium opposing work is magic.

Mephistopheles arranges for subtle changes in the aesthetic production, the masque that was to have been the court's pleasant diversion from the problem of thesaural scarcity in the empire. The Herald of the masque, a proctophantasmiac (4158–60), suspects rightly that ghosts (*Gespenster*; 5501) are disrupting the show. He notes, for example, that Zoilo-Thersites (played by Mephistopheles) interrupts the goddess of all activities (*Tätigkeiten*; 5449–60). Although he claims to be able to "make the high low" and vice versa (5467), the Herald is unable to interpret, or mine below the surface meaning of, three allegorical figures that appear on stage: Boy Charioteer; Plutus, or Wealth (played by Faust); and Starveling (played by Mephistopheles). Boy Charioteer introduces Plutus to the courtiers as the answer to the desire for gold (5569–71), and in a riddling poem he calls himself "Poetry" and describes his relationship to Plutus in terms of dispensation:

> I am Dispensation [*Verschwendung*], I am Poetry; I am the Poet,
> who fulfills himself when he dispenses his own [*eigenst*] good.

---

17. Georg Simmel, *The Philosophy of Money*, trans. Roberta Ash, in *On Individuality and Social Forms*, ed. Donald Levine (Chicago, 1971), p. 180; cf. Georg Simmel, *The Philosophy of Money*, trans. Tom Bottomore and David Frisby (London, 1978), p. 328.

Also I am immeasurably rich and treasure myself as the like
[*gleich*] of Plutus. I enliven and adorn his dance and feast, and
whatever he lacks, that do I parcel out.   (5573–79)

In *Faust*, as in *Pandora* (meaning "all gifts") and *Hermann und Dorothea* (*Dorothea* meaning "gift of the gods"), poetry is identified with
cornucopian dispensation.[18] This association is as old as Aristotle and
Alcidamus, and was common among many eighteenth-century thinkers, such as Alexander Gottlieb Baumgarten.[19] Goethe's Boy Charioteer seems to refer to the Longinian theory in which sublimity or dispensation is the polar opposite of orderly disposition. The effect of
sublime language is irresistible transport, while the effect of disposition
is persuasion. "Sublimity flashes forth at the right moment, scatters everything before it like a thunderbolt, and displays the power of the orator in all its plenitude." The sublime precipitates a sense of production
by the reader. "Our soul is naturally uplifted by the truly [sublime]; we
receive it as a joyous offering; we are filled with delight and pride as if
we had ourselves created what we heard." Longinus' polar opposition
of economy to sublimity, moreover, involves a corresponding opposition of work or resistance to beauty. The audience, like the writer, may
be inventive and skillful, and may work hard at understanding the
events that it sees or reads. The audience, however, cannot control its
reaction to the sublime.[20] As in the philosophy of Immanuel Kant, the
beautiful is that which can, indeed must, be comprehended without
work, so the sublime here is that which we in the audience believe,

18. Cf. 236. As Boy Charioteer is associated with poetry and dispensation, so the
Starveling (5646–65), played by Mephistopheles, is associated with avarice and greed
(5665, 5767–82). Cf. *Faust*, Paralipomen, 102, in *Goethes Werke*, editing commis-
sioned by Sophie von Sachsen, 133 vols. (Weimar, 1887–1919), 15.2:191–92. Hereafter this edition of Goethe's works will be referred to as Weimar Edition.

19. Emil Staiger (*Goethe*, 3 vols. [Zurich, 1952–59], 3:287) suggests that the association of dispensation with poetry was common in the eighteenth century and cites
Goethe's *Maskenzug* of 1798 and *Divan* (III). Wilhelm Emrich (*Die Symbolik von
Faust II: Sinn und Vorformen* [Berlin, 1943], esp. pp. 176–81) considers Faust's double role as Plutus and poet, and suggests that the idea of worth provides Plutus and
poetry with their common ground. Kuno Francke ("Mantegna's Triumph of Caesar in
the Second Part of *Faust*," *Studies and Notes in Philology and Literature* 1 [1892]:
125–28) argues that Goethe was influenced by Mantegna's painting of Plutus. Cf. figure 13.

20. The first quotation is adapted from W. Rhys Roberts, ed. and trans., *Longinus
on the Sublime* (Cambridge, 1899), sec. 1; the second, from G. M. A. Grube, trans.,
Longinus: On Great Writing (New York, 1957), sec. 7.

however erroneously, that we ourselves have created or produced effortlessly. It is the sublime that Goethe depicts in many productions (compare 236) and that, finally, Goethe shows to be unworthy of credit. Without work there is no production; without resistance there is no justifiable feeling of liberation from resistance. In *Faust* the opposition between disposition (Longinus' "body") and dispensation (Longinus' "soul")[21] creates a tension between creditable, real activity and uncreditable, unreal activity. As we shall see, such figures as Homunculus (a soul without a body), Boy Charioteer (who calls himself "Dispensation"), and the poet Euphorion end in a sublime manner.

Boy Charioteer's attempt to explain the relationship of Poetic Dispensation to wealth (Plutus) is not successful. The courtiers do not understand his riddle about aesthetic and economic production, and they are enraged when Boy Charioteer's apparently valuable gifts are metamorphosed into insects (5699, compare 6592–603, 1516–17). The annoyed Herald exclaims: "How much the scamp seems to promise, yet only gives what glitters like gold!" (5604–5). But, as Boy Charioteer argues, the Herald fails properly to interpret the transformation (5609). The Boy must appeal to Plutus, who thus upholds the credentials of Poetry.

> You are the spirit of my spirit [*Geist von meinem Geiste*]. You always proceed after my own mind, and you are richer than I am myself. . . . To everyone let a true word be known: my dear son, I am pleased with you.   (5623–29)

Plutus calls the boy his son, but the latter soon raises questions about this supposed kinship. The "father" and "son" differ along the lines that defined the wager between Faust and Mephistopheles (the opposition between rest and activity). Boy Charioteer asks Plutus:

> Should one give himself over to you or to me? Your followers may rest idly [*ruhn*], it is true, while mine rejoice that they always have something to do [*tun*].   (5702–4)

In *Faust*, Goethe thus considers the kinship between wealth and poetic dispensation, as in *Torquato Tasso* he considers the implications of pat-

---

21. "If you take away the sublime, you will remove . . . the soul from the body." Grube, trans., *Longinus*, sec. 11.

ronage in the arts, and as in *Wilhelm Meister's Apprenticeship* he considers the opposition between commerce and poetry.[22]

Plutus dismisses Boy Charioteer after the Boy has brought a casket from the chariot to the appropriate area on stage. Like other caskets in the works of Goethe, the one carried by the Boy in *Faust* is full of dangers.[23] The courtiers believe they see in it all things, including rolls of coins and ducats that jump as if stamped (*geprägt*; 5715–26). They see the answer to all desire. The Herald is disturbed that the audience takes the seeming for the real. He argues that what they see is mere seeming (*Schein*) or play (*Spiel*), that the contents of the casket are *Goldschein*.[24] "Do you think one would give you gold?" (5730). His warning goes unheeded.

The finale of the masque is signaled by the arrival of Pan (played by the Emperor). Accompanying him are gnomes who mine, or bring to the light of day, gold, "so that man may steal and pimp [*kuppeln*]"

22. In *Torquato Tasso* the relationship of economics to poetry is explored in terms of patronage. Cf. *Pandora* and *Hermann und Dorothea*, in which this relationship is explored in terms of giving and receiving, possession and dispossession: Epimetheus, for example, tries to "fasten" again onto the figure of Pandora, who has disappeared. In these and other works of Goethe, we are reminded that those who cannot give cannot be free or happy (e.g., *Wahlverwandtschaften* [Elective Affinities], pt. 2, chap. 5, Hamburg Edition, 6:396; and *Faust*, 857).

In *Wilhelm Meisters Lehrjahre* [Wilhelm Meister's Apprenticeship] (bk. 1, chap. 10; Hamburg Edition, 7:35–40), the relationship of economics to poetry is explored in an elaborate conversation about commerce (or Plutus in his feudal or postfeudal role). In his "The Youth at the Parting of the Ways," the young poet Wilhelm personified business as a shriveled, wretched-looking sibyl. Werner, on the other hand, considers the goddess Commerce to be (like double-entry bookkeeping) an essential agent of order and balance, and regards Wilhelm's theatrical "Deliverance of Jerusalem" only as a potential box-office hit. Wilhelm is interested in poetic dispensation. Werner extolls the productive aspect of capitalism: "What a drama it will be for you when you see the happiness that accompanies bold undertakings distributed to men!"

23. See *Pandora*, *Natürliche Tochter* [Natural Daughter], and *Zauberflöte zweiterteil* [Magic Flute, Part Two]. Note that the casket (2731) that Gretchen mistakes for a *Pfand* (2786) on a loan in her mother's care is a gift horse (2828), which fails to ensnare her. Cf. the second casket delivered to Gretchen (2875), the casket delivered to Helen by Lynceus (9273–345), and the caskets full of money of which Mephistopheles speaks (3666–69).

24. For an exploration of the relationship of economics to poetry in terms of aesthetic falseness and the counterfeit nature of *Scheingold*, see the first paragraphs of *Wilhelm Meisters Wanderjahre* [Wilhelm Meister's Travels], (Hamburg Edition, 8:7), in which "Felix" (a Latin equivalent of "Faust") discusses cat's gold (*Katzengold*, cf. *Katzengeister* in 2484). See also the diagram in which Goethe carefully relates *Gold* with *Schein* ("Auslegungen des Märchens aus den 'Unterhaltungen Deutscher Ausgewanderten,'" Weimar Edition, 42.2:445).

(5857). Seeming to do the work required to satisfy desire, they would bleed the veins of the mountains for golden blood (5850–51). Instead of actually digging, however, the gnomes flatter Pan as a potential source of all things:

> Here we now discover a wondrous source [*Quelle*] promising to furnish easily what before was hardly reached. (5906–9)

The gnomes promise that the Emperor can introduce, or himself become, a cornucopian source of wealth. "Speak the word only," they implore Pan. One of the gnomes (later to be identified as the Chancellor) makes a plea for the Emperor to do something (later to be identified as certifying a credit note) that will profit all the world. Whatever else the Emperor does, he is taken with and in by the fiery source (*Feuerquelle*) in the casket. His close approach to this source precipitates an explosion that ends the masque. This explosion becomes an important focus in the remaining scenes of Part Two, in which Mephistopheles will seem to establish a fiduciary economy that reveals the secrets of nature.[25] As Kenneth Burke suggests, the masque is an allegorical exploration of a lack of aesthetic and economic funds.[26]

In the following episode, generally called the "Paper Money Scene," what was presented in the *Schein* of the masque as plenty of *Gold* issues as paper money or *Geldscheine*. When the scene opens we learn that the creditors of the Emperor are somehow paid; the army is rehired, and there is fresh blood in the soldiers' ranks (6047). The Chancellor explains what has happened when he reads aloud a text inscribed on a leaf of paper:

> Be it known to anyone who desires it: the ticket [*Zettel*] here is worth a thousand crowns. To it is secured [*gesichert*] as certain guarantee [*Pfand*] the measureless buried goods in the Emperor's land [*Kaiserland*]. It is now being arranged that the rich treasure, as soon as it is elevated [*gehoben*], will redeem this [*deine zum Ersatz*]. (6057–62)

25. In *Maximen und Reflexionen* [Maxims and Reflections], no. 904 (Hamburg Edition, 12:493), Goethe writes that "poetry points to the secrets of nature and seeks to reveal them by means of images [*durchs Bild*]." See Karl Viëtor, *Goethe: The Thinker* (Cambridge, Mass., 1958), esp. pp. 174–77.

26. Kenneth Burke, "Faust II," *Language as Symbolic Action* (Berkeley and Los Angeles, 1966), pp. 163–85.

During the masque the Emperor set his signature to this negotiable paper with a feather pen (*Federzügen*; 6064–70), just as Faust in Part One set his signature to the contract with Mephistopheles with a feather (*Feder*). (Faust's words mocking Mephistopheles' demand in Part One that their contract be a written one—"An inscribed and sealed parchment is a ghost" [1726–27]—make us leery of this "ghost money"[27] in Part Two.) The monetary bargain, which promises delivery of assigned underground goods, is thus the foil to the contract between Mephistopheles and Faust, which seemed to promise delivery of a soul. As a "magic mantle" (1122) seemed to redeem Faust's situation in Part One, so the "magic leaves" (*Zauberblätter*; 6157) of money seem to redeem the political economy of the empire in Part Two. They are "gilded leaves" that, like the "leaf" on which Faust wrote his pact, seem able to transform all that is bad into good. The "poem" on the paper seems to turn it into a "golden leaf."[28]

Unlike the contract in Part One, this signed document promising delivery is reproduced thousandsfold with a stamp (6074). The wonderful technology brings to mind mechanical reproduction by the coin maker's anvil die and the printer's press; Mephistopheles' amazing technique recalls achievements like those of the medieval printer and moneylender Fust.[29] Printing in Fust's medieval world surpassed the old alphabet, but the new monetary sign (*Zeichen*) that is paper money does more: it makes all other symbols supernumerary and at the same time elicits belief in the greatest treasure (6081–82). "Hoc signo victor eris" reads the legend on a coin circulated by the successors of the Roman emperor who was both son of Helena and husband of Fausta (compare 4997–98).[30] In this part of *Faust* the new and ideologically

27. For "ghost money," see chapter 1.
28. In a letter to F. J. Soret (September 30, 1830), Goethe calls the *assignats* that he enclosed in a letter to Soret as an honorarium for Soret's translation of his *Metamorphose der Pflanzen* [Metamorphosis of Plants] not "golden apples" but "gilded leaves." In a letter to Schiller (January 30, 1796) in which he considers *Faust*, Goethe compares poems to golden leaves.
29. Johann Fust (?–1466), often confused with "Faust" (even by his grandson, in a dedication to the Emperor Maximilian), was a printer accused of robbing Gutenberg of the fruits of his invention and of being a moneylender or banker.
30. Constantine the Great (A.D. 288–337), son of Helena and husband of Fausta, saw a vision of a flaming cross with the legend *en toutoi nika* ("by this conquer") just before the Battle of the Milvian Bridge (A.D. 312), a vision that is said to have led to his conversion to Christianity. The legend soon appeared, as HOC SIGNO VICTOR ERIS ("you

subversive mode of symbolization is linked with the historical advent of paper money.

Paper Money and Language

Understanding the significance of paper money in *Faust* requires both consideration of historical and literary antecedents and exploration of the theoretical problems of aesthetic and philosophical—as well as economic—inflation that the Paper Money Scene poses.

In the Paper Money Scene, Goethe imitates Marco Polo's brilliant description of paper money in China, in which Polo tries to explain Chinese financial institutions, which his European audience did not believe to exist, in terms of alchemy and flight.[31] Goethe himself dis-

---

will be victorious through this sign"), impressed into designed coins, including Vetranio's issue of about A.D. 350, in which Victory crowns the emperor. See figure 14.

For Goethe's interest in coins and numismatic terminology, see *Venetianische Epigramme* [Venetian Epigrams], no. 25 (Hamburg Edition, 1:180); *Anhang zur Lebensbeschreibung des Benvenuto Cellini* [Appendix to Benvenuto Cellini] (Weimar Edition, 44:323); and various remarks on coins and medals (Weimar Edition, 49: 99–124). On Goethe's lost essay "Münzbelustigungen" ["Money Pleasures"], see Bernard Pick, "Goethes Münzbelustigungen" (in *Jahrbuch der Goethe-Gesellschaft* 7 [1920]: 195–227), and Hermann Kuhn (*Geprägte Form: Goethes Morphologie und die Münzkunst* [Weimar, 1949]).

31. Marco Polo writes that "the great Kaan causes sheets to be spent for money. . . . The great lord has the alchemy perfectly" (Marco Polo, The *Description of the World*, trans. A. C. Moule and Paul Pelliott [London, 1938], pp. 238–40). Block printing and paper money may have been seen by Polo not only in China but also in Persia, which he probably visited during a short-lived, catastrophic paper money experiment (*The Book of Ser Marco Polo*, ed. and trans. with notes by Henry Yule, 2 vols. [London, 1903], 1:428–30; and Karl Jahn, "Das Iränische Papiergeld: Ein Beitrag zur Kultur- und Wirtschaftsgeschichte Irän's Mongolenzeit," *Archiv Orientální* 2 [Prague, 1938]: 308–40). Goethe knew about the monetary institutions of China from Jean-Baptiste du Halde (*Description géographique, historique, chronologique et physique de l'Empire de la Chine et de la Tartarie chinoise*, 4 vols. [Paris, 1735]; translated as *Ausführliche Beschreibung des chinesischen Reichs* [Rostock, 1747–56], as well as from Marco Polo.

Stuart Atkins (*Goethe's Faust: A Literary Analysis* [Cambridge, Mass., 1958], p. 148) is mistaken in saying that the paper money of which Goethe writes in Part Two may be that of antiquity, since there were no bank notes in ancient Greece. (But see A.-N. Bernardakis, *Le Papiermonnaie dans l'antiquité*, extract from *Journal des Économistes* [March 15, 1874].)

W. Cohn-Antenorid ("Die Quellen des Faustischen Papiergeldes," *Goethe-Jahrbuch* 24 [1903]: 221–24) and Max Reinitz ("Säkularerinnerungen an den Wiener Bankozettel [Beethoven, Goethe und Pratobevera]," *Österreichische Rundschau* 31 [1912]: 365–70) are among those who have addressed the question of literary sources.

liked and distrusted paper money.[32] In *Faust* he recalls such disastrous European monetary experiments as the issuing of *notes de confiance* by John Law (see figures 15–18), the "Don Quixote of finance" (see figure 19).[33] He alludes to the hypothecal and land-secured *assignats* issued during the French Revolution (see figure 20)[34] and to the Austrian redemption notes (called "Scheingeld").[35] And he takes into consideration Shakespeare's account of how Richard II, more "Landlord of England" than its king, issued "blank charters" and "rotten parchment bonds."[36]

The theoretical relationship between aesthetic and monetary theory was explored by several European and American writers during the first part of the nineteenth century,[37] but only Goethe seriously con-

32. On the Prussian banknotes (*Tresorscheine*), for example, see Johann Peter Eckermann, *Gespräche mit Goethe* [Conversations with Goethe], ed. E. Beutler (Zurich, 1948), pt. 2: December 27, 1829. See also Eckermann, *Gespräche*, pt. 3: February 14, 1830; and "Betrachtungen im Sinne der Wanderer," from *Wilhelm Meisters Wanderjahre* (Weimar Edition, 42.2:172).

33. John Law, a Scottish financier and monetary theorist, founded the Banque Générale in France (1716). The bank issued paper money, prospered, and finally collapsed (1720). For an English literary analysis of the French monetary experiment, see Daniel Defoe, *The Chimera: or, The French Way of Paying National Debts, Laid Open. Being an Impartial Account of the Proceedings in France, for Raising a Paper Credit, and Settling the Mississippi Stock* (London, 1720), and George Paston, "Popular Delusions and Impostures," *Social Caricature in the Eighteenth Century* (London, 1905; rpr. New York, 1968). For figures 15–18, see Benjamin Betts, *A Descriptive List of the Medals Relating to John Law and the Mississippi System* (Boston, 1907). Washington Irving, in "The Great Mississippi Bubble: 'A Time of Unexampled Prosperity'" [1840], in Irving, *The Crayon Papers* (New York, [1883]), p. 39, calls John Law a "commercial Quixote."

34. For Goethe's remarks on the *assignats*, see his *Campagne in Frankreich* [Campaign in France], October 13 (Hamburg Edition, 10:278).

35. Alexander Del Mar (*Money and Civilization: or, A History of the Monetary Laws and Systems of Various States Since the Dark Ages, and Their Influence upon Civilization* [1867; rpr. New York, 1969], p. 330): "The 'redemption' or 'anticipation' notes were issued by the Austrian Government [in 1810]. . . . The name of these notes was derived from the expectation that they would be redeemed in coins from the proceeds of certain anticipated revenues." After "the resumption law of 1825 or 1826" these notes came to be called "'Wiener Währung' or 'Vienna currency'" and also "Scheingeld" (p. 335).

36. William Shakespeare, *Richard II*, ed. Matthew W. Black (Baltimore, 1957), 2. 1. 113, 1. 4. 48, and 2. 1. 64.

37. Thomas L. Peacock (*Paper Money Lyrics* [1837]), for example, argues against the introduction of paper currency in England and explores some of the implications of the comparison between literary poems and the "money-men's" "promises to pay." An anonymously authored book entitled *Ein Blick in die Geschichte der Zettelbanken in Europa und auf die Errichtung einer Nationalbank in Baiern* (n.p., 1822) includes

sidered the connection between economic symbolization in paper money and aesthetic symbolization in poetry. In *Faust* this connection involves the inflation that follows from the Emperor's allowing the printed papers to pass for gold.

> With the people it is valid [*gilt's*] as good gold? The court, the army, take it as full pay? However much amazed, I must let it stand as valid [*gelten*]. (6083–85)

His own Marshall reassures the astonished Emperor by describing the widespread circulation of the "flying moneys":

> They scattered everywhere, like wildfire blazing, these winged bills [*Flüchtigen*], and no one could stop their course. Each moneychanger's shop stays open, and every leaf is honored duly with gold and silver—though with discount, truly. (6086–90)

Although the Emperor seems not to notice, the Marshall's words imply that inflation is already affecting the economy of the empire. Just as verbal inflation serves to damn the Student from Part One, so the monetary "kites"[38] (see figure 21) lead the empire toward political disaster in Part Two. The Emperor might have been better counseled by Thomas Gresham, the English contemporary of both Faust and Fust, who explored the general problem of inflation. If the amount of gold is unmeasurable in the same way that Boy Charioteer's gifts are supposed to be, then the inflationary discount must increase infinitely. All moneys, including crowns, will become worthless, as will the crown itself.

Mephistopheles, who had argued earlier in Part Two that belief was all that the court needed to obtain golden wealth, now allies aesthetic with monetary symbolization. Through the medium of the dummy-like Faust, he suggests that the *Kaiserland* is a poetical reserve and that the treasure in the land is, like the fantastical goods parceled out by Poetic Dispensation or Boy Charioteer (5576–79), infinite and unquantifiable. Faust himself compares mining with imagining:

---

a poetic prayer that the land be saved from the "plague of paper" (quoted in Albert Pick, *Papiergeld* [Brunswick, Germany, 1967], pp. 129–30).

38. *Kite* is commercial slang for "exchange bill" (*Oxford English Dictionary*, s.v. "Kite," 3; hereafter this dictionary will be referred to as *OED*). On the financial institution called "flying money" (*fei-ch'ien*) in China (ca. 750), see Lien-sheng Yang, *Money and Credit in China: A Short History* (Cambridge, Mass., 1952), p. 52, and Yang. "Das Geld und seine Bezeichnungen in der chinesischen Geschichte," *Saeculum* 8 (1957): 335.

The surplus of wealth, that, petrified, in your land lies buried in
the ground, lies unused. The most immense thought is to such
wealth [*Reichtum*] a miserable barrier. . . . (6111–14)

Thought cannot measure buried wealth. The winged bills, he says
with some irony, fly higher than fantasy can imagine.

> Fantasy, in its highest flight, exerts itself, but cannot quite grasp it.
> Yet choice spirits fit to see what is deep, in limitless things have
> limitless trust. (6115–18; cf. 640-51)

To Faust's apparent advocacy of credit, Mephistopheles adds reminders
of the ability of paper money to take the place of gold and to help one
know exactly what one possesses (6119–20), just as writing, which he
praised to the Student in Part One, helps one know what one knows.
Mephistopheles and Faust thus formulate a false and inflationary economics of thought. The inadequacy of that economics is later revealed
in a flight of fantasy by Euphorion, the son of Faust and Helen, akin to
the Boy Charioteer.[39] In act 1, however, only the fool (whose role in
the foolish court Mephistopheles until now has usurped) openly questions the insubstantiality of the paper money notes. He asks that he be
allowed to translate the papers given to him by the Emperor into real
estate (*Grundbesitz*; 6171), what Kant calls *Substanz*. As the fool suspects, it will turn out that the *Pfand*, or pledge, that the banknote represents is an idealist *Pfänderspiel* (5194), or play of forfeits.[40]

The Paper Money Scene is part of a critique of the idealist philosophy that operates without material guarantees or substantial securities. As early as 1844 Wilhelm von Schütz considered the philosophical significance of Goethe's description of money in terms of German
idealism.

> It is with seeming money [*Scheingeld*] as it is with seeming phi-
> losophy [*Scheinphilosophie*]—phenomenology. All this is incom-
> parably delineated [in *Faust*], although it remains in the back-
> ground . . . an ingenious knotting together of the real with the
> ideal, or better, as their bilateral confrontation. The fundamental

---

39. Compare Faust's early comments on bold flights of fantasy (640–51). On the
kinship between Boy Charioteer and the flying Euphorion, see note 72.
40. On the fool's request, see Eckermann, *Gespräche* [Conversations], pt. 2: December 20, 1829.

Goethean thought is here; that idealism is paper money [*Papiergeld*] and paper money is idealism; a view that, before *Faust* Part Two appeared [*erscheinen*], was articulated several times.[41]

Von Schütz thus linked Hegelian phenomenology (or logic of appearances) with paper money as it is presented in Goethe's *Faust*. No one, to my knowledge, has gone beyond this analysis, but as we shall see at the end of this chapter and in chapter 5, there is a further connection: Goethe has it that phenomenology promises an "Absolute" through intellectual *Aufhebung* ("sublation") in the same way that Mephistophelian paper money promises "solid" gold through mining, or material *Hebung* ("elevation"; 6062).

In *Faust* the tension between promise and delivery is presented as an opposition between the ideal and the real. What seems to guarantee a promise—Faust's conditional promise to deliver his soul, for example, and the Emperor's promise to deliver underground treasure—is a creditable deposit, a *sumbolon* or hypothec. As Kant argues in a discussion of money and contractual transference of ownership (*translatio/Übertragung*), some contracts require an immediate cash transfer that connects purchase with sale and thus serves as a secure guarantee. In other contracts, alienation of property depends on an exchange of a cautionary pledge or of collateral. Money that changes hands in cash transfers should not be confused with caution money: caution money is not part of the purchase price.[42] (The role of caution money in guaranteeing exchange does not differ in kind from that of a ring broken into two parts for the purpose of later identification of the buyer by the seller and vice versa.) In *Faust* Mephistopheles hopes that paper money—which is insubstantial in the sense that real estate is substantial—will entirely replace both cash transfer and real collateral. His conceptual conflation of monetary *sumbola* with their linguistic counterparts leads toward a devilishly insidious confusion between monetary hypothecs in economic transactions and dialectical hypotheses in idealist philosophy.

41. Wilhelm von Schütz, *Göthe's Faust und der Protestantismus: Manuscript für Katholiken und Freunde* (Bamberg, 1844), p. 236. See too G. Lukács, *Goethe*, p. 200.

42. Immanuel Kant, *Die Metaphysik der Sitten*, [Metaphysic of Morals] in *Kants Werke* (Berlin, 1907–14; rpr. Berlin, 1968), 6:271–86. See the discussion of *ousia aphanēs* ("invisible substance") as "money" and as "property transferred without witnesses" in Marc Shell, *The Economy of Literature* (Baltimore, 1978), pp. 31–35. For Karl Marx's interpretation of money as a pledge, see "The Dead Pledge (*Faustpfand*)" later in this chapter.

In *Faust*, moreover, the word of the Emperor on the banknote seems to substantiate credit and exchange just as the word of God in some English idealist philosophies substantiates the credibility of human discourse.[43] In *The World as Will and Representation* (1819), Arthur Schopenhauer considers idealism and realism in similarly monetary terms:

> By reducing the external world to a matter of faith [*Glaube*], [Friedrich Heinrich Jacobi] wanted merely to open a little door for faith in general and to prepare the credit for that which was afterwards actually to be offered on credit; just as if, to introduce paper money, we tried to appeal to the fact that the ringing coin depended merely on the stamp the State put on it. In his philosopheme on the reality of the external world assumed on faith, Jacobi is precisely the "transcendentalist realist playing the part of the empirical realist" whom Kant censured in *The Critique of Pure Reason*.[44]

In *Faust*, Mephistopheles teaches a monetary as well as a linguistic immaterialism. The "Absolute" (6736) in many German idealist philosophies—one of which the damnable Student, who disdains empirical knowledge (6758), has adopted as his own—is associated by Mephistopheles not only with a lack of substance but also with an *absence* of monetary solvency or of *solida* (Roman coins of "solid" gold).[45]

Why is paper money more to Mephistopheles' liking than coin?

---

43. In English idealism, monetary theory often plays this role. Jean-Joseph Goux (*Économie et symbolique* [Paris, 1973], p. 197) says about the idealist Berkeley what is true of Mephistopheles in *Faust*—that he disassociates symbol from what is supposed to be symbolized. "La philosophie de Berkeley est l'expression extrême, unilatérale, de cette négation de la nature et de la matière qui se réalise dans la circulation signante et monétaire développée. Si elle exprime sur le plan de la conceptualisation philosophique la forclusion de la référence matérielle (négation pure et simple de l'existence de la matière), elle s'exclame dans la même geste: 'Ce compte en banque ne s'est-il pas révélé meilleur qu'*une mine d'or à Amsterdam?*'" (cf. Goux, p. 184).

44. Arthur Schopenhauer, *The World as Will and Representation*, trans. E. F. J. Payne [New York, 1958], 2:7–8. Schopenhauer refers to Immanuel Kant, *Kritik der reinen Vernunft*, A 369; translated as *Immanuel Kant's Critique of Pure Reason*, trans. Norman Kemp Smith (London, 1970), pp. 345–46. For references to the *Kritik der reinen Vernunft*, numbers preceded by A refer to pages of the first edition (Riga, 1781), and numbers preceded by B refer to pages of the second edition (Riga, 1787).

45. In 6735–36, Mephistopheles connects the meanings of *absolut* (including "bald" and "penniless") with those of *resolut* (including "bald"). On the "absolute" currency of the *solidus* (its metallic purity and weight matched, or were adequate to, the claims made for it by its inscriptions), see R. S. Lopez, "The Dollar of the Middle Ages," *Journal of Economic History* 11 (1951): 209–34.

During its historical metamorphosis from commodity (a lump of gold) to coin (a commodity impressed with the stamp of the state) to paper money (a mere impression), *solid* metal undergoes and participates in culturally and philosophically subversive changes. The widespread use of coins, which are both symbols and commodities, may precipitate some conceptual misunderstanding of the relationship between signs and things, but it does not encourage its users to believe that symbol and commodity, or word and concept, are entirely separable. (In his essay on translation, Antoine de Rivarol thus argues that "words are like moneys: they have a proper value before they express all the kinds of value.")[46] Paper money, on the other hand, does appear to be a symbol entirely disassociated from the commodity that it symbolizes.

A theory of coin and paper money that treats them both as kinds of inscriptions may shed further light on the difference between their modes of symbolization, a difference that Mephistopheles uses to his own ends. On the one hand, it is clear that a coin is a composition of a numismatic inscription and a metallic ingot into which the inscription is impressed and to which the inscription refers as a valuable commodity. On the other hand, it is unclear whether paper money should be conceived as a composition of an inscription and an inscribed paper (*Zettel*), whose reference to an untold, unmined, and perhaps nonexistent commodity is ultimately irrelevant to its validity, or whether it should be conceived as a composition of an inscription, an inscribed thing, and a commodity for which the inscription and the inscribed thing, taken together, are an ersatz. Thus the paper money, or *Ersatz* gold (6057–62), in *Faust* raises questions crucial to understanding not only symbolization, but also the epigram, which Gotthold Ephraim Lessing and Johann Gottfried von Herder define as a genre in which the inscription and the inscribed thing are to be thought of as two theoretically inseparable parts of the same whole.[47]

46. "Les mots sont comme les monnaies: ils ont une valeur propre avant d'exprimer tous les genres de valeur" (Antoine de Rivarol, "Des Traductions" [ca. 1785], in *Rivarol* [Paris, 1906], p. 125). See Daniel Droixhe, *La Genèse de la linguistique scientifique de 1650 à 1800*, Ph.D. dissertation, University of Liège, 1974. Umberto Eco argues that "the only difference between a coin (as sign-vehicle) and a word is that the word can be reproduced without economic effort while a coin is an irreproducible item (which shares some of the characters of its commodity-object)" (Eco, *A Theory of Semiotics* [Bloomington, Ind., 1979], p. 25; cf. F. Rossi-Landi, *Il linguagio come lavoro e come mercato* [Milan, 1968]).

47. G. E. Lessing, *Zerstreute Anmerkungen über das Epigramm* [On the Epigram] (in *Lessings Werke*, Vollständige Ausgabe, ed. J. Petersen, W. v. Olhausen, et al., 25 vols. [Berlin, 1925], 14:118–208), argues that with the epigram the inscribed writing

Goethe's analysis of the relationship between language and money had a remarkable influence on social theorists from Wilhelm von Schütz to Oswald Spengler. The theorist for whom *Faust* was a dominant influence throughout his life, however, was Karl Marx. In his ideological analyses of the alienation that obtains in linguistic and monetary appropriation, Marx returns again and again to *Faust*; and many works by Marx can be understood as attempts to interpret and develop Goethe's concern with the relationship between linguistic and monetary alienation and with Hegelian idealism (which Marx calls "mind's coin of the realm").[48] Like Goethe, Marx compares linguistic translation with monetary transaction. In the *Grundrisse*, for example, he argues that

> to compare money with language is not less erroneous [than to compare money with blood]. Language does not transform ideas, so that the peculiarity of ideas is dissolved and their social character runs alongside them as a separate entity, like prices alongside commodities. Ideas do not exist separately from language. Ideas which have first to be translated out of their mother tongue into a foreign [*fremde*] language in order to circulate, in order to become exchangeable, offer a somewhat better analogy; but the analogy then lies not in language, but in the foreign quality [*Fremdheit*] of language.[49]

In *Capital*, Marx redefines the connection between linguistic estrangement (*Entfremdung*) and monetary alienation (*Entäußerung*). Here the commodity Gold, personified as the hero of a series of historical episodes, is transformed first into coin and then into paper money. In explaining the first transformation, Marx associates Faust's translation of John's *logos* as *Tat* ("act") with the assumption by one com-

---

refers to and is not to be thought of apart from that into which it is properly inscribed. Cf. Johann Gottfried Herder, *Anmerkungen über das griechische Epigramm*, in *Herders Sämmtliche Werke*, ed. B. Suphan (Berlin, 1888), 15:337–92.

48. On Marx's critique of Hegel, see chapter 5.

49. Karl Marx, *Grundrisse der Kritik der Politischen Ökonomie (Rohentwurf)* (Moscow, 1939), p. 80; translated as *Grundrisse: Foundations of the Critique of Political Economy*, trans. Martin Nicolaus (New York, 1973), p. 163. In another consideration of the "manifestation of capitalism in the sphere of immaterial production," Marx suggests that only analogies like the ones between hack writers and exploited workers and between teachers and wage laborers are accurate (Karl Marx, *Theorien über den Mehrwert*, MEW, 26.1:385–86; translated as *Theories of Surplus Value*, trans. Emile Burns, 3 vols. [Moscow, 1975], 1:410–11).

modity of the power to measure or to purchase—in effect to translate—all others. For barterers in a premoney economy, writes Marx, no commodity acted as a universal equivalent. In order to facilitate trade, barterers began to think like Faust; they conjured forth an agent of transfer.

> "In the beginning was the act." They therefore transacted before they thought. Instinctively they conformed to the laws imposed by the nature of commodities. They could not bring their commodities into relation as values and therefore as commodities, except by comparing them with some one other commodity . . . as the universal equivalent. . . .[50]

But, as Marx notes, a commodity becomes the universal equivalent by a social act (*Tat*), which, theoretically speaking, consists of the assumption by this commodity of the power to measure or purchase all the others and, practically speaking, consists of the minting (*Beprägung*) of coins. The act of monetary exchange, like the act of linguistic translation, depends on a socially recognized (*gültige*) universal equivalent, which seems to homogenize everything, or to reduce everything to a common denominator.

(This homogenization is like that practiced by the infernal Mephistopheles when he uses his seal to stamp the souls of the damned [11662]. In John's Revelation such a seal is called the monetary mark [*character*] of the "beast" to whom damned men have translated, or given over [*tradere*], their power, a transfer that turns each man into a monetary token for circulation in hell.[51] Lewis Mumford writes that the capitalist economy, which he conflates with other monetary economies, is such a "translation of all goods, services, and energies into abstract, pecuniary terms.")[52]

50. Karl Marx, *Das Kapital* (MEW, 23:101; trans. Moore and Aveling, 1:86, adapted). Marx had integrated the sentence from the Gospel of John, which Goethe's Faust translates, into his unfinished novel *Scorpio and Felix*, chap. 16, which he wrote before 1837.

51. "[The ten kings, or commodities] have but a single purpose among them and will translate [*tradunt*] power and authority to the beast. And no one was allowed to buy or sell unless he bore this beast's mark [*characterem*] either name or number" (Rev. 17:13 and 13:17; quoted in Marx, *Das Kapital* [MEW, 23:101; trans. Moore and Aveling, p. 86]). Cf. Marshall McLuhan's discussion of "Media as Translators" and of "Money: The Poor Man's Credit Card" (McLuhan, *Understanding Media: The Extensions of Man* [New York, 1966], pp. 56–61, 131–44).

52. Lewis Mumford, *The Myth of the Machine* (New York, 1967), "The Mechanization of Mammon," p. 274; cf. "The Linguistic Economy of Abundance," p. 96.

Following Goethe, Marx calls the transformation of coin into paper money more ideologically perverse than that of gold into coin because the former transformation is less visible and hence more easily misunderstood. As paper money, Marx explains, the commodity (gold) seems to use only its exchange value as a means of purchase and to have lost its commodity value. Referring, in *Contribution to a Critique of Political Economy*, to Chamisso's Peter Schlemihl, an analogue to Goethe's Faust, Marx reflects ironically on this development of gold into paper money. ("Gold, unlike Peter Schlemihl [who sold his shadow for money], has not sold its shadow, but merely uses its shadow as a means of purchase.")[53] Similarly Marx reminds us of the topsy-turvy, and hence Mephistophelian or apparently negative, qualities of paper money. Paper money, he argues, upsets our notions of symbolization: "In the circulation of tokens of value [*Wertzeichen*] all the laws governing the circulation of real money seem to be reversed and turned upside down [*auf den Kopf gestellt*]. Gold circulates because it has value, whereas paper has value because it circulates." To many economists exchange value appears, like price, to be an imagined, ideal entity that possesses no reality in commodities. In their confused understanding, Marx writes, "the exchange value of commodities assumes in the price merely a nominal [*ideele*] existence, and in money merely an imaginary or symbolic existence." Marx notes that "the state, whose mint price merely provided a definite weight of gold with a name and whose mint merely imprinted its stamp on gold, now seems [in the printing of paper money] to transform paper into gold by the magic of its imprint." Paper money, however, is actually the token of coined money. The irony is that "in the case of purely imaginary money everything should depend on the physical [*materiellen*] substance whereas in the case of

---

53. Karl Marx, *Zur Kritik der Politischen Ökonomie*, MEW, 13:95; translated as *A Contribution to the Critique of Political Economy*, trans. S. W. Ryazanskaya (New York, 1970), p. 115. Hereafter cited as *Krit. Pol. Ök.* In *Peter Schlemihls Wunderbare Geschichte* [The Wonderful Story of Peter Schlemihl] (Leipzig, 1814), Adelbert von Chamisso (orig. C. A. de Chamisso) tells the story of a man who sells his shadow for gold. Chamisso suggests that a shadow stands in the same relation to gold as does a soul to reputation, and he associates soul with shadow (*umbra*). Marx (*Krit. Pol. Ök.*, MEW, 13:94; trans. Ryazanskaya, p. 115) writes that from the point of view of personified commodities the situation looks like this: "As far as commodities are concerned the token of value represents the *reality of their price* and constitutes a token of their price [*signum pretii*] and a token of their value, only because their value is expressed in their price."

the corporeal [*sinnlich*] coin everything should depend on a numerical relation that is ideal." [54]

The persuasiveness of Mephistopheles' linguistics depends on this ideal or nominal relation. Credit money, an extreme form of paper money, [55] divorces the name entirely from what it is supposed to represent and seems to allow an idealist transcendence (perhaps even a conceptual annihilation) of commodities. [56] As the Student is confused about the relationship between words and concepts (1868–2048), so such economists as the political theorist Pierre Proudhon and the theorist of paper money Adolph Wagner are confused, in their studies of the German *Zettelbank*, about the relationship between paper money and commodities. In *Capital* Marx scores rhetorical points by associating Proudhon's utopian theory, which abolishes the polar opposition between money and commodities and consequently abolishes money itself (which exists only in virtue of this opposition), with Mephistopheles' linguistic doctrine, which disassociates words and concepts. He quotes Mephistopheles' devilish advice to the Student to illustrate the economist Proudhon's faulty mode of argument: "With words a dispute can be won, / With words a system can be spun" (1997–98). In an essay about Adolph Wagner's philological interpretation of the problem of value, Marx quotes the same lines to mock the errors that Adolph Wagner, like Goethe's Wagner, makes about language and about the language of economics. [57]

54. Marx, *Krit. Pol. Ök.*, MEW, 13:93–100; trans. Ryazanskaya, pp. 113–22.

55. Cf. Marx, *Das Kapital*, MEW, 23:141; trans. Moore and Aveling, 1:125–26. The money depicted in *Faust* Part Two is a kind of *Kreditgeld* ("credit money"), which, as Marx writes in *Krit. Pol. Ök.* (MEW, 13:95; trans. Ryazanskaya, p. 116), "belongs to a more advanced stage of the social process of production and conforms to very different laws [from paper money]. Symbolic paper money indeed [*in der Tat*] does not differ at all from subsidiary metal coin except in having a wider sphere of circulation."

56. What Goux (*Économie*, p. 197) writes of George Berkeley might properly be written of Mephistopheles, who empties words of meaning. "On voit [qu'il] pousse jusqu'à ses limites extrêmes une conception de l'arbitraire de l'instrument monétaire. A la limite d'ailleurs, s'il en est ainsi, la monnaie fiduciaire elle-même peut disparaître, s'évanouir. *Le compte courant*, ou *le compte en banque* est encore plus abstrait et plus économique. On se passera de la matière même du jeton: une simple trace, une marque réduite au minimum suffira."

57. For Proudhon, see *Das Kapital* (MEW, 23: 82n–83n, cf. 96n, 99n, 102n; trans. Moore and Aveling, 68n, cf. 81n–82n, 84n, 87n). Adolph Wagner's name makes him the butt of witty comparisons with Goethe's philologist Wagner, and Marx sometimes calls Adolph Wagner the "famulus" of the contemporary "scientist" of lan-

Confusions in the economics of language continue to influence current thought about thought. Problems like those that arise from Goethe's probable reference to "Viennese Currency" (*Wiener Währung*, another name for Austrian *Scheingeld*) inform interpretations of philosophical verification (*Bewahrung*) and validity (*Geltung*). For example, Ludwig Wittgenstein, working from David Hume's theory that language and money are both conventions-without-promise[58] and from German theories of economics and metaphysics,[59] suggests that thought is a kind of validity, that it has the same relation to a sentence that *Geltung* (the agency that lends paper *Geld* its worth) has to unmonied paper. In *Zettel*, Wittgenstein writes that thought is (like) what distinguishes a piece of paper money from any other printed slip of paper, or *Zettel* (cf. 6058).

> One might say: in all cases one means by thought what is living in the sentence. That without which it is dead, a mere sound sequence or sequence of written shapes [*Figuren*]. . . . Or what if we spoke of a something that distinguishes paper money from mere printed slips of paper [*Zetteln*] and [that] gives [paper money] its meaning, its life.[60]

Is it etiquette—politic custom or political economy—that gives a printed paper its epigrammatically numismatic validity and that transforms it into current ticket? Is this what transforms pieces of paper into Mephistopheles' winged bills or into literary flights of fantasy like *Faust*? Focusing on the relationship between paper money and coin, Faust comes to believe that numismatic validity, which is proposed by

---

guage, Meyer. Marx, in his *Randglossen zu Adolph Wagners "Lehrbuch der politischen Ökonomie"* [Critical Notes on Adolph Wagner's "Treatise on Political Economy"] (MEW, 19:355–83), argues that contemporary philology needs change as much as does contemporary economics.

58. David Hume writes that "languages [are] gradually established by human conventions, without any promise" and that "in like manner do gold and silver become the common measures of exchange and are esteemed sufficient payment for what is of a hundred times their value" ("Of the Origin of Justice and Property," in *David Hume's Political Essays* [New York, 1953], p. 33). The anti-Hobbesian Hume compares language and money to "a [political] convention entered into by all the members of the society," which is similarly "not of the nature of a promise" (pp. 32–33).

59. On verification and validity in Lotze, Heidegger, and others, see chapter 6.

60. Ludwig Wittgenstein, *Zettel*, ed. G. E. M. Anscombe and G. H. von Wright (Berkeley and Los Angeles, 1967), sec. 143. The book was given its title by the editors. Cf. Wittgenstein, *Philosophische Untersuchungen / Philosophical Investigations*, trans. G. E. M. Anscombe (New York, 1958), 1. 121 (p. 49) and 1. 268 (p. 94).

a coin (as its own inscription) is derived from the coin itself (as ingot), yet in the end he discards this belief when he comes to consider paper money and inflation.

Georg Lukács alleges that there is a confusion in *Faust* between coin and paper money,[61] but Lukács is dazzled by Mephistopheles' monetary theory and fails to notice that it is the general tendency of *Faust* to put the devil in his place. Goethe does not confuse paper money with coin. In *Faust* paper money is more subversive than coin insofar as it appears to represent the value of the commodity directly. Paper money is a token of gold, but it appears to be a token of exchange value. This value appears to exist only in the commodity and to be expressed by the price. Paper money thus doubly enforces the illusion that exchange value has an independent existence. It is this doubleness that informs Mephistopheles' shadowy "purchase" of the soul of Faust.

The Evocation of Helen

At a magic mirror before which he stands in Part One, Faust sees the image (*Bild*) of a beautiful woman (2429–30, 2436, 2600). Images, like words, may be deceptive. Mephistopheles, who remarks that "man usually believes [*glaubt*] if he hears only words" (2565), hopes that Faust will soon be deceived into seeing a beautiful Helen (in general) in every woman (in particular; 2603–4). The heart of Faust, indeed, is soon impressed (*geprägt*) by the image of Gretchen. (Similarly, in Part Two the courtiers are stamped by the sight of the things in the casket [5719].) Mephistopheles, hoping to use the magic image (*Zauberbild*; 4190) for his own ends, decides to mediate between Faust and the woman he believes that Faust seeks. Acting the pimp (*Kuppler*; 3030, 3338), he argues that the value of a woman's love is measurable by gold (3156, 3314), just as he argued earlier that love, the feeling that for Faust was ineffable, "measures up to" a word. If Mephistopheles could convince Faust of this theory of measurement or payment as he convinced the Student of his linguistic theory, then the love of Gretchen would no longer seem to Faust to be immeasurable or inexpressible in words.

The problem of translation is thus linked with that of prostitution.

---

61. Lukács (*Goethe*, p. 184) is correct in saying that paper money in *Faust* is related to the downfall of feudalism, but is wrong in his belief that Goethe does not distinguish between coin and credit moneys.

Mephistopheles, whose metamorphosis from poodle to devil accompanied Faust's linguistic translation of word to act, plays the intermediary. Goethe often remarks that linguistic translation is itself a kind of pimping or coupling:

> Translators are to be viewed as busy bawds [*Kuppler*] who ballyhoo [*anpreisen*] for us a half-veiled beauty as most worthy of love: they arouse an irresistible inclination for the original.[62]

Part One of *Faust*, then, depicts Mephistopheles' attempt to convince Faust that Gretchen is a whore, which is what Valentine calls her (3730, compare 3767), and that Faust and he are an inseparable duo: "I am the broker and you [Faust] are the suitor" (4071).[63] (When Marx calls money the pimp [*Kuppler*] between human desire and its satisfaction,[64] he is thinking in part of Mephistopheles.)

The motif of pimping continues into Part Two. During the masque, for example, Mephistopheles, who plays the role of Avarice, breaks through a redeemable security or hypothecary pledge of order (*Ordnung Unterpfand*; 5761), erected by Plutus, and delivers a propagandistic speech in favor of paper money, which is supposed to represent, even to produce, gold. He promises the members of the court the golden treasures of the bowels of the earth and the sexually satisfying treasures of an erotic find. (In *Faust* the social production of gold through mining the earth is associated with the individual production of valuable earthen ingots through defecation.)[65] Mephistopheles forms the "gold" contained in the casket into a phallus, a quintessential symbol of male desire. Gold, like sexual desire, is omnimorphous; it can

---

62. Goethe, *Maximen und Reflexionen* [Maxims and Reflections], no. 947 (Hamburg Edition, 12:947). On the translator as middleman (*Vermittler*), see note 71.

63. Mephistopheles imitates Satan, who, in a deleted section of *Faust*, sings these words about money and sex to one who seeks the "life of deepest nature": "Euch gibt es zwei Dinge / So herrlich und groß: / Das glänzende Gold / Und der weibliche Schoos" (Paral. 50, Weimar Edition, 14:306).

64. Karl Marx, *Ökonomisch-philosophische Manuskripte*, MEW, Ergänzungsband, pt. 1, p. 563; trans. Bottomore, pp. 189–90.

65. In Goethe's day the association of coined money with feces was popular throughout Europe. For an example, see figure 22; George Cruikshank's caricature entitled "The Blessings of Paper Money" depicts a figure of Napoleon withdrawing a large pan filled with gold coins from underneath John Bull, who is being dosed with paper money (*Scourge and Satirist: or, Literary, Theatrical and Miscellaneous Magazine* 2 August 1, 1811]: 87). Cruikshank and others, including Goethe, were careful to distinguish coin from paper money. It is remarkable, I think, that in its Mephis-

be metamorphosed or translated into anything (5781–82, compare 4977–92). The phallus, like money, is architectonic. "This metal can be transformed into everything" (5782).

In his praise of paper moneys, moreover, Mephistopheles associates banknotes with love letters. Seeming to recall his praise of the possessibility and portability of written words delivered to the Student in Part One (1966–67), he suggests that both letters and moneys are mediators between whore and client:

> One need not carry purse or sack. A little leaf is light to carry on the bosom and fits well with lovers' letters. . . . Your Majesty will pardon, if I seem to belittle the lofty work.   (6103–10)

The lofty work to which Mephistopheles here refers is the printing of paper money in Part Two. The other productions called works in *Faust* are the creation of the world, to which reference is made in the "Prologue in Heaven," and the creation of Helen herself in Part Two. Throughout Part Two we ponder the status of Hellenic beauty. Is Helen a prostitute like the one that Mephistopheles and Valentine wrongly assume Gretchen to be? Is she a mere ghost like paper money? Or is she somehow real?

In Part Two Helen appears twice, first as a ghost and then, apparently, in reality. These appearances recapitulate the Gretchen and paper money episodes.

Helen's first appearance follows the Emperor's request that Faust bring forth Paris and Helen, the prototypic images (*Musterbilder*) of man and woman (6185). In the masque, as we have seen, Faust and Mephistopheles produced the *Schein*, or appearance, of gold. (What was presented artfully in the masque as plenty of gold was represented in the Paper Money Scene as the cornucopia of monetary *Geld-*

---

tophelian association of money with feces Freudian psychoanalysis makes little distinction between coin and paper money. For example, Ernest Jones does not distinguish conceptually between the coins in Fores' caricature entitled "The Rival Gardeners," which depicts a wheelbarrow filled with coins and labeled "Manure from Italy and Switzerland" beside figures of Napoleon and George III, and the paper money in George Cruikshank's "Blessings of Paper Money" (Ernest Jones, "Anal-Erotic Character Traits," *Papers on Psychoanalysis* [Boston, 1961], p. 426n). Cruikshank's "Paper Money" emphasizes the fundamental differences between coin and paper money that, a few years later, Goethe's Mephistopheles was to use to his own ends in *Faust*. Among psychoanalysts who do try to distinguish between coin and paper money is Sandor Feldman, "Contributions to the Interpretation of a Typical Dream: Finding Money," *Psychiatric Quarterly* 26 (1952): 663–67.

scheine.) The Emperor's present request for ideals makes Faust remark: "First we made him rich, now we are supposed to amuse him" (6191– 92). The production of aesthetic ideals, he suggests, is part of the same structure as that of monetary wealth. Mephistopheles, however, insists that to produce Helen (a love "treasure"; 6315, 6323) is not so easy as to produce paper money. Helen, he insists, is not so easy "to evoke as the paper ghosts of guilders" ("hervorzurufen / Wie das Papiergespenst der Gulden" [6197–98]). Mephistopheles pretends that the machines of the devil are not able to pass (*gelten*; 6202) for heroines, but pro- poses nevertheless to translate Helen from Greece to Germany if Faust visits the Mothers (6216), who, like the "mothers" in John Law's paper money system, seem to confer rights of subscription.[66] Faust, who re- marked, "For every means you want a new fee" (6206), agrees to the contract.

The artful production of Helen does not require extra magic. The Herald notes that the room is already inhabited by spirits (6378). The astrologer introduces the playlet, but he is interrupted by Mephis- topheles, who rises from the prompter's box and reminds us that prompt- ing is the "devil's art of speaking" (6400). Mephistopheles presents an Aristotelian theory of probability and possibility, and, arguing "ven- triloquistically" through the astrologer, suggests that the tension be- tween probability and possibility is resolvable by credit: "Be it now shown with the eyes what you have boldly desired; it is impossible, hence worthy of credit."[67] If one were to restrain reason with a magical word, then daring fantasy could make the impossible appear probable (*glaubenswert*; 6415–20).

In the following playlet, Helen in particular is supposed to be cred- ited as the Beautiful (*Schönheit*) in general. The allegory is a kind of cornucopian dispensation. "In rich dispensations the bold magician, full of confidence, shows to everyone what he wishes, that which is

66. The significance of the Mothers in *Faust* has been considered from many points of view. To my knowledge, however, no one has studied their relationship to the *mères* ("rights to subscribe," literally "mothers") issued by John Law. "[John Law] re- quired subscribers to his new issues [of shares and paper money] to be holders of a certain number of old shares, and . . . there was always a headlong rush to obtain the shares of the old series, called 'mothers' (*meres*) [*sic*] in order to be able to subscribe to the new, called 'daughters' (*filles*)" (Elgin Groseclose, *Money and Man: A Survey of Monetary Experience* [Norman, Okla., 1976], p. 130).

67. On Goethe's theory of probability and possibility in art, see "Prelude in the Theatre" in *Faust*, and *Über Wahrheit und Wahrscheinlichkeit der Kunstwerke* [On Truth and Probability in Art Work] (Hamburg Edition, 12:67–72).

worthy of wonder" (6436–38). As it turns out, Faust is more taken by the image of Helen than other members of the court. To him she seems a blessed boon, the source of beauty (*der Schönheit Quelle*; 6488). The image he saw in the magic mirror, he now says, was a mere smoke image (*Schaumbild*; 6497) of Hellenic beauty.

Faust is so enraptured that Mephistopheles must prompt him to keep to his part (6501). He reminds Faust that Paris, whose seizure of Helen Faust would now repeat, is a mere ghost; that Faust himself is the author of the phantasmagoria entitled "Der Raub der Helena" ("The Rape/Robbery of Helen"; 6546–48). The German Faust, however, still wants to appropriate to himself the Greek Helen. Like the Emperor at the end of the masque, he oversteps the bounds of art, and, holding the key brought from the Mothers, tries to seize Helen.

> What robbery [*Raub*]! Is it for nothing that I am here? Is not this key in my hand! Through terror, waste and waves it led me, through solitudes, here to firm shore. Here I fasten [*fass'*] my foot! Here are realities.   (6549–53)

The German Faust would appropriate the Greek Helen from the Trojans and thus hold fast to reality. He ignores the arguments, like that of the stranger in Goethe's *Collector*, that *Schönheit* such as hers is mere *Schein*.[68] Like the Emperor at the end of the masque, Faust grabs for the ideal as though it were real. "Der Raub der Helena" ends, like the masque, in an explosion.

Faust, however, does not cease to attempt to appropriate, or translate, Helen to himself. Classical Walpurgisnacht (act 2) depicts his dreamlike search for her, and the Helena Act (act 3) depicts its apparent success. In act 3 Goethe makes what is impossible appear probable to Faust and to us. (We replace the courtly audience from act 1.) The German man acquires the Greek woman; the German devil Mephistopheles travels with this man from Germany to Greece, to which the devil is alien, and the devil is translated (*übertragen*; 8013) into the Greek Phorkyas; and Helen, speaking German in Greek syntax,[69] is united with Faust in a kind of matrimony. Faust, it seems, accomplishes in a medieval castle, perched amid ancient Troy/Greece and Goethe's Germany, the kind of appropriation of the Hellenic that he

68. See, for example, the argument in *Der Sammler und die Seinigen* [The Collector and His Own], fifth letter (Hamburg Edition 10:73–78).
69. Cf. *Pandora*, in which Pandora speaks German with Greek syntax.

sought. It appears that Faust accomplishes in the central act of Part Two what Goethe sets forth as two complementary maxims for translators: with the help of a middleman Faust brings himself to an alien (*fremde*) nation and also brings that alien nation to himself in such a way as to find its property (*Eigenheit*) in himself.[70]

Helen sings of the marvelous union between herself, Faust, and their child Euphorion as a bond (*Bund*); Faust sings of their being bound together (9705); and the chorus, too, sings to their union (*Verein*; 9710, 9736). For a while everyone credits the union as a treasured possession and boon (*Schatz, Hochgewinn, Besitz,* and *Pfand*). But they are ultimately deceived. Although the aim of some translation is to make familiar what was strange, no middleman (*Vermittler*) can translate or appropriate the Hellenic treasure (*Schatz*) to Germany in such a way that the alien Helen can become homely fare (*Hausmannkost*).[71] In *Faust*, the apparent union of the German and the Greek falls apart. Its product and sign, Euphorion, is too much an outburst of divine spirit, which, as Longinus noted, is difficult to bring under control. Prefigured in the masque as Boy Charioteer, or Poetic Dispensation,[72] Euphorion is as little at home in Germanic Greece as was the Boy in the masque. His end, like that of the child of Faust and Gretchen in Part One, is swift. Euphorion flies too high (9821), as does paper money, and, like Homunculus, he ends in the sea. The bond between Helen and Faust is shattered. Poetry, it turns out, is illusive and inflationary. Whatever necessity impelled Euphorion to break the lawful but dreamy bond (9883), his leave-taking precipitates that of Helen herself.

Helen may represent "reality" in Faust, as Lukács suggests.[73] Once

---

70. Goethe writes: "Es gibt zwei Übersetzungsmaximen; die eine verlangt, daß der Autor einer fremden Nation zu uns herüber gebracht werde, dergestalt, daß wir ihn als den Unsrigen ansehen können; die andere hingegen macht an uns die Forderung, daß wir uns zu dem Fremden hinüber begeben und uns in seine Zustände, seine Sprachweise, seine Eigenheiten finden sollen" (*Zu brüderlichem Andenken Wielands*, Weimar Edition, 36:329–30).

71. In a letter to the younger J. H. Voss (July 22, 1821) Goethe wrote: "Wie hoch haben wir daher den Übersetzer als Vermittler zu verehren, der uns jene Schätze herüber in unsere täglichen Umgebungen bringt, so wir vor ihnen nicht als fremden seltsamen Ausgeburten erstaunen, sondern sie als Hausmannskost benutzen und geniessen."

72. Eckermann (*Gespräche* [Conversations], pt. 2: December 20, 1829) reports that Goethe said that Euphorion and Boy Charioteer are ghosts of each other.

73. Lukács (*Goethe*, p. 187) calls "real" the second raising of Helen.

Helen learns to speak German, however, Mephistopheles has some control over her. Mephistopheles, Goethe says, is a director of the Hellenic ghosts in act 3; he can stop the action. (See stage directions at 8929–30 and 8936–37.) He knows that Helen is a ghost as "petrified" (8930) as the golden treasure in the underground to which Faust elsewhere refers (6111). Goethe himself wrote of Byron, on whom Euphorion is modeled, that he was "much money and no authority."[74] Like the *Schein* of the masque, in which gold appears to be discovered, Helen is a paper model.

The Law of the Fist (Faustrecht)

Faust Part Two, as Hegel might note, depicts allegorically the downfall of a society typified by feudal dueling and the rise of a society typified by modern warring.[75] The political allegory begins with the spiritual dueling between Faust and Mephistopheles in Part One, and occupies many scenes of Part Two. War informs *Faust* Part Two from "Der Raub der Helena" to the politically significant conflations of such concepts as robbery and contribution (*Raub* and *Kontribution*) or deceit and exchange (*Täuschung* and *Tausch*).

In Classical Walpurgisnacht, a Hellenic version of the Germanic Walpurgisnacht of Part One, insectiform animals and pygmies mine golden treasure from an island mountain that seismic forces have raised above sea level. The griffon (*Greif*), a political tyrant, supervises

74. Cf. Lukács (*Goethe*, p. 189) and Goethe's review of Byron's Faustian *Manfred* (Weimar Edition, 44.1:189–93).

75. G. W. F. Hegel, in his *Phänomenologie des Geistes* (in *Werke*, 20 vols. [Frankfurt, 1970], 3:271–72; translated as *The Phenomenology of Mind*, trans. J. B. Baillie [New York, 1967], pp. 384–85), comments on the individualism of Faust's struggle in Part One and suggests that Faust holds that the only true reality is the reality of individual consciousness. In the *Philosophie des Geistes*, par. 432, Zusatz (*Werke*, 10:222; translated as *Hegel's Philosophy of Mind*, trans. William Wallace [Oxford, 1971], pp. 172–73), Hegel deals directly with the transition from the situation of feudal duel (the one between Faust and Mephistopheles and the one between God and Mephistopheles) to that of modern politics. "The feudal system was supposed to be a society based on law, but was so only to small degrees. There the knight, no matter what he might have done, wanted to be esteemed [*gelten*] as without stain and without reproach, and the duel was supposed to prove this. Although the rule of might [*das Faustrecht*] was elaborated into certain forms, yet its absolute basis was egotism. Consequently its practice was not a proof of rational freedom and civic honor, but rather a proof of barbarism and the shamelessness of a desire which, in spite of its vileness, was ambitious for outward honor."

the mining and guarding of the treasure, and, like Faust, he tries to grasp (*greifen*) "women, crowns, gold" (7102; see figure 23.) The griffon speaks of gold in leaves as Mephistopheles spoke of paper money (7582, 6104). He implores his pygmy miners not to allow their enemies to rob them (7584), and encourages them to swarm "only with the gold herein!" (7600).[76] Similarly, he expounds a theory of etymology, or digging for verbal sources (7094–98). But as the Centaur Chiron, who carries Faust through classical antiquity, tells Faust, who is seeking the Hellenic ideal of woman, it is erroneous to seek literal sources. Helen's age, for example, Chiron compares to a fact that philologists would unearth but that is unimportant to Helen's timeless form, which poets alone can bring to show (*Schau*; 7429).

Two philosophers, Anaxagoras and Thales, watch the geographic and political events on the island mountain. Anaxagoras makes an offer to a foil to Faust, the chrysaloid Homunculus: "If you can accustom yourself to mastery [*Herrschaft*], I will have you crowned as king" (7879–80). The clever Thales, who better understands the workings of symbolic appropriation,[77] urges Homunculus to reject the devilish offer. Thales' advice is prudent, for the island mountain is destroyed in the night of its birth. This destruction suggests to the spectator a possible end to a Faustian attempt to make all things one's own property (*Eigentum*) and to establish over it the kind of mastery that Hegel calls "law of the fist" (*Faustrecht*).[78]

At the beginning of act 4 we know that Faust wants mastery, which he associates with property. "I would gain mastery, property. The act is all, not reputation" (10187–88). Mephistopheles does not understand the human desire that impels Faust, and offers him "the riches of the

76. The mining episode in Part Two has its counterpart in the works of Mammon in Part One. See 3664–65 and 3912–35.

77. Thales was famous for his use of economic contracts, especially the *sumbolon* (Aristotle, *Politics* 1. 4. 6–8). At one point in Classical Walpurgisnacht, Homunculus, who has become Thales' follower, suggests that philosophers often break their heads in trying to explain what to Homunculus seem to be mere pots. Thales tries to explain how nonsensical (if aesthetically necessary) symbols, like the potlike "Cabiri," can come to be more highly prized than even the golden fleece (8215). To explain intellectual evaluation, he resorts to a monetary metaphor. "It's rust that first gives the coin its worth" (8224). The value of money, explains Thales, derives not so much from its intrinsic worth as from suppositions about its patina or age.

78. For Hegel on *Faust* and *Faustrecht*, see note 75. For Schiller, who makes the same connection, see Schiller's letter to Goethe (September 13, 1800). "Fist-law" is the English translation of *Faustrecht* (OED, s.v. "Fist," 4).

world and its mastership" (10131). Jesus refused the same offer in Matthew 4:8–10, and Homunculus refused Anaxagoras' similar offer in Classical Walpurgisnacht. Here Faust, who in Part One expressed his disinterest in amounts of wealth, eschews the devil's offer. Faust wants neither to dig in the earth nor to raise earthen islands from the sea, but to appropriate to himself a new shore between the land and the sea. He wishes to harness the force of the sea itself: "Then would my mind dare to overfly itself; here would I fight, this would I subdue" (10220–21). In formulating this plan for subduing the ocean and making new real estate, Faust recalls the terms of the original wager with Mephistopheles: "This is my wish, dare to expedite it!" (10233).

Mephistopheles too assuredly concludes that the expedition of Faust's command will be easy for him (10234). From the conditions of war he believes he can win shore rights for Faust. As it happens, the Emperor (*Kaiser*) is warring against a counter-emperor (*Gegenkaiser*).[79] Mephistopheles and Faust plan to form an alliance with the Emperor in order to gain land rights, seize booty, and otherwise gain their own ends. (In this sense, they are allies of the counter-emperor against whom they seem to struggle. The Emperor thus has a relation to Faust and Mephistopheles like that of Faust to Mephistopheles; Faust pities the Emperor as Mephistopheles pities Faust [297–98], and Mephistopheles himself suggests that Faust and the Emperor are akin to each other [10244].) Faust, who earlier conspired with Mephistopheles in the showing of false wealth and in the subsequent conflation of government and pleasure (10245, 10251), knows that the victory that he and Mephistopheles plan to promise the Emperor is deceit, magic delusion, or hollow *Schein* (10300).

When the besieged Emperor appears on stage, he expresses fear that he acted wrongly in making paper money (10422), and again describes his experience at the end of the masque. In the casket, he says, he saw a mirrorlike source (*Quelle*) that revealed to him a counter-emperor. Somehow his own breast was sealed. "I felt my breast sealed [*besiegelt*] when I stood mirrored [*bespiegelt*] in that fiery realm" (10417–18). In the forms in which they are used, *Spiegel* ("mirror") and *Siegel* ("seal") rhyme with each other, and with *Geld* ("money"). (The description of

79. Goethe, in *Aus meinem Leben, Dichtung und Wahrheit* [From My Life, Poetry and Truth], pt. 1, bk. 1 (Hamburg Edition, 9:20–21), discusses Charles the Great, Charles IV, Maximilian ("the last 'kaiser'"), and Gunther von Schwarzburg as counter-emperors and emperors.

the sealing of Faust's breast by the image of Helen in Part One contains similar associations of *Spiegel* with *Siegel*.) A mirror, which produces a counterfeit image, is as much an agent of personal alienation, or translation out of oneself, as is money. The mirror, and the seal described by the Emperor, who now faces the counter-emperor, reveal to us, as did the Paper Money Scene, the material, spiritual, and aesthetic results of the Emperor's signing promissory notes.

Faust, appearing in court as a necromancer supposedly obligated to the Emperor (10447), promises to supply military weapons and personnel. The church berates such means, and the Emperor himself wonders to whom he will be obligated for such help (10603). The General accuses the king of making a union (*vereinigen*; 10693) with devilish forces, but even he gives up command of the situation.[80] Mephistopheles believes that he is now in control. To Faust's "What's to be done [*zu tun*]?" he gives an answer that Faust hardly believes: "It is done [*getan*]" (10710).

The true nature of Mephistopheles' "mighty men" (10329), with whose aid the Emperor seems to win victory, is revealed allegorically when they rob the tent of the counter-emperor. One seizes (*greifen*; 10788) the goods of the counter-emperor; another is overly dispensative (*verschwenderisch*; 10816) and loses his stolen treasure. To answer the followers of the Emperor, who accuse them of robbery, the "mighty men" use Mephistophelian logic: their booty, they say, is not illegal *Raub* but rather legal *Kontribution* (10828). As in Gresham's Law, the bad (*Raub*) drives out, or replaces with counterfeit near-synonyms, the good (*Kontribution*). "To change the sense of the words of a language," says Rivarol, "is to alter the value of the moneys in an empire."[81]

In the following scenes the Emperor himself, while in the tent of the apparently defeated counter-emperor, contributes the Empire legally to those who seem to have helped him in battle.[82] The treaties by which the Emperor parcels out various rights—including the right to

80. At first the Emperor refuses to give Mephistopheles the cross-shaped staff that symbolizes the leadership of the imperial army. Compare the unwilling sharing of the sceptre by Herald and Plutus in the masque.
81. "Changer le sens des mots d'une langue faite, c'est altérer la valeur des monnaies dans un empire" (Rivarol, "Sur le style" [ca. 1788], in *Rivarol*, p. 122.)
82. For historical information about the act by which Faust seems to receive the fief, see the *Golden Bull* issued by Charles IV in 1356, reprinted in an edition of 1766, and discussed by Goethe in *Aus meinem Leben* [From My Life], pt. 1, bk. 4 (Hamburg Edition, 9:158).

mint money—depend on signs and signatures, as did Faust's contract with Mephistopheles and the Emperor's paper money:

> The word of the Kaiser is great and secures every gift [*Gift*]. But to empower it there is necessary the noble writ, the signature is necessary. (10927–29, compare 10966)

The Arch-Chancellor refers to a holy signature or seal:

> With good will, I confide the important statute to parchment, for the good of the realm [*Reich*] and our own good. The chancery will obtain fair copy and seal it; with holy signature will you, the master, empower it. (10971–74)

In private conference, the Archbishop accuses the Emperor of being in league (*Bunde*) with Satan (10982, compare 10871). To redeem the sin of the Emperor, he argues, it is necessary to erect an ecclesiastical monument and bell tower on the spot where the sin was perpetrated (11005–16). The Emperor is willing to sign the documents: "Bring me a formal document, conveying [*eignen*] this gift to the church and I will sign [*unterzeichen*] it with joy" (11021–22). The Archbishop also demands "some booty-gold" (11028) and the tithes, quitrents, and taxes from the rich shore (*Reiches Strand*) that the Emperor has granted to Faust. Although the land does not yet exist, the Archbishop assumes that the church will eventually get everything that it demands, and he cites scripture to his purpose (11040). At the end of act 4 we hardly know to whom will belong the real estate yet to be uncovered by Faust.

At the beginning of Act 1, the Chancellor warned the Emperor that "When everyone destroys, when all suffer, majesty itself is set to robbery [*Raub*]" (4810–11). At the end of act 4, the Emperor expresses his fear that this robbery or rape could well occur, as legitimate contribution, through the medium of signature: "I could sign [*verschreiben*] over the whole realm" (11042). The Emperor, victim of the designs of the devil, fears that he has written off, or translated to others, the empire that he once possessed.

The Dead Pledge (Faustpfand)

At the beginning of act 5, Faust seems to have transformed the old shoreline into his own real estate. A plot of land tenured by two old peasants, however, mars his proper self, or property (11151–55, compare 10187). He complains that his "magnificent possession [*Hochbesitz*] is not clear" (11156). Some things are not his own (*eigen*), and the richer he becomes the more he understands how much he lacks (11241–52). Faust's goal is to translate all alien things into his own property. In the *Zueignung* (meaning both "dedication" and "appropriation") to *Faust*, however, we learn the ambiguity in all possession: "What I possess [*besitzen*] seems far away to me, and what is gone becomes reality" (31–32). The difficulty of self-appropriation, which Goethe here expresses as he commences in 1797 the reworking of forms (*Gestalten*; 1) he first explored in the *Urfaust* of 1775, becomes for Faust in act 5, which Goethe composed as late as 1831, a fundamental problem of political alienation and appropriation.

As in act 1 Poetic Dispensation (Boy Charioteer) claims to be able to provide Wealth (Plutus) with what he lacks, so in act 5 Mephistopheles provides Faust with the peasants' land he wants. But Faust is displeased at the murderous means of the devilish appropriation: "Were you deaf to my words? Exchange [*Tausch*] I wanted, not robbery [*Raub*]" (11370–71). Faust wanted *Tausch* ("exchange"); Mephistopheles translated this into his own discourse or way of acting as *Täuschung* ("deceit"). In *Faust*, however, exchange is the polar opposite of deceit, just as contribution is the polar opposite of robbery. In *Faust*, position is counterbalanced by negation in a dynamic union of mutual dependency. One of Goethe's epigrams, "Totalität," expresses the impossibility of separating what we admire (perhaps a man like Faust) from what we despise or pretend to despise (an ass like Mephistopheles): "And if he has no behind, how is the noble man to sit down?"[83] A *Mensch* cannot progress without somehow allying himself with an *Unmensch*.[84] Faust, then, may try to ignore the necessity of such an alliance, but Mephistopheles' agents defend their murderous actions by referring to laws, like those of Gresham about language and those of

83. Goethe, "Totalität," Weimar Edition, 2:263. Quoted by Friedrich Engels, *Die wahren Sozialisten*, MEW, 4:258.
84. Karl Marx (*Kritik der Hegelschen Rechtsphilosophie* [Critique of Hegel's Philosophy of Right], MEW, 1:378) defends the "unholy" alliance between Faust and Mephistopheles in the following way: "Der Mensch, der in der phantastischen Wirklichkeit des Himmels, wo er einen Übermenschen suchte, nur den Widerschein [cf. "Gleichnis," *Faust* 512] seiner selbst gefunden hat, wird nicht mehr geneigt sein, nur den Schein seiner selbst, nur den Unmenschen zu finden, wo er seine wahre Wirklichkeit sucht und suchen muß" (cf. *Faust* 3349, 490). More than once, Faust wishes

Marx about capitalism, which seem to legitimate the conceptual exchanges of *Kontribution* for *Raub* and *Täuschung* for *Tausch*.

Faust can no longer derive pleasure from the accumulation of things. Even the sight of merchant ships and of the caskets of booty that they carry does not delight him as it delights the Faust imagined by Oswald Spengler in his *Decline of the West*.[85] They serve only to remind him of what is behind, or the behind of, his merchant-mastership.

Finally, blinded by care, a declining Faust must depend on a hidden

---

that Mephistopheles were remetamorphosed or retranslated into a dog (*Faust*, "Trüber Tag. Feld." p. 137, lines 16–20), to which he compared himself (*Faust* 376). According to Marx, however, Mephistopheles is the unwitting means of Faust's salvation, conferring on Faust both the alienating and alien power of money and the "radical chains of servitude" by the overcoming of which, according to Marx's dialectic of master and slave, the German proletariat can be emancipated (*Kritik der Hegelschen Rechtsphilosophie* [Critique of Hegel's Philosophy of Right], MEW, 1:391).

85. This is how Spengler's Faust praises the connection between Faustian money and the mind: "The Faustian money-thinking 'opens up' whole continents, the water-power of gigantic river-basins, the muscular power of the peoples of broad regions, the coal measures, the virgin forests, the laws of Nature, and transforms them all into financial energy, which is laid out in one way or another—in the shape of press, or elections, or budgets, or armies—for the realization of masters' plans. Ever new values are abstracted from whatever world-stock is still, from the business point of view, unclaimed, 'the slumbering spirits of gold,' as John Gabriel Borkman [Henrik Ibsen's dramatic character] says; and what the things themselves are, apart from this, is of no economic significance at all" (Oswald Spengler, "Money," in *Decline of the West* trans. C. A. Atkinson, 2 vols. [New York, 1926–28], 2:485–86). Spengler argues that the "bodily money of the Apollinian style [that is, the stamped coin] is as antithetical to relational money of the Faustian-dynamic style [that is, the booking of credit units] as is the Polis to the State of Charles V" (2:477). (Spengler associates Charles V with cheques based on credit, which were invented by Frederick II [2:489].) He holds that in the modern world (and in *Faust*) "the act, by which the function is fulfilled in writing [modern paper money]" is most significant (2:490). Of this act Spengler writes that "it *is* money—Faustian money, namely, which is not minted, but *thought of as an efficient centre* coming up out of a life which elevates the thought to the significance of a fact. *Thinking in money generates money*—that is the secret of the world-economy" (2:492).

In Spengler's thought, as Adorno suggests, "mind and money go together" and economic matters express a particular "state of soul." "Economics becomes a 'form-world' like art, a sphere which is the pure expression of a soul that is as it is, a sphere which constitutes itself essentially independently of the need to reproduce life. It is no accident that in matters of economics Spengler remains a helpless dilettante. He speaks of the omnipotence of money in the same tone that a petty bourgeois agitator would use to rant about the international conspiracy on the stock market. He fails to see that in economics the decisive factor is not the medium of exchange but production" (Theodor W. Adorno, *Prisms* [London, 1967], pp. 25, 67–68).

light within his individual self (11499–510). He believes that his imperial word is sufficient to handle a thousand hands: "The word of the master alone confers power" (11502). But Faust is deceived. He imagines, for example, that servants of his are building a paradisiacal land (11569), but, as one of the peasants earlier predicted, servants of Mephistopheles are actually building a paradisiacal image (11086). Once again the informing tension in *Faust* is the difference between the symbol and the thing: the image and the land, the word and the concept, the ticket and the gold.

Faust's last monologue, perhaps, overcomes this difference. He imagines that servants are building a land where men will live "though not secure [*sicher*], yet free for active toil [*tätig-frei*]" (11564). The construction and maintenance of dikes ensures that the citizenry will work in ceaseless activity: "He only earns his freedom and existence who must daily conquer them anew" (11575–76). He envisions in the future a free people that, significantly, will need neither mastery nor a master's word: "Such a throng I would like to see standing on free ground [*Grund*] with a free people." Faust seems to fulfill the terms of the wager: "Then I'd dare hail the fleeting moment, Ah, linger still, you are so fair!" (11581–82, compare 1706, 2710, 11600). With this statement Faust dies.

Mephistopheles and his servants believe that Faust mortgaged his soul in order to receive from them a short-term loan of power (11610). Although he pities Faust, Mephistopheles fully believes that Faust will now have to pay off his creditors, or believers (11611). On this account he takes the "deed written in blood" (11613) from his pocket and waves it before the audience as if it were a *mortuum vadium*, not on visible real estate, but on an invisible soul—as if it were a *gage morte*, or dead pledge.[86]

In most earlier versions of the Faust legend, Faust is carried off to hell.[87] In the "Prologue" to Goethe's *Faust*, however, God foretold a

86. Sir. Edward Coke (*The First Part of the Institutes of the Lawes of England: or A Commentary upon Littleton* [London, 1628], p. 205) writes: "It seemeth that the cause why it is called mortgage is, for the Lessor will pay at the day limited such summe or not, & if he doth not pay, then the Land which is put in pledge upon condition for the payment of the money is taken from him forever and so dead to him upon condition, etc. And if he doth pay the money, then the pledge is dead as to the Tenant, etc."

87. Gotthold Ephraim Lessing's lost *Faust* is the exception. At the end of Lessing's drama, says Johann Jakob Engel in a letter to Karl Lessing, the angels put Faust into a deep sleep; it is only a phantom (*Phantom*) of Faust that disappears from the devils (in

new role for the devil, who is the apparent marplot of the divine design, and hence predicted a new finale:

> Of all the spirits that negate, the rogue gives me least to do. For man's activity [*Tätigkeit*] can easily abate, he soon prefers uninterrupted rest [*Ruh*]. Hence it seemed best to give him this companion who entices and brings things about and must, as devil, create. (338–43)

Mephistopheles, the unwitting agent of God, loses the hypothecated soul for which he struggled throughout *Faust*. He is about to seal the soul of Faust with his stamp (11662), when heavenly spirits translate to heaven the soul that he believed to be a treasure that was pledged (*verpfändet*) to him (11829–30).[88]

Mephistopheles hardly understands losing his investment (11837), and many readers take his side. Some critics suggest that a gratuitous *deus ex machina* saves Faust. They suggest, in other words, that God is the mortmain of the mortgage, the security of which is the soul of Faust. This soul He redeems by raising it above the down-to-earth hypothecation in the pactual bond (*Pfand*), so that it becomes a heavenly chrysalis (*Unterpfand*; 11984) from which Faust is born a heavenly angel. Other readers suggest that the power of woman is the mortmain of the mortgage, and that Gretchen plays the major role in saving Faust (compare 12110). (If Gretchen is what saves Faust from bondage to Mephistopheles, then she has to have overcome her belief that everything and everyone is bound to gold: "All contend for gold, and all depend on gold" [2802–4]; figures 27 and 28.)

In an early version of *Faust*, Mephistopheles argues with God about the outcome of the bond, much as Shylock might have argued with lawyers in the Venetian court.[89] Mephistopheles has wrought in the court a change no less than that of Hans Sachs' alchemist,[90] but, like Shakespeare's usurer, he has victimized himself as well as the court.

Lessings Werke, ed. Julius Petersen and Waldemar v. Olshaufen [Berlin, 1925; rpr. Hildesheim, 1970], pt. 10, vol. 8, p. 221). Christian Friedrich von Blankenburg noted in 1784 that in Lessing's *Faust* the angels say to the disappointed devils, "What you saw and now believe you possess is nothing but a phantom [*Phantom*]" (ibid., p. 218).

88. On the spiritual translation of souls, cf. *OED*, s.v. "Translation," 1. 1. c.

89. Goethe, *Faust*, Paral. 69, 70, 95, 96, and 206. (Weimar Edition, 15.2:181, 187–88, 246).

90. Sachs, "Geschicht Keyser Maximiliani."

Mephistopheles, who throughout the drama stood by the bond, is, in the end, stood up by it. He it was who described to others the future amortization of paper money (6126), but as it turns out, Mephistopheles can receive the mortgaged soul of Faust no more than the people of the Empire, former believers (*Gläubiger*) who have become creditors, could amortize their money.[91]

Mephistopheles' failure to comprehend his loss involves a misunderstanding of monetary and contractual translation. In the *Nicomachean Ethics*, Aristotle defines money as "a guarantee of exchange in the future for something not given."[92] In the *Grundrisse*, Marx shows how money can appear in the form of collateral (*Pfand*). Men place their faith in this collateral "because it is an objectified, mutual relation between their productive activity [*Tätigkeit*]. Every other collateral may serve the holder directly in the function of objectified exchange value. Money, however, serves him merely as 'the dead pledge or mort-gage [*Faustpfand*]' of society, but it serves as such only because of its social (symbolic) property; and it can have a social property only because individuals have alienated their own social relationship from themselves so that it takes the form of a thing."[93] As *Faust* turns out, Faust, who sought what Hegel calls *Faustrecht* ("law of the fist"), is saved by Mephistopheles' misunderstanding of what Marx calls a *Faustpfand* ("dead pledge").

The Dialectical Plot

Goethe's *Faust*, as we have seen, exposes apparent similarities among linguistic, propertal, sexual, spiritual, and other kinds of translation. Translation not only is depicted by the plot of *Faust* as its content, but also is internalized in the plot as an informing element. *Faust* conflates its content, which includes the hypothecal contract depicted in the wager scene, with its form, which includes the series of apparently dialectical hypotheses that allow Faust to progress and that Faust finally seems to overcome. In Goethe's drama, as we have seen, Faust lays down his soul conditionally (hypothetically) as a deposit (hypothec) to

91. Cf. Marx, *Krit. Pol. Ök.* (MEW, 13:117; trans. Ryazanskaya, p. 140): "The former believer becomes a creditor and turns from religion to jurisprudence. 'I stay here on my bond' [*Merchant of Venice* 4. 1. 242]."
92. Aristotle, *Nichomachean Ethics* 5. 5. 14. Cf. *Politics* 3. 5. 10.
93. Marx, *Grundrisse*, p. 78; trans. Nicolaus, p. 160, adapted.

Mephistopheles, a negative motive spring (*Triebfeder*)[94] or prompter (*hupothētēs*) of subsequent action. The conflation of spiritual deposition, on which the making of the wager depends, and economic deposition, on which the movement of the plot (*hupothēsis*) depends, is the motor of progress in *Faust*.[95]

Wilhelm von Schütz noted in 1844, by which time hypothecal banks were widespread in the German states (see figure 24), that the *Ersatz* in the paper money contract in *Faust* (6062) depends on a hypothecal deposition. "Faust counsels [the Emperor] to make paper money . . . as a hypothec [*Hypothek*] of the subterranean treasure that is not yet brought up to the light of day through mining industry."[96] All the hypotheses of *Faust* are contracts of alienation, which tend both to ensnare by hypothecation and to offer the means by which to transcend hypothecation. In both the intellectual and economic aspects of *Faust*, man progresses or acts by setting forth (depositing) something, using it to translate himself over a spiritual or material barrier, and ultimately transcending what was originally set forth. Throughout *Faust*, spiritual and material deposition are comprehended in a single vision, a vision often called dialectical.

Scholars adduce various kinds of evidence to show that *Faust* is dialectical in the Hegelian sense. They point out, for example, that in

94. In German thought *Triebfeder* was associated both with money and with dialectic. Friedrich Ludwig Schröder, for example, writes "Geld ist die Triebfeder aller seiner Handlungen" (*Die heimliche Heirath*, 1.2, in *Dramatische Werke*, ed. E. v. Bülow, introd. Ludwig Tieck [Berlin, 1831], vol. 1). Schröder's work is a version of George Colman and David Garrick, *The Clandestine Marriage* [1766], in which Lovewell says, "Money (you will excuse my frankness) is the spring of all his actions" (act 1). (Cf. P. A. Caron de Beaumarchais, *Le Barbier de Séville* [1775], 1.6: "Gold, my God! gold, that is the nerve of the plot [*le nerf de l'intrigue*]"). *Triebfeder* is a critical term for Immanuel Kant; see, for example, his *Kritik der reinen Vernunft* [Critique of Pure Reason], A 15 = B 29, A 555 = B 583, A 589 = B 617, A 812 = B 841, A 853 = B 881.

95. On hypothesis and hypothecation in the dialectic of Plato, see Marc Shell, *The Economy of Literature*, chap. 1. The association between philosophical and propertal processes suggested by the historical development of such terms as *hupothēsis* and *hupothēkē* recalls the Hebrew (or Aramaic) *asmakhta*, which, in the Talmud, both "applies to such contracts in which one of the parties binds himself to an unreasonable penalty, which presumes that there was a lack of deliberate intention on the part of the person entering into it" and "denotes the use of a biblical text merely as a 'support' for a *halakhah* ["law"] without suggesting that the *halakhah* is thus actually derived from this exegesis" (*Encyclopaedia Judaica*, 16 vols. [Jerusalem, 1971–72], 3:751–54).

96. Von Schütz, *Göthe's Faust*, p. 36. On the hypothecal banknote in Germany, see Albert Pick, *Papiergeld*, p. 162.

his *Phenomenology* and *Philosophy of Right* Hegel adapts Mephistopheles' account of Faust's going over to the devil (1851–52, 1866–67),[97] or that one section of the *Phenomenology* begins with an explanation of the spiritual development of Faust in Part One.[98] In fact, however, the *Faust* drama informs only a small part of the *Phenomenology*, a part in which Hegel explores the inability of Faust to reach the goal set for him. Hegel argues generally that going over to the devil is not a dialectical procedure, that the devil can never be the agent of dialectical negation. Dialectical negation, argues Hegel, depends on a relationship between logical categories (such as true and false, or good and evil) lacking in Goethe's tale of man and the devil:

> Evil and falsehood are indeed not so bad as the devil, for in the form of the devil they get the length of being particular subjects; *qua* false and evil they are merely universals, though they have a nature of their own with reference to one another.[99]

The particularity of Mephistopheles disallows dialectic. Mephistopheles is merely the comic spirit of a dueler who always denies.

Other aspects of *Faust* suggest its undialectical qualities. The protagonist, for example, goes directly to heaven without passing through the hell, whence came Mephistopheles, or, as Hegel says, without holding fast to the negative and death.[100] Moreover, the opposition of act to rest, which informs the terms of the wager and the distinction between Poetry and Wealth, is undialectical. In Hegel only the opposition of movement in one direction to movement in another is or can become dialectical.

The most significant difference between Hegelian and Faustian dialectics, however, concerns the means and ends of progress. Although

97. Hegel, *Phänomenologie* (*Werke*, 3:271; trans. Baillie, p. 384) and *Philosophie des Rechts* (*Werke*, 7:19; translated as *Hegel's Philosophy of Right*, trans. T. M. Knox [Oxford, 1952], p. 6).

98. Hegel (*Phänomenologie* [*Werke*, 3:270; trans. Baillie, p. 384]) considers the state of mind of one like Faust: "Insofar as he has risen from out of the substance of ethical life and [out of] the quiescent [*ruhigen*] state of thought, and attained [his] conscious independence, [he] has left behind the law of custom and of substantial existence, the kinds of knowledge acquired through observation, and the sphere of theory: these lie behind [him] as a gray shadow that is just vanishing." Cf. *Faust* 2038–39.

99. Hegel, *Phänomenologie* (*Werke*, 3:40; trans. Baillie, p. 98).

100. Ibid. (*Werke*, 3:36; trans. Baillie, p. 93).

the hypothecation of a soul in *Faust* and the hypothesis of a concept in the *Phenomenology* seem identical, the Faustian Act differs fundamentally from what motivates the *Phenomenology*. In *Faust*, on the one hand, the hypothecal bond is finally a useless item to Mephistopheles, however useful it has been to *Faust*. Only the mistaken devil holds that the bond ought to be exchangeable for the soul of Faust. The bond in *Faust* is not cashed in by the devil, but rather is dismissed from *Faust* much as Malvolio's claim is dismissed from Shakespeare's *Twelfth Night*. In the *Phenomenology*, on the other hand, the hypotheses that are the counterparts to the hypothecal bonds in *Faust* continue to be useful after each *Aufhebung* ("sublation") of thesis and antithesis into synthesis. Each hypothesis is cashed in for a synthesis that is both homogeneous and heterogeneous with it. At the moment of being redeemed the hypothesis has a value like that Mephistopheles holds his bond should have, but which in *Faust* it lacks. *Aufhebung* in Hegel's *Phenomenology* has for its counterpart in Goethe's *Faust* the *Hebung* ("elevation") of solid treasure that the paper money inscription promises but never delivers (6062).

This talk of cashing in bonds may seem too metaphorical a way to distinguish between *Faust* and the *Phenomenology*. Contemporary criticism has it that *Aufhebung*—which I am now translating as "cashing in"—refers only to the cancellation or equation of opposite forces to a relative zero, as it does in Kant, or to the cancellation and transcendence of opposites, as it does in Hegel. In its strictly mathematical sense, of course, *Aufhebung* does refer only to magnitudes that reduce each other to zero, or that mutually annul or suppress each other, and therefore become indifferent to their equation. As scholars of eighteenth-century commercial language have noticed, however, an *aufgehobene* note or bond still has positive value as a receipt or a discharge from debt. This positive value of the negative bond is explicit in the philosophy of Hegel, in which the zero is at once negative and positive.

In *Faust*, dialectical movement (if it exists at all) does not consist of forces that anyone, much less Faust or Mephistopheles, can cash in according to the ways of dialectic. The positive value of the negative bond is absent from *Faust*, in Part One of which, Hegel says, Faust is engaged merely in the search for individual pleasure. The individual Faust, if not the masterless progeny that he foresees in his last monologue in Part Two, lacks the universal viewpoint of man and the absolute knowledge to which philosophical dialectic is supposed to offer access.

Faust, who contracted with a devilish behind, is left behind in the development of the spirit. It is as though the whole plot of *Faust*—the interest, as it were, on the principal that is the original wager between Mephistopheles and Faust—can pass beyond the confrontation between Faust and his counterpart Mephistopheles neither logically nor dialectically, but only by way of divine mechanics.

In an autobiographical remark Goethe seems to have recognized the lack of qualitative difference between the original hypothesis of *Faust* and its final result. He describes his own life in terms of making, as did Faust, the most of a single hypothec. "I am in the position of a man who in his youth has a great many silver and copper coins which in the course of his life he changes for ever larger denominations, until at last all his youthful possession lies before him in coins of pure gold."[101] Gold counts more than silver and copper. As money rather than as metal, however, the gold coins are homogeneous with the coins of smaller denomination from which they are changed. Goethe admits no qualitative distinction between the wealth of his youth (Part One) and that of his age (Part Two). The changings of age merely repeat in greater denominations those of youth. Part Two, like Part One, delivers to the attentive reader no satisfactory sublation of the series of interrelated hypothecs and hypotheses that inform the plot of *Faust* and that it depicts.

Nor, perhaps, is *Faust* supposed by Goethe to satisfy such a reader. His contemporary Hegel argued that literature can depict dialectical struggle in some stages, but cannot work through the contradictions of partly negative hypotheses and discover truth. Some readers of *Faust*, like the courtly spectators of the masque, may see in the masked ending of Goethe's work the pure gold—the true victory of Faustian Man—that they desired from the beginning. Others, like the fool at the end of the Paper Money Scene, are wise enough to cash in *Faust* for the search for wisdom that led Goethe to write it.

101. Eckermann, *Gespräche* [Conversations], pt. 2: December 6, 1829. Cf. Lessing's *Briefe antiquarischen* 52, quoted in chapter 6, note 8.

5 / Money of the Mind

DIALECTIC AND MONETARY FORM
IN KANT AND HEGEL

ACCORDING TO Plato and Hegel, dialectic comprises two related ways of thinking, the *division* of a whole into parts and the *generation* of a whole from partial hypotheses. These dialectical methods are exemplified and informed by monetary representation and exchange. Plato, for example, argues that most men unwittingly divide up the conceptual and political world in which they live by a kind of division that is formally identical with money changing. His dialogues show how the dialectical relationships of the whole Idea (the One) to its special parts (the many) differ from the relationships of a coin of large denomination to the coins of smaller denomination into which it may be changed. They show how monetary differs from dialectical differentiation.[1] Plato stresses that ignoring or relying uncritically on deceptive interconnections between economic and linguistic categories (rather than taking them into account) renders the intellectual disease of which they are symptomatic more difficult to diagnose and more politically dangerous. In the thought of such modern philosophers as Arthur Schopenhauer[2] and Immanuel Kant[3] there is still some un-

1. On the relationship between division (*diairēsis*) and money changing in the Platonic dialogues (in which both the intellectual process and the financial one are signified by *kermatidzein*), see Jakob Klein, *A Commentary on Plato's Meno* (Chapel Hill, N.C., 1965), p. 81. Cf. Seth Benardete, "Eidos and Diairesis in Plato's *Statesman*," *Philologus* 108 (1963): 212.

2. "Every *general* truth is related to special ones as gold to silver in so far as we can convert it into a considerable number of special truths that follow from it, just as gold coin can be turned into small change" (Arthur Schopenhauer, "On Logic and Dialectic," in *Parega and Paralipomena: Short Philosophical Essays*, trans. E. F. J. Payne [Oxford, 1974], 2:21).

3. Immanuel Kant sometimes considers even the idea of virtue, which Socrates in the *Meno* seems to conflate with the One, in terms of money changing. "All human

questioned dependence on formal relationships between division and money changing.

Plato argues that dialectical generation, or the production of the whole from partial hypotheses, may be connected with monetary processes in the same way as dialectical division. Socrates, for example, is said to deposit in his interlocutors partial falsehoods or likenesses of the whole Idea that the god has deposited with him. These seminal parts are homogeneous with the Idea in the same way that monetary interest is homogeneous with its principal or that a child is homogeneous with its progenitor.[4] Socrates' maieutic art ensures that from these likenesses are generated, by a series of intellectual births and rebirths from the minds of his interlocutors, intellectual offspring ever more like the Idea. (In the same way the hypotheses figured on the divided line approach the Idea ever more closely.) Thus Socrates husbands the Idea as if he were a midwife, and he draws intellectual hypotheses out of and to the Idea as if he were a banker drawing out compound interest from a financial deposit or hypothec.[5]

Greek dialecticians thus articulate the relationship of genuses with species in terms of monetary differentiation and elucidate intellectual hypothesizing in terms of monetary hypothecation. That articulation, as we shall see in this chapter, involves tropologies of division and hypothesizing that are similar to (and which perhaps influenced) the tropologies of adequation (*adequatio*) and sublation (*Aufhebung*) proposed by Kant and Hegel. In Hegelian dialectic, for example, differentiation (division) and hypothesizing similarly involve the generative potential of parts (hypotheses and antitheses) and the absolute whole. They involve the mutual cancellation of two partial *Hypotheses* in polar opposition to each other, and their incorporation and transcen-

---

virtue in exchange is fractional currency," says Kant. "He is a child who takes it for genuine gold [*ächtes Gold*].—But it is better to have fractional currency [*Scheidemünze*] than to have no medium in circulation: fractional currency can be changed for cash money [*baares Geld*], albeit with considerable loss" (*Immanuel Kant's Anleitung zur Menschen- und Weltkenntnis, nach dessen Vorlesungen im Winterhalbjahre 1790–91*, in *Immanuel Kants Menschenkunde*, ed. Fr. Ch. Starke [Hildesheim, 1976], p. 82).

4. For Plato's analogy from intellectual offspring both to animal offspring (*tokos*) and to monetary interest (*tokos*), see Plato, *Republic* 507, 509, 534.

5. In English, as in Greek, *hypothec* (from *hupothēkē*, literally "deposit") and philosophical *hypothesis* (from *hupothēsis*) are cognate. On Socrates' divided line, see Marc Shell, *The Economy of Literature* (Baltimore, 1978), pp. 39–45.

dence by a third. This transcendence, Hegel implies, is the sublative cashing in (*Aufhebung*) of an already canceled or annulled financial bond, or exhausted *Hypothek*.[6] The moderns—Kant and Hegel—shift dialectic, as we shall see, away from the Platonic division of the Ideal One towards the cancellation (*Aufhebung*) of things to zero. The modern movements from division to sublation and from One to none, however, do not eradicate the "economics" in dialectic. The modern concept of sublation, indeed, seems to express the historical fact of the internalization of economic form in philosophy.

Suppression and Adequation in Kant

In *An Attempt to Introduce the Concept of Negative Quantities into Mundane Wisdom* (1763), Kant discovers suppression (*Aufhebung*) to zero in Newtonian physics and in credit economics.[7] Kant considers two kinds of opposition. Logical opposition is contradiction, affirming and denying something about a single subject. (Such affirmation and denial, as Kant says, are of no consequence: *nihil negativum repraesentibile*.) Real opposition, on the other hand, arises when two predicates of a single subject are opposed, but without logical contradiction. Real opposition occurs, for example, when a single body is pulled in different directions by two forces so that one force tends to suppress (*aufheben*) the other.[8] One direction in which the body is pulled may be called "negative" and the other "positive," but these words are meaningful only when the directions are taken in relation to each other.[9]

6. In German philosophy the association of *Hypothek* with *Hypothesis* is suggested by the discussions of both words in Johann Georg Walch, *Philosophisches Lexicon*, 4th ed. (Leipzig, 1775; rpr. Hildesheim, 1968).

7. Kant, *Versuch, den Begriff der negativen Grössen in die Weltweisheit einzuführen*, in *Werke in zehn Bänden*, ed. Wilhelm Weischedel (Darmstadt, 1968), 2:775–819. Unless otherwise noted, references to Kant's *Werke* are to this edition. The relation between this *Versuch* and other works of Kant is a theme of Susan Meld Shell, *The Rights of Reason: A Study of Kant's Philosophy and Politics* (Toronto, 1980); and Hans Saner, *Kant's Political Thought: Its Origins and Development*, trans. E. B. Ashton (Chicago, 1973).

8. "In its mathematical sense, [*Aufhebung*] is used of magnitudes which reduce each other to zero [or which] mutually annul or suppress each other, and therefore become indifferent to their equation (W. T. Harris, "Note," in *Hegel: Selections*, ed. J. Loewenberg [New York, 1929; rpr. 1957], p. 102).

9. Some thinkers on the left ignore the significance of the distinctions that Kant makes between logical and real opposition. Lucio Colletti ("Marxism and the Dialec-

The principal example of nonphysical suppression that informs Kant's concept of negativity is mutual suppression by credit and debt. (The example is not surprising; the opposition of positivity to negativity was first "discovered" by Brahmagupta when he studied the unique interaction of credit and debt in the monetary economy of India in the seventh century A.D.)[10] Throughout *The Concept of Negative Quantities*, Kant refers to "negative" debt and "positive" credit as real opposites. In this way he allies *Aufhebung* with a zero sum:

> A person who owes a debt to another person of 100 florins must find this sum. But suppose that the same person is owed 100 florins by another. The latter is then held as reimbursing the former. The two debts united form a ground [*Grund*] of zero. There is no money to give and no money to receive.[11]

In economics, as in physics, the zero is supposed to be a relative nothing, the final result of *Aufhebung*. In Kant's thinking, an *Aufhebung* is the cancellation to zero, or stasis, of a debt (*Aktivschuld*) by a credit (*Passivschuld*) when both *Schulden* are "predicates belonging to a single subject and are quantitatively equal to each other." The *Grund* is zero.

Kant seems to generalize this notion of reciprocal exchange infinitely.[12] In *The Concept of Negative Quantities*, he applies the notion of mathematical negativity and reciprocity to psychology, to the estimation of the total values of pleasure and displeasure, to crime and pun-

---

tic," *New Left Review*, no. 93 [September-October 1975], pp. 3–30) suggests that this distinction is necessary to understanding "the relationship between Marxism and science." The distinction also pertains to the historical development of dialectic from Plato to Marx and to thinking about the relationship between money and commodity, as well as about the oppositions between and contradictions within social classes.

10. H. G. Zeuthen (*Geschichte der Mathematik im Alterum und Mittelalter* [Copenhagen, 1896], esp. p. 280) argues that the Indians invented negative numbers by observing an economy of debts and credits. Cf. J. Ruska ("Zur ältesten arabischen Algebra und Rechenkunst," *Sitzungsberichte der Heidelberger Akademie der Wissenschaften Philosophisch-historische Klasse* [1917], 2 Abhandlungen, esp. pp. 35, 49, 60–61, 104, 109–10, 113–14) on Indian sources of Greek "algebra"; and Morris Kline (*Mathematical Thought from Ancient to Modern Times* [New York, 1972], p. 185), who notes that the "first known use [of negative numbers] is by Brahmagupta about [the year] 628."

11. Kant, *Versuch*, in *Werke*, 2:784; cf. 2:785–89.

12. On a similar generalization of the concept of reciprocal exchange, see Gregory Vlastos, "Equality and Justice in Early Greek Cosmologies," *Classical Philology* 42 (July 1947): 173–74.

ishment, and so on. For Kant, the sum total of such opposites is or should be zero. The concept of zero and of negativity is thus crucial to Kant's studies of morality and human intentions. Numerical mathematization informs the Categorical Imperative of his later works on morality. And in *Perpetual Peace* (1795) the notion that different forces cancel each other informs a modern political theory of the balance of powers in which, as in Adam Smith's economics, a cunning historical ruse is seen to balance out and perfect the separate tendencies of individuals, larger groups, or nations. The end of this historical balance is a mutual cancellation, which becomes a dynamic equilibrium that is supposed to move history forward.[13] The theory of negative quantities, which began by associating equation with mutual suppression, ends with a metaphysical and political justification of the liberal free-market system.

Plato tried to show how opposites, such as pleasure and pain, participate in each other as species of one genus or as parts of a single unity. Kant, however, tries to show that such opposites mutually suppress each other to zero. The Being of unity in Plato, then, is replaced by the *Grund* of a relative zero in Kant.

This replacement, which relies on a theory of equilibrium or equation, affects the Kantian theory of truth. The Platonic conception of truth is connected with the one way to One (*alētheia*). The Kantian conception of truth, however, is connected with the double way of equation towards zero. In the *Critique of Pure Reason* (1781, second edition 1787), for example, Kant adopts the Thomist definition of truth as the equation or adequation of *intellectus* and *res*.[14] He assumes as granted "the nominal definition of truth, that it is the agreement [*Übereinstimmung*] of knowledge with its object."[15] Thus he associates

13. Kant, *Zum ewigen Frieden*, in *Werke*, 9:191–251. The transformation of "mutual cancellation" into "dynamic equilibrium" is already treated in Kant's cosmological *Allgemeine Naturgeschichte und Theorie des Himmels* (1755), in *Werke*, 1:219–400.

14. For Plato, see the ironic Socrates' etymological explanation of truth (*alētheia*) as "the wandering way of the god" (*theia alē*) (*Cratylus* 421b). For Thomas Aquinas, see his *Quaestiones disputatae de veritate*, question 1, art. 1. Aquinas borrows the phrase *adequatio res et intellectus* from Isaac Israeli (ca. 855–955).

15. Kant, *Kritik der reinen Vernunft*, A 58 = B 82; translated as *Immanuel Kant's Critique of Pure Reason*, trans. Norman Kemp Smith (London, 1933), p. 97. (For references to the *Kritik*, numbers preceded by A refer to pages of the first edition [Riga, 1781] and numbers preceded by B refer to pages of the second edition [Riga, 1787].) The "object" in question is the object of knowledge, not the thing-in-itself.

logical truth with an adequation implying the existence of two things that are (in some essential way) adequate or equal to each other. As a matter of course, an equal subtracted, or lifted up (*aufgehobene*), from an equal leaves zero.[16] The tropic movement towards zero is essential to the concept of truth as adequation.

Kant argues that the general logic of truth can be either analytic or dialectic. Analytic logic is a negative touchstone that touches properly only the form of truth or that tests only whether our knowledge contradicts itself. General logic, however, has "no touchstone for the discovery of such error as concerns . . . the content." Kant criticizes the "dialecticians" who believe that general logic can be treated as "an *organon* for the actual production of at least the semblance of objective assertions." He argues that "dialectic" is a logic of illusion, and that "dialecticians" do not understand that "logic teaches us nothing whatever regarding the content of knowledge, but lays down only the formal conditions of agreement with the understanding," and that "since these conditions can tell us nothing at all as to the objects concerned, any attempt to use this knowledge as an instrument [*Werkzeug*] or organon which professes to extend and enlarge our knowledge can end in nothing but mere talk. . . ." Kant thus argues that the formal laws of logic cannot provide such adequation; knowledge is nothing more than the combinatory activity of the understanding.[17] In Kant, then, the *Grund* of a relative zero becomes, like Being itself, a kind of unknowable source.

Plato argued that the universe is subject to government by number, and he recognized a general similarity between number (*numerus*) and coined money (*nummus*): the theory of number and the theory of coined money concern both symbols (numbers as numerals [*Zahlen*] and the inscriptions in ingots) and things (numbers as groups of things [*Anzahlen*] and the ingots themselves), which the symbols represent as, or homogenize into, one genus. Kant distinguishes his from the

16. The connection between "equation" and *Aufhebung* is commonplace in German mathematical discourse. Thus Andreas Reyher, in a widely used textbook (*Arithmetica oder Rechen-Büchlein* [Gotha, 1653; 4th ed., 1657], p. 72) writes: "Wie die grosse gebrochene Zahlen in Kleinere *gleichgeltende* zu reduciren, *auffzuheben* oder zu bringen."

17. Kant, *Kritik*, A 60–61 = B 85–86; trans. Smith, pp. 98–99. I do not consider, for the time being, transcendental logic.

Platonic position by an elaborate disengagement of the intellectual *Zahl* from the *Anzahl* of things.[18]

The Kantian concept of truth, however, is relative to another numerical concept, the zero obtained from discourse about economics and physics. In *The Concept of Negative Quantities*, Kant argued that the *Grund* of being is associated with an equation that is the mutual cancellation (*Aufhebung*) to zero of opposite and real (i.e., not logically contradictory) objective forces, such as physical attraction and repulsion or monetary debt and credit. In *The Critique of Pure Reason*, he argues similarly that truth is associated with the adequation of *intellectus* and *res*, and refers the relationship or affinity of subject with object to a transcendental *Grund*.[19] (Note, however, that credit and debt, of which he wrote in *The Concept of Negative Quantities*, are homogeneous, and that the knower and the known, of which he writes in the *Critique of Pure Reason*, are heterogeneous.) In his theory of truth, then, Kant both uses *Aufhebung* (as adequation) and decries dialectic (which would confirm the truth of objective assertions). That *Aufhebung* is crucial both to the zero in the adequation of analytic logic (which is confined to mere forms) and to the zero in real equation (which may consider quantities and forces of objects) suggests, however, an unavoidable problem in the Kantian critique of dialectic. As it happens, the Kantian relationship between *Aufhebung* and truth is one of the problems with which the dialectician Hegel takes issue.

Against Formalism

Hegel criticizes the infinite generalizations of wayward Kantian systems of reciprocities like those of Friedrich Wilhelm Joseph von Schelling and Johann Gottlieb Fichte. In *The Phenomenology of Mind* (1807), for example, Hegel attacks the formalism of Schelling: "The predicate may be subjectivity or objectivity, or again magnetism, electricity, and so on, contraction or expansion. . . . With a circle of

18. On "the calculating character of modern times" and the Kantian conception "of the world as a huge arithmetical problem," see Georg Simmel, *The Philosophy of Money*, trans. T. Bottomore and D. Frisby (London, 1978), esp. pp. 443–46. On the relationships between *numerus* and *nummus*, and the Greek root *nem-*, see Chapter 6, note 28.

19. Kant, *Kritik*, A 57–64 = B 82–88; trans. Smith, pp. 97–101.

reciprocities of this sort it is impossible to make out the real fact in question."[20] According to Hegel, Kant's formalism of real opposites degenerates with Schelling into a schematizing system of pseudoclassification or pseudodifferentiation like the system of labeled boxes in a merchant-grocer's stall. Schelling employs mathematical relations, such as "$0 = 1 + 1 - 1 + 1 - 1 \ldots$," to define his notion of differentiation and cancellation (*Aufhebung*).[21] Hegel, in his *History of Philosophy*, claims that for Schelling all difference is only quantitative, as is money in its role as measure, and he makes his famous assertion that philosophical "difference must really be understood as qualitative."[22] Similarly, in *Faith and Knowledge* (1802), Hegel attacks the formalism of deduction in Fichte as "nothing but a transformation of signs, of the *minus* sign into *plus* sign." He mocks Fichte's formalism, as presented in his *Vocation of Man* (1800), by an ironic observation that "an empty money-bag is a bag with respect to which money is already posited, to be sure, though with the *minus* sign; money can immediately be deduced from it because, as lacking, money is immediately posited."[23] Hegel thus accuses post-Kantian formalists of a tendency to differentiate among the things of the world as though thinking were merely double-entry bookkeeping.

This accusation informs Hegel's discussion of "the opposition of

20. Hegel, *Phänomenologie des Geistes*, in *Werke*, 20 vols. (Frankfurt, 1970), 3:48–49. Unless otherwise noted, references to Hegel are to this edition. Translations of the *Phänomenologie* are from the translation by J. B. Baillie (*The Phenomenology of Mind* [New York, 1967], here p. 108). I have also consulted the translation of the Preface by Walter Kaufmann (*Hegel: Texts and Commentary* [New York, 1965]).

21. Joseph L. Esposito (*Schelling's Idealism and Philosophy of Nature* [Lewisburg, Pa., 1977], esp. pp. 178–85) suggests that Hegel misunderstands Schelling and is confused about the relationship between quantity and quality. Esposito notes that "Schelling's Absolute first *appears* as simple (absolute) indifference, as [Lorenz] Oken . . . had interpreted it, and progressively moves toward greater differentiation. . . . However, this differentiation is not, in fact, conceived as *real*. . . . To explain this Schelling would use the . . . mathematical relation [$0 = 1 + 1 - 1 + 1 - 1$]. Hegel prefers to characterize this motion of cancellation [*Aufhebung*] as 'the life of the Concept,' but for Schelling this metaphor and all those involving 'movement' [which] Hegel uses [are] deceptive" (p. 180; cf. F. W. J. von Schelling, *Sämmtliche Werke*, 14 vols., ed. K. F. A. Schelling [Stuttgart, 1856–61], 2:41).

22. Hegel, *Vorlesungen über die Geschichte der Philosophie*, in *Werke*, 20:440–54; translated as *Lectures on the History of Philosophy*, trans. E. S. Haldane and F. H. Simson (London, 1896), 3:512–45.

23. Hegel, *Glauben und Wissen*, in *Gesammelte Werke*, ed. Hartmut Buchner and Otto Pögeler (Hamburg, 1968), 4:391–92; translated as *Faith and Knowledge*, trans. W. Cerf and H. S. Harris (Albany, N.Y., 1977), p. 159.

Being and Nothing" in his *Logic* (1812–16). Here Hegel offers a critique of the Newtonian physics that (as he argues) Kant incorporated wholesale into his philosophy, and he makes a related attack on Kant's ontology and theory of the creditability of Being, or on Kant's attempt to demonstrate the impossibility of the Cartesian and Leibnizian proofs of the existence of God.[24] In the *Critique of Pure Reason*, Kant compared the actual and potential worths of certain moneys (*Taler*), and pretended that Descartes had argued that because we have the idea of God He must exist in the same way that if we have the idea of money it can be spent. Kant wrote that "the attempt to establish the existence of a supreme being by means of the famous ontological argument of Descartes is merely so much labor and effort lost; we can no more extend [*reicher werden*] our stock of [theoretical] insight by mere ideas [*Ideen*], than a merchant can better his position by adding a few noughts [*Nullen*] to his cash account."[25] Hegel criticizes Kant's supposed demonstration of the impossibility of the ontological argument by ridiculing his identification of "ideas to be extended" with "noughts to be cashed in." Hegel, for whom the possibility of ontology is crucial, argues that "what above all has made successful the Kantian critique of the ontological proof of the existence of God is without doubt the example which Kant added to make it more striking." He argues at length that a coin is different from God; in terms of the attachment of predicates to subjects, they operate differently.[26]

Sublation and the Modus Tollens

Hegel's position against formalism accounts for his redefinition of *Aufhebung*. In Hegel *Aufhebung* is not "suppression," as it is in the

24. Hegel, *Wissenschaft der Logik*, in *Werke*, 5:88–92; translated as *Science of Logic*, trans. W. H. Johnston and L. G. Struthers (London, 1929), 1:98–102. Cf. Hegel, *Jenenser Logik, Metaphysik und Naturphilosophie aus dem Manuskripte*, ed. G. Lasson (Leipzig, 1923); and *Enzyklopädie der philosophischen Wissenschaften im Grundrisse, Erster Teil: Die Wissenschaft der Logik*, in *Werke*, 8:135–37.

25. Kant, *Kritik*, A 630 = B 658; trans. Smith, p. 507. Compare Kant's quite different *Der einzig mögliche Beweisgrund zu einer Demonstration des Daseins Gottes* (1763), in which he relies on the theory of *Aufhebung* presented in his essay on the concept of negative quantities (1763). Kant writes: "Das Dasein ist gar kein Prädikat, und die Aufhebung des Daseins keine Verneinung eines Prädikats, wodurch etwas in einem Dinge sollte aufgehoben werden" (in *Werke*, 2:642).

26. Hegel, *Enzyklopädie*, in *Werke*, 8:135. See the ironic remark, in Hegel's 1831 revision of the *Wissenschaft der Logik* (originally published 1812), "that man should

Kantian definition, but rather "sublation." In the *Logic*[27] Hegel defines his new meaning for *Aufhebung* with a reference to the Ciceronian pun, "Tollendum esse Octavium," which may be translated as "Octavian is to be raised/rased." (*Sublation*, the term I use to translate Hegel's *Aufhebung*, is derived from the Latin verb *tollo, tollere, sustuli, sublatum.*) In the Latin pun *tollere* has two of the three meanings of *Aufhebung* in Hegelian dialectic. It means "keeping or preserving" and "making to cease or to finish," but it does not mean "qualitatively transcending," the third movement of *Aufhebung*, which Hegel usually has in mind.[28]

In his reworking of *Aufhebung* Hegel criticizes Kant's dismissal of arguing by the *modus tollens* and Kant's consequent limitation of the boundaries of human knowledge. Kant, in his discussions of contradiction in the *Critique of Pure Reason* and in his *Logic* (1800), defined the *modus tollens*, which he associates with *Aufhebung*, as one mode of reasoning which "proceeds from consequences to their grounds." For Kant, the *modus tollens*, or apagogic mode, is "the mode of conclusion according to which the consequence can only be a negative and indirectly sufficient criterion of the truth of cognition." (Compare "If A then B; not-B, therefore not-A" with "If A then B; B, therefore A.") If we allow this definition to stand unqualified (as Hegel does not), then it is common sense to distrust the *modus tollens* because, as Kant notes, it is "only negative."[29]

---

raise himself to this abstract generality in his mind, so that in fact it becomes a matter of indifference to him whether the hundred dollars . . . are or are not" (*Wissenschaft der Logik* [*Werke*, 5:91]; trans. Johnston and Struthers, 1:101). Hegel does not consider in what sense moneys, such as *Taler*, may differ in respect to "predication," not only from God but also from other things. In his discussion of this section of Hegel's *Logic*, Charles Taylor (*Hegel* [Cambridge, 1975], pp. 246–52) misconstrues Hegel's understanding of quantity by misinterpreting his "100 *Taler* [units of money]" as "100 units [of anything]."

27. Hegel, *Logik*, in *Werke*, 5:114; trans. Johnston and Struthers, 1:119–20.

28. In a letter to Cicero, D. Brutus writes that "Labeo Segulius . . . told me . . . that Caesar [i.e., Octavian] himself had made no complaint at all about you, except as to the remark which he said you had made 'that the young man should be praised, honoured and *immortalized* [*tollendum*]'" (in Cicero, *Letters to his Friends*, trans. W. Glynn Williams, 3 vols. [Cambridge, Mass., 1929], vol. 2, p. 479, 11. 20). From Velleius Paterculus (Oxford Classical Text, ed. R. Ellis [Oxford, 1898], 2. 62) it would seem that *tollendum* was to have a double meaning like the one that Hegel ascribes to it, but D. R. Schackleton (*Cicero: Epistulae ad Familiares* [Cambridge, 1977], 2:541) suggests that such a meaning would have been "forced." Cf. *Suetonius*, trans. J. C. Rolfe, 2 vols. (Cambridge, Mass., 1913), 1:137.

29. Kant, *Kritik*, A 790–91 = B 818–19; trans. Smith, pp. 625–26. And Kant,

For Kant the *modus tollens* is "permissible only in rhetoric and in those sciences in which it is impossible mistakenly to substitute what is subjective in our representations for what is objective, that is, for the knowledge of that which is in the object." Nevertheless Kant does allow one use of hypotheses "in the domain of pure reason." One may use hypotheses, he says, "for the purpose of defending a right, not in order to establish it." In this case,

> we must always look for the opposing party [which we may attack by using hypotheses] in ourselves. For speculative reason in its transcendental employment is *in itself* dialectical; the objections which we have to fear lie in ourselves. We must seek them out, just as we do in the case of claims that, while old, have never become superannuated, in order that by annulling [*Vernichtigung*] them we may ground [*grunden*] a permanent peace [*ewigen Frieden*].[30]

Only in argument where the opposing party is "ourselves" does Kant hold that dialectical hypotheses are tolerable to pure reason.

Hegel seeks to extend the territory within which to allow annulment by the *modus tollens* and by dialectic. He does so by reinstating and adopting Thomas Aquinas' conception of the *modus tollens*, or *sublatio*, as mediation between opposites.[31] Hegel introduces a new *modus*

Logik, in *Kants gesammelte Schriften*, ed. Königliche Preussische Akademie der Wissenschaften (Berlin, 1923), 9:1–150, esp. sec. 7; translated as *Logic*, trans. Robert Hartman and Wolfgang Schwartz (Indianapolis, 1974), pp. 57–58. On the *modus tollens*, cf. note 57.

30. Kant, *Kritik*, A 777 = B 805; trans. Smith, pp. 617–18. Kant's attitude to the *modus tollens* may be compared with his Newtonian suspicion of hypotheses: "Everything . . . which bears any manner of resemblance to an hypothesis is to be treated as contraband [*verbotne Ware*]; it is not to be put up for sale even at the lowest price, but forthwith confiscated immediately upon detection" (Kant, *Kritik*, A xv; trans. Smith, p. 11). According to Aristotle, there are other proofs by refutation of hypotheses (*anairoumenon hypothēsin*) (Aristotle, *Eudaimonean Ethics* 1222b; cf. *Sophistical Refutations* 1177a).

31. In his consideration of whether evil destroys good entirely, Thomas Aquinas writes that "the good which is directly opposite to an evil is wholly made away with [*tollitur*], as we have said, but other goods are not wholly made away with [*tollentur*]" (*Summa Theologiae*, 1a. 48. 4). Related examples of the way the Hegelian concept of *Aufhebung* militates against that of Kant include his discussion of giving and receiving hypothecs or deposits (*Phänomenologie*, in *Werke*, 3:316–23; trans. Baillie, pp. 446–53) and his refutation of the Kantian reciprocity theory of crime and punishment: "The annulment [*Aufhebung*] of the crime is retribution [*Wiedervergeltung*] in so far as (a) retribution in conception is an 'injury of the injury,' and (b) since as existent a crime is something determinate in its scope both qualitatively and quantitatively, its negation as existent is similarly determinate. This identity rests on the concept, but is

tollens (the dialectical *Aufhebung*), which becomes his principal mode of argument.

Checkers and Checks

Sublation in Hegelian dialectic comprises both the cancellation or equation of opposing forces to a relative zero, as it does in Kant, and the transcendence of opposites, as it does in J. C. Friedrich von Schiller.[32] The presentation of Hegel's theory, moreover, associates logical procedures, such as cancellation and transcendence, with uniquely monetary ones. If Hegel conceives of money as a purely quantitative measure (as opposed to, say, a commodity with value in its own right), then the association of logic with money may be symptomatic of, and may even inform, problems in his notion of *Aufhebung*. Thus locating "the logical place of money"[33] in Hegelian dialectic helps to situate the "quality" of Hegelian *Aufhebung*.

In this section I shall consider three traditions on which Hegel draws, traditions in which *Aufhebung* is associated with counting, exchange, and interest.

1.   In its initial stages Hegel's intellectual method is similar to the arithmetic one of contemporary German accountants. In German states in the eighteenth century, most merchants did their accounts by manipulating tallies or checkers on a board. (In Hegel's time the English chancellor of the exchequer still used this method; compare fig-

---

not an equality between the specific characteristics of the crime and that of its negation; on the contrary, the two injuries are equal only in respect of their implicit character, i.e., in respect of their 'value'" (*Philosophie des Rechts*, in *Werke*, 7:192; translated as *The Philosophy of Right*, trans. T. M. Knox [Oxford, 1952], p. 71).

32. J. C. Friedrich von Schiller (*Über die ästhetische Erziehung des Menschen in einer Reihe von Briefen* [Letters on the Aesthetic Education of Man], letter no. 18, in *Sämmtliche Werke* [Munich, 1962], 5:625) writes that "beauty unites [the] two opposed states and thus sublimates [*aufhebt*] the opposition. But because both states remain eternally opposed to each other, they cannot be united in any other way than by being sublimated." See also Schiller's use of *Aufhebung* in letter no. 20, where he observes that "the scales balance when they are empty; but they also balance when they contain weights" (Schiller, *Sämmtliche Werke*, 5:633).

33. Cf. Bruno Liebrucks, "Über den logischen Ort des Geldes," *Kantstudien* 61 (1970): 159–89; and Alfred Sohn-Rethel, *Warenform und Denkform* (Frankfurt, 1971).

ures 40, 41, and 42.) In reckoning, "the tallies or counters used for working out problems on a board were 'picked up [*aufgehobene*]' when dealt with; thus if one was picked up from either side, the result that remained was unaffected."[34] The money token, or checker, was canceled without changing the total. The cancellation of the opposing part became a partial means towards indicating the one whole.

The historical transition from reckoning with this checkerboard to figuring with Arabic numerals, algorithm, and the sign for nought (the cipher "o") was a significant turning point in Western thought.[35] (See figure 43.) The new "algebra" of double-entry bookkeeping had been "discovered" by ninth-century Arabs who needed an efficient method to calculate inheritance shares. Their discovery influenced analysis of simple and dialectical opposition. Al-Khowārazmi's *Concise Calculation of Restoration and Confrontation* was, "in effect, a new way of solving equations, first by 'restoring' normalcy to an equation by bringing its negative terms up to a positive value through addition, a process which was repeated on the other side of the equation; and second by 'confronting' similar and congruent terms on either side of the equation and eliminating them."[36] This way of using equation and adequation to zero especially intrigued thinkers who lived during the transition from the old system of accounting to the new one. Among these thinkers were Shakespeare, who lived during a period of rapid economic and financial development in Elizabethan England,[37] and Kant

34. See Johann Eisenhut, *Ein künstlich Rechenbüch auff Zyffern, Linien und Wälschen Practica* (Augsburg, 1538), G 2b. On the synonymity of *Aufhebung* with *elevatio* in the discourse of German accountants, see Karl Menninger, *Kulturgeschichte der Zahlen* (Königsplatl, 1934), p. 265. According to Felix Müller ("Zur Terminologie der ältesten mathematischen Schriften in deutscher Sprache," *Abhadlungen zur Geschichte der mathematischen Wissenschaften* 9 [1899]: 319), the meaning of *aufheben* in mathematical discourse derives from its significance in the commercial discourse of accounting with reckoning pennies.

35. For an early comparison of calculation by checkerboard (abacus) and by algorithm, see Gregor Reisch, *Margarita Philosophica* (Freiburg, 1503). Reisch includes a vignette depicting the opposition between the old and new arithmetic (figure 43).

36. Muhammad al-Khowārazmi, *The Concise Calculation of Restoration and Confrontation*, composed in Baghdad ca. A.D. 825; the quotation is from F. E. Peters, *Allah's Commonwealth: A History of Islam in the Near East 600–1100 A.D.* (New York, 1973), pp. 334–35. For the connection with inheritance, see *The Algebra of Mohammed ben Musa*, ed. and trans. F. Rosen (London, 1831), esp. p. 2; and S. Gandz, "The Algebra of Inheritance," *Osiris* 5 (1938): 319–91.

37. On the significance of the old and new arithmetic in Shakespeare's plays, see Henry W. Farnam, *Shakespeare's Economics* (New Haven, Conn., 1931), esp. pp. 108–14.

and Hegel, who lived in economically and financially backward, although philosophically advanced, states.

2. Discussion about the relationship between economic theory and philosophy in Hegel's time was largely centered on the issues of changing money and redeeming monetary notes. Kant, in "What is Money?" (1797), discusses money as an intellectual concept or rational form.[38] Fichte, in his "Theory of the Right of Exchange" (1800), presents an argument by which the withdrawal of money from a bank account and the drawing of conclusions from logical forms may be allied. "The form," writes Fichte, is the draft [*Trasse*]."[39] The works of economic theory that Fichte adapts to idealist philosophy—Carl Grattenhauer's *Procuration in Exchange* (1800), for example, and Gottlieb Hufeland's *Protestation in Exchange* (1799)—were themselves adapted to economic theory from works of idealist thinkers such as the Schlegel brothers and other "idealist transcendentalists."[40]

In *The Difference Between Fichte's and Schelling's System of Philosophy* (1801), Hegel criticizes Fichte's theory of exchange by zeroing in on his apparently innocent proposal that checks be cashable by the bearer only upon the bearer's signing his name and presenting a passbook or identity card.[41] (Fichte believed that such signing would avoid counterfeiting.) Hegel harshly criticizes the "closed" medieval money system that Fichte proposes.[42] Hegel rarely treats problems of reforming the monetary system[43] or of defining the "aura" of monetary tokens

38. Kant, "Was ist Geld?" in *Die Metaphysik der Sitten*, in *Werke*, 7:400–404; translated as *Kant's Philosophy of Law*, trans. W. Hastie (Edinburgh, 1887), pp. 125–29.

39. Fichte, "Theorie des WechselRechts" in *Gesamtausgabe*, ed. Reinhard Lauth and Hans Gliwitzky (Stuttgart, 1979), 2. 5. 211. On the specifically German *Trasse*, or "bill of exchange" (cf. Italian *tratta*), see Alfred Schirmer, *Wörterbuch der deutschen Kaufmannssprache* (Strasbourg, 1911), p. 193.

40. Carl Grattenhauer, *Ueber die Wechselprocura* (Berlin, 1800), pp. 12 and 16; cf. Gottlieb Hufeland, *Primae lineae doctrinae de protestione cambiali* (Jena, 1799).

41. Hegel, *Differenz des Fichte'schen und Schelling'schen Systems der Philosophie*, in *Werke*, 2:84–86; translated as *Differenz* (*The Difference Between Fichte's and Schelling's System of Philosophy*, trans. W. Cerf and H. S. Harris [Albany, N.Y., 1977], pp. 146–47). Hegel here refers to Fichte's *Grundlage des Naturrechts nach Principien der Wissenschaftlehre* (1797); in *Sämmtliche Werke*, ed. I. H. Fichte, 8 vols. (Berlin, 1845–46), 3:292.

42. See Fichte's *Der geschlossene Handelsstaat* [The Closed Commercial State] (1800), in *Sämmtliche Werke*, 3:387–513.

43. There are some exceptions. See, for example, Hegel, *Über die englische Re-*

in a particular culture;[44] even more infrequently does he make such treatments an occasion for defining the logical place of money per se; yet, in his critique of Fichte, he emphasizes the connection between the logical problem that in Fichte's system of philosophy "the intellect is bound to fall into the making of endless determinations" and the economic dilemma that "in Fichte's state [with its complex series of state-issued passbooks] every citizen will keep at least half a dozen people busy with supervision, accounts, etc., each of these supervisors will keep another half dozen busy, and so on, ad infinitum, [with the result that] the simplest transaction will cause an infinite number of transactions."[45]

Hegel would transform the "financial" procedure of Fichte's formalist logic into a unique and powerful process of philosophic cancellation and redemption. In eighteenth-century commercial discourse and practice, a canceled (*aufgehobone*) bond or note still had positive value as a receipt or discharge from debt. (Henry C. Brokmeyer uses *cancel* in both financial and logical senses to translate *aufheben* in his translations of Hegel's works on logic.)[46] In Hegelian dialectic the nought of cancellation (*Aufhebung*) is, like this bond, both null and positive. (Although *Aufhebung* can denote "cashing in a bond," it can also denote "preservation" and hence "not cashing it in." Thus the inscription in the bottom border of the emergency money depicted in figure 44 cleverly opposes *Aufhebung* as "preservation of the banknote" to *Einlösung* as "cashing it in": "Heb' mich gut auf und lös' mich niemals ein!!") In Hegel the nought that is the bond is neither simple negativity,

---

formbill (1831), in *Werke*, 11:84–87. Karl Rosencranz (*Georg Wilhelm Friedrich Hegels Leben* [Berlin, 1844; rpr. Darmstadt, 1971], p. 61) notes that Hegel did a study of the finances of Berne during the 1790s. See what is probably Hegel's first publication, his anonymously published German translation of J. J. Cart's *Lettres confidentielles* (*Vertrauliche Briefe über das Vormalige staatsrechtliche Verhältnis des Wadtlandes [Pays de Vaud] zur Stadt Bern* [Frankfurt, 1798]). Hegel's introduction to this translation is included in *Dokumente zu˙Hegels Entwicklung*, ed. J. Hoffmeister (Stuttgart, 1936; rpr. Stuttgart, 1974), pp. 247–57.

44. On coinage in Rome, however, see Hegel, *Vorlesungen über die Philosophie der Religion*, in *Werke*, 17:169–70; and Hegel, *Aphorismen aus Hegels Wastebook* (1803–6), in *Werke*, 2:544.

45. Hegel, *Differenz*, in *Werke*, 2:84–86; trans. Cerf and Harris, *Differenz*, pp. 146 and 148.

46. I thank the Missouri Historical Society for making the still unpublished manuscript of Brokmeyer (1828–1906) available to me.

as in Kant, nor apparently simple unity, as in Plato; rather the bond ought to be cashed in, with interest, by the appropriate teller. This "tally-man" is the dialectician.[47]

3. That the cashiered bond to be cashed in (*aufgehobone*) is interest bearing brings us to another traditional association of *Aufhebung* with money, its connection with the institution of monetary interest. The use of *Aufhebung* to mean "to collect interest of the monetary kind" is as old as the fourteenth century.[48] This is one of its principal meanings in the works of Martin Luther.[49] In such writers as Schiller, Goethe, and Hegel, the collection of monetary interest is extended conceptually to include "interest of the spiritual or intellectual kind."[50]

In Hegelian, as in Platonic, dialectic, economic hypothecation informs intellectual hypothesizing: a monetary hypothec (or principal) from which interest is drawn is like a philosophical hypothesis from which a deduction is drawn, and just as mature bonds are homogeneous with the sums of their principals and interests, so dialectical syn-

---

47. For the role of the tally (*Tale*) in Fichte's understanding of absolute knowledge, see Fichte, *Darstellung der Wissenschaftlehre (Aus dem Jahre 1801)* (in *Sämmtliche Werke*, 2:17–18): "Beyond all knowing, according to our present representation, freedom and being come together and permeate one another, and only this intimate permeation and identification of the two into a new being brings about knowing—now truly in the form of knowing—as an absolute *Tale*."

48. For example: "Die vff gehabene czinse" (*Meissner Urkunde von 1398*) in Lorenz Diefenbach and Ernst Wülcker, *Hoch- und nieder-deutsches Wörterbuch der mittleren und neueren Zeit* (Basel, 1885), p. 103. Cf. the English *raise*, which can mean "to collect (rents or other charges)" (*Oxford English Dictionary*, s.v. "Raise," v., 25).

49. For *Aufhebung* in Martin Luther as "the collection of interest and of fees for indulgences," see the German writings of Luther in the Jena edition, pt. 1 (Jena, 1564), 195^a, 298^b, and pt. 2 (Jena, 1563), 263^b. See too Luther's use of "gleich aufheben mit einem" to mean "beide theile fahren lassen, auf eine linie zu stehn kommen" (Luther, pt. 5 [Jena, 1575], 340^a; discussed by Jacob and Wilhelm Grimm, *Deutsches Wörterbuch* [Leipzig, 1854–1960], s.v. "Aufheben," 10) and his use of *aufheben* to mean "aufheben und behalten" ("to pick up and to lay aside for future use"). Keith Spalding (*Dictionary of German Figurative Usage* [Oxford, 1952–], s.v. "Aufhebung") discusses Luther, pt. 1, 40^a, together with Luther's translations of Matt. 14:20, Matt. 16:9, Mark 6:43, and Luke 9:17.

50. For Schiller, see his letter to Goethe (August 17, 1797): "Mit meinem Protégé . . . habe ich freilich wenig Ehre aufgehoben" (*Schillers Werke*, Nationalausgabe, ed. L. Blumenthal and B. v. Weise [Weimar, 1977], 29:117–18). For the argument that *Aufhebung* in Schiller's letter is to be connected with collecting interest or rent, see *Trübners Deutsches Wörterbuch* (Berlin, 1939–57), s.v. "Aufhebung." Compare Goethe's use of *einwechseln* in Johann Peter Eckermann, *Gespräche mit Goethe* [Conversations with Goethe], ed. E. Beutler (Zurich, 1948), pt. 2: December 6, 1829.

theses are, in a way, homogeneous sublations of their hypotheses. In Socrates' exposition of dialectic in the *Republic*, this apparent homogeneity between hypotheses and Idea poses no problem, since there is a mythic leap from the partial hypotheses to the Idea figured on his divided line. In Hegel (and in the later dialogues of Plato), however, theory has to confront directly the problem of homogeneity and heterogeneity, of sameness and difference, that motivates every dialectical process.

The Difference

Sub-lation is connected grammatically with *dif-ference. Tollo, tollere, sustuli, sublatum* borrows its principal parts from *fero, ferre, tuli, latum*. Thus Hegelian *Aufhebung*, associated with the Ciceronian and the Thomist *sublatio*, has the same conceptual relationship to the German proverb "Aufgeschoben ist nicht aufgehoben" ("Deferral is not doing away with") that the *modus tollens* has to the Latin witticism "Quod differtur non aufertur" ("Deferral is not removal").[51] Such grammatical connections and puns, of the kind that Hegel has in mind when he refers us (in his *Logic*) to the dictionaries, suggest the logical connection between *Aufhebung* and *Differenz* that motivates Hegelian dialectic.

This connection between sublation and difference is also apparent in Hegel's consideration of the concept of truth. Kant, as we have seen, relies on a definition of truth in which the *intellectus* is supposed to become "adequate" to the *res*: the pertinent difference between them is annulled (becomes nought) as they become "equal" to each other. Hegel, however, argues in the *Phenomenology* that truth does not involve "the rejection of the discordance, the diversity, like dross from pure metal, nor, again, does truth remain detached from diversity, like a finished article from the instrument [*Werkzeug*] that shapes it. Difference itself continues to be an immediate element within truth as such, in the form of the principle of negation."[52] Thus Hegel attacks those who reject dialectical negation or mediation in philosophy.

51. For the German proverb, see Georg Büchmann, *Geflügelte Worte, der Zitatenschatz des deutschen Volkes* (Berlin, 1927), p. 436; for the Latin witticism, see Arnobius, *Commentarii in Psalmos Davidis*, Psalm 36.
52. Hegel, *Phänomenologie*, in *Werke*, 3:41; trans. Baillie, p. 99. One topos that Hegel attacks—that wisdom is like a pure metal (usually gold)—informs much of the

Hegel himself begins with illusion and negation. "The system of the experience of the spirit," he writes in the *Phenomenology*, "deals only with the negative appearance [*Erscheinung*] of the spirit, a spirit that gains its truth only by finding itself in absolute dismemberment" and then "looking the negative in the face and abiding with it."[53] Hegel explains the need to focus on negativity by emphasizing the distinction between negativity and the ordinary conception of falsehood. This distinction is summarized by Hegel's description of the process of the generation of truth. "Dissimilarity [*Ungleichheit*; of knowledge with its substance] is dissimilarity which is an essential moment. Out of this differentiation [*Unterscheidung*] their identity comes, and this resulting identity is truth."[54] This relationship between negativity (or nonidentity) and truth, which Hegel posits against nondialectical thinkers such as Kant, is the way by which phenomenology (the "logic of illusion") becomes logic.

Throughout his writings Hegel is careful to distinguish his concept of truth from mathematical and monetary relations. In the *Phenomenology*, for example, he insists that "true and false are [not] among the determinate thoughts which are considered immobile separate essences, as if one stood here and the other there, without community, fixed and isolated. Against this view, one must insist that truth is not a minted coin [*ausgeprägte Münze*] which can be given or pocketed ready-made."[55] In a fragmentary essay of 1793, Hegel already had claimed that the conventional use of syllogisms and of other logical exchanges constituted a deceptive intellectual currency, and he tried to

---

Western tradition in philosophy and mathematics. See for example, François Vieta, *In artem analyticem isagoge*; in *Francisci Vietae opera mathametica*, ed. F. van Schooten, (Leyden, 1646), p. 1. A few thinkers, however, do argue that truth cannot be separated from falsehood in the same way that gold can be separated or refined from dross. Jakob Boehme, for example, relies on the images of alchemy, but does not believe in the complete separation of the false from the true; and G. W. von Leibniz, in his crucial essay on truth, argues that "distinct notions," while they are like those unreliable ones that "assayers [*Docimastae*] have of gold," are hardly sufficient for understanding "cognition, truth and ideas." On Boehme, see Hegel, *Vorlesungen über die Geschichte der Philosophie*, in *Werke*, 20. For Leibniz, see his *Meditationes de cognitione, veritate et ideis* [*Reflections on Knowledge, Truth and Ideas*], in *Philosophischen Schriften*, ed. C. J. Gerhardt, 7 vols. (Berlin, 1875–90; rpr. Berlin, 1960), 4:423.

53. Hegel, *Phänomenologie*, in *Werke*, 3:25; trans. Baillie, p. 93.
54. Ibid., in *Werke*, 3:40; trans. Baillie, p. 99.
55. Ibid., in *Werke*, 3:40; trans. Baillie, p. 98. For the allusion to Lessing's *Nathan the Wise*, see chapter 6.

distinguish "authentic wisdom" from the "inauthentic" knowledge of "mere argument [*Räsonnement*]."

> Wisdom does not begin from concepts with a "mathematical method," and arrive at what it takes for truth through a string of syllogisms [*Schlußen*] like Barbara and Baroco—it has not purchased its conviction at the general market where they give out knowledge to everyone who pays the fair price, nor would it know how to pay for it in the current hard cash [*in blanker Münze*] that gleams on the counter—it speaks rather from the fullness of the heart.[56]

The syllogistic inferences that the pietistic young Hegel singles out for special attention—Barbara and Baroco—are associated with the *modus tollens* and with the problems of negativity and differentiation in general.[57]

In dismissing the traditional use of syllogistic inferences, Hegel would raise himself above (and/or erase) the conventional distinction between the genuine and the counterfeit. It is Hegel's conviction in the *Phenomenology* that "counterfeit instead of genuine coin may doubtless have swindled individuals many a time . . . but in the knowledge of that inmost reality where consciousness finds the direct certainty of its own self, the idea of [such] delusion is entirely baseless."[58] Hegel argues that truth can be separated from falsehood no more than an instrument can be separated from the finished product that it helped to make. The two parts of being are interrelated in a way different from that of oil and water in a heterogeneous mixture. "The false," writes Hegel, "is no longer something false as a moment of the true."[59]

56. Hegel, Fragment: "Religion ist Eine . . . ," in *Werke*, 1:25; translated as "Religion is One," in H. S. Harris, *Hegel's Development* (Oxford, 1972).

57. "Barbara" indicates the mood AAA in the first figure of syllogisms, M—P / S—M // S—P. "Baroco" indicates the mood AOO in the second figure of syllogisms, P—M / S—M // S—P. The proper names are mnemonic devices from a hexameter verse that aids the student to remember the nineteen "valid" syllogistic modes. Cf. Wilhelm T. Krug, *Allgemeines Handwörterbuch der philosophischen Wissenschaften* (Leipzig, 1832), s.v. "Schlußmoden." All second figures, including Baroco, must have a universal major, premises opposed in quality, and a negative conclusion; they are thus associated with the *modus tollens*. Second figures, such as Baroco, may seem to be reduced to (or exchanged for) first figures, such as Barbara.

58. Hegel, *Phänomenologie*, in *Werke*, 3:408, trans. Baillie, p. 570.

59. Ibid., in *Werke*, 3:41; trans. Baillie, p. 99. Cf. Heraclitus, Fragment 67, in Hermann Diels, *Die Fragmente der Vorsokratiker*, 5th ed. (Berlin, 1934), with additions by Walter Kranz; and Marc Shell, *The Economy of Literature*, esp. pp. 53–54.

The motive force of the *Phenomenology* is the inequality or dissimilarity that obtains in consciousness between the Subject and the Substance.[60] This negative force allows Hegel's system (and, as Marx also suggests, the systems of the Greek atomists)[61] to begin, by arguing *modus tollens*, with a consequential falsehood:

> A so-called fundamental proposition or first principle of philosophy, even if it is true, is yet none the less false just because and in so far as it is merely a fundamental proposition [*Grundsatz*], merely a first principle. It is for that reason that it is easily refuted. The refutation consists in bringing out its defective character; and it *is* defective because it is merely the universal, merely a principle, the beginning. If the refutation is complete and thorough, it is derived and developed from the nature of the principle itself, and not accomplished by any other counter-assurances [*Versicherungen*] and chance fancies.[62]

The refutation of a first and false principle is both positive and negative. That the truth must always be realized in this form is expressed in the idea that "represents the Absolute Spirit—the grandest conception of all."[63] This absolute, alone and without the counter-assurances of a credit economy, replaces both the Kantian zero and the Platonic One, which Hegel discusses as the two major precursors to his dialectic.

Putting Hegel Down

The remarkable tension in Germany between the development of thought and that of material production—and, I think, of financial reckoning, or calculation[64]—helps to explain German philosophers'

---

60. Hegel, *Phänomenologie*, in *Werke*, 3:22–23; trans. Baillie, p. 80.

61. Karl Marx, *Differenz der Demokritschen und Epikureischen Naturphilosophie*, in Karl Marx and Friedrich Engels, *Werke*, ed. Institut für Marxismus-Leninismus beim ZK der SED (Berlin, 1956–68), Ergänzungsband, pt. 1, pp. 257–375. (Hereafter this edition of Marx and Engels will be referred to as MEW.) Marx, like Hegel (*Phänomenologie*, in *Werke*, 3:27; trans. Baillie, p. 97), allies this kind of negation with negation in the systems of Leucipidus and Democritus.

62. Hegel, *Phänomenologie*, in *Werke*, 3:27; trans. Baillie, p. 85.

63. Ibid., loc. cit.

64. Hegel, for example, ignores the calculus introduced by Leibniz and Newton (of whose physics he offers nevertheless a scathing attack in the second part of the *Logik*, in *Werke*, 6) and thus sidesteps problems in probability theory and in moral arithmetic (later to become econometrics). These problems, however, ought properly to have influenced both his understanding of infinitesimal smallness (and the naught) and infinite largeness, and his theory of opposition and difference. See Appendix 2.

fascination with the relationship between money and ontology and it elucidates the influence of the economists James Steuart and Adam Smith on Kant and Hegel.[65] Monetary theory ties together symbol and commodity, as well as universal and particular, in a knotty conception of the relationship between thought and matter. (Thus Hegel, in *The Philosophy of Right* [1821], presents a theory of money, and of the contemporary problem of paper money in particular, which involves the dialectic of symbol and commodity.)[66] Tension between the development of thought and that of material production, however, does not explain away dialectic. My reference to historical contexts—the development at the same time and place of both coined money and Greek dialectic, for example, Brahmagupta's discovery of dialectical negativity in the credit economy of India, and Al-Khowārazmi's discovery of algorismic algebra among a people uniquely concerned with inheritance shares[67]—is not meant to put dialectic down to material condi-

---

65. On Adam Smith and Hegel, see Guy Planty-Bonjour, "Introduction," in Hegel, *La Première Philosophie de l'esprit,* trans. G. Planty-Bonjour (Paris, 1969); P. Chamley, *Économie politique et philosophie chez Steuart et Hegel* (Paris, 1963); and Jean Hyppolite, *Genèse et structure de la Phénoménologie de l'esprit de Hegel* (Paris, 1946), 2:382.

66. Like Adam Smith and Kant, Hegel argues that "money is not one particular type of wealth amongst others, but the universal form of all types so far as they are expressed in an external embodiment and so can be taken as 'things'" (Hegel, *Philosophie des Rechts,* in *Werke,* 7:467; trans. Knox, pp. 194–95). Hegel also insists that "a bill of exchange . . . does not represent what it really is—paper; it is only a symbol of another universal—value. . . . Money represents any and every thing, though since it does not portray the need itself but is only a *symbol* of it, it is itself controlled by the specific value [of the commodity]. Money, *as an abstraction,* merely expresses this value" (Hegel, *Philosophie des Rechts,* ed. Eduard Gans, in Hegel, *Sämtliche Werke: Jubilämsausgabe in zwanzig Bänden,* ed. Hermann Glockner [Stuttgart, 1964], 17:119; trans. Knox, p. 240). Cf. Hegel, *Philosophie des Rechts, nach der Vorlesungsnachschrift von H. G. Hotho, 1822/23,* in *Vorlesungen über Rechtsphilosophie, 1818–31,* ed. Karl Heinz Ilting, 6 vols. (Stuttgart, 1973–), 3:234–43. In the *Rechts-, Pflichten- und Religionslehre für die Unterclasses (1810ff.)* (in *Werke,* 4:240), Hegel discusses money as *die allgemeine Ware* and as "abstract value."

67. There are many other instances, for example, "the modern sign of . . . equality [which was] first used in [a book] of [Robert] Recorde that is dedicated to the 'governors and the reste of the Companio of Venturers into Moscovia' with the wish for 'continualle increase of commodities by their travell'" (Robert Recorde, *The Whetstone of Witte* [London, 1556]; cf. Simon Stevin, *De thiende* [Leyden, 1585; facsimile rpr., The Hague, 1924]). The position that mathematics follows trade is expressed by Edgar Zilsel ("The Sociological Roots of Science," *American Journal of Sociology* 47 [January 1942]: 547), who argues that the "classical mathematical tradition . . . could be revived in the sixteenth century because the new society had grown to demand calculation and measurement." Cf. Alexander Koyré, *Newtonian Studies* (Cambridge, Mass., 1965), pp. 5–6.

tions. Even when historically accurate and inclusive, such observations differ from, and may even obscure the way towards, accounting thoughtfully for idealist dialectic.

Ideology, or the study of the expression of the connection between spirit and matter, generally focuses, as does Henri Storch in *Course of Political Economy* (1815), on the relationship between "internal goods [*biens internes*] or elements of civilization" and "material goods, components of material production."[68] (It includes consideration of how the material interests of a particular class are expressed or promoted through religion and philosophy: Jean-Jacques Rousseau in his *Discourse on the Origin and Foundations of Inequality among Men* [1755], for example, studies how the dogmas of the priests support the institution of private property;[69] David Hume in A *Treatise on Human Nature* [1739] interprets property as a "species of causation";[70] and Moses Hess in *Twenty-One Sheets from Switzerland* [1843] associates the "estrangement" of all the physical and mental senses, which he remarks in modern European civilization, with capitalist ways of "having" and "alienating" properties.)[71] Within a decade of Hegel's death, many students of ideology concentrated their focus on specifically monetary "alienation": the reactionary Wilhelm Schulz in *The Movement of Production* (1843),[72] for example, and the radical Moses Hess, who, in his remarkable "On the Essence of Money" (1844), initiated a systematic study of spiritual money (*geistiges Geld*) rather than material money, money of the person rather than money of the purse.[73]

68. Henri Storch, *Cours d'économie politique, ou Exposition des principes qui déterminent la prosperité des nations*, ed. with notes by J.-B. Say (Paris, 1823), 3:217. Among the analogies between spirit and matter adduced by Storch is the one that "internal goods are susceptible of being accumulated like wealth, and of forming capitals that can be used in reproduction" (3:236). Cf. Karl Marx, *Theorien über den Mehrwert*, MEW, 26.1:258; translated as *Theories of Surplus Value*, trans. Emile Burns (Moscow, 1975), 1:286.

69. Jean Jacques Rousseau, *Discours sur l'origine et les fondements de l'inégalité*, in *Oeuvres complètes* (Paris, 1959–), 3:111–223.

70. David Hume, *A Treatise on Human Nature*, ed. L. A. Selby-Bigge (Oxford, 1888 and 1896), pp. 310 and 505–6.

71. Moses Hess, *Einundzwanzig Bogen aus der Schweiz*, pt. 1 (Zurich, 1843), p. 329. Hess suggests that in modern society "an object is 'ours' only when we have it—when it exists for us as capital or when it is directly eaten, drunk, worn, inhabited, etc."

72. Wilhelm Schulz (or Schulz-Bodmer), *Die Bewegung der Production* (Zurich, 1843).

73. Moses Hess, "Über das Geldwesen," in *Philosophischen und sozialistischen Schriften: 1837–1850*, ed. Auguste Cornu and Wolfgang Mönke (Berlin, 1961), p.

In "On the Essence of Money," Hess considers the interrelations among money, language, and German philosophy, arguing that in German thought "God is merely idealized capital, and heaven the theorized merchant world" and suggesting that "theological and philosophical speculation will cease only with the cessation of commercial speculation, and only then will religion give way to genuine politics."[74] Karl Marx, adopting Hess's words and arguments,[75] attempts to state some of the general and supposedly necessary similarities between negativity and monetary alienation that would help to explain such tropes as *adequatio* and *Aufhebung*. In his sweeping "Critique of Hegelian Dialectic and Philosophy as a Whole" (1844), Marx attempts to do to Hegel what Hegel did to Kant, or, rather, he attempts to do more. "[Hegelian] logic," writes Marx, "is mind's coin of the realm [*das Geld des Geistes*], the speculative or thought value of man and nature— their essences grown totally indifferent to all real determinateness, and hence their unreal essences."[76] And, in an afterword to *Capital*, Marx explains that "with [Hegel, the dialectic] is standing on its head" and that he is trying "to turn [the dialectic] right side up again."[77]

If Marx's attempt literally to put down[78] Hegel were to prove wholly

---

346. Cf. Jean-Joseph Goux's discussion (*Les Iconoclastes* [Paris, 1978], p. 162) of the "merchant teleology of reason."

74. Hess, "Über das Geldwesen," pp. 337 and 347.

75. On Marx's use (some say "plagiarism") of Hess's work on money, see Georg Lukács, "Moses Hess und die Probleme der idealistischen Dialektik," *Archiv für die Geschichte des Sozialismus und der Arbeiterwegung*, ed. Carl Grünberg, 12 (1926): 108, 124, 138; Edmund Silberner, *Moses Hess: Geschichte Seines Lebens* (Leiden, 1966), esp. pp. 191–92; and Elisabeth de Fontenoy, *Les Figures juives de Marx* (Paris, 1973), esp. pp. 61–65.

76. Marx, "Kritik der Hegelschen Dialektik und Philosophie überhaupt," MEW, Ergänzungsband, pt. 1, p. 571; translated as "Critique of the Hegelian Dialectic and Philosophy as a Whole," in Marx, *The Economic and Philosophic Manuscripts of 1844*, trans. Martin Milligan (New York, 1964), p. 174 (adapted). Elsewhere Marx allies money with mind by way of an ironic restatement of Mephistopheles' offer of twenty-four horses' legs to Faust in Goethe's *Faust* (1824–27): "I am *stupid* [*geistlos*]," states Marx's version of Faust, "but money is the *real mind* [*Geist*] of all things and how then should its possessor be stupid?" (Marx, *Ökonomisch-philosophische Manuskripte* (1844), MEW, Ergänzungsband, pt. 1, p. 564; trans. Milligan, p. 167).

77. Marx, *Das Kapital*, MEW 23:27; translated as *Capital*, trans. S. Moore and E. Aveling (New York, 1967), 1:20. On Marx's inversion of Hegel's position, see Louis Althusser, "On the Young Marx" and "Contradiction and Over-Determination," in *For Marx*, trans. Ben Brewster (New York, 1970).

78. As "picking up" is one literal translation of *Aufhebung*, so "put-down" is one literal translation of *hypothēsis* ("hypothesis").

appropriate, it would have to outdo Hegel in the same way Hegel began to outthink traditional logic. In his *System of Ethical Life* (1802–3), Hegel already had defined money as a middle term that makes for "the indifference of all labor,"[79] and, in his *First Philosophy of Spirit* (1803–4), he called money an abstraction of need and labor that makes for a "monstrous system," or "life of the dead body," which requires "continual dominance and taming like a beast," a taming that Hegel's State would accomplish much as would Marx's communist society.[80] And, following in the wake of Kant and Fichte, Hegel tried, in his *Philosophy of Right* (1824–25), to explain money as one expression of reason.[81]

This study of *Aufhebung* in Kant and Hegel is not the place to settle the Marxist claim to have surpassed philosophy. As that claim appears in "The Critique of Hegelian Dialectic and Philosophy as a Whole," in *Capital*, and elsewhere, however, it is certainly misleading. Thus many thinkers, following what they interpret to be Marx's lead but ignoring the significance of the differences between the kinds of oppositions and sublations that we have considered, assert that "mind's coin of the realm" plays no part at all in their own thinking. They fail even to inquire whether some money of the mind, like the one they suppose to pervade Hegelian logic, participates in their own supposedly superior dialectics.[82] Marx's critique of Hegel may fail to acknowledge

79. Hegel, *System der Sittlichkeit*, in Hegel, *Schriften zur Politik und Rechtsphilosophie*, ed. G. Lasson (Leipzig, 1918), p. 478; translated in Hegel, *System of Ethical Life* (1802–3) and First Philosophy of Spirit (1803/4), trans. H. S. Harris and T. M. Knox (Albany, N.Y., 1979), p. 154.

80. Hegel, *Philosophie des Geistes* (Jenaer Systementwürfe I), ed. Klaus Düsing and Heinz Kimmerle, in *Gesammelte Werke* (Hamburg, 1975), 6:324; trans. Harris and Knox, p. 249. That one prerequisite for the advancement of enlightened learning is the transcendence (*Aufhebung*) of private property was already the argument of Carl Wilhelm Frölich, *Über den Menschen und seine Verhältnisse* (1792), ed. Gerhard Steiner (Berlin, 1960), esp. the section about the "Aufhebung des Privateigentums" (pp. 84–107).

81. Hegel, *Philosophie des Rechts, nach der Vorlesungsnachschrift K. G. v. Griesheims 1824/25*, in *Vorlesungen über Rechtsphilosophie*, 3:229. Cf. *Vorlesungen*, 3:230 on "Geistiges Eigentum."

82. For example, Louis Althusser (*Essays in Self-Criticism*, trans. Grahame Lock [London, 1975], pp. 178–79) asserts a clear boundary between "the category of origin [that gives] classical bourgeois philosophy . . . from Descartes to Kant . . . the means of *guaranteeing* its ideas" and genuine "dialectic." "When you reject the category of origin as a philosophical issuing bank," writes Althusser, "you have to refuse its cur-

Hegel's critiques of Kant and Fichte, but it does warn that the thinking which fails to account for or even to encounter its own internalization of economic form remains insensitive to a sting that goads thought into becoming philosophy and, perhaps, into surpassing it.

---

rency too, and put other categories into circulation: those of the dialectic." Althusser admits that Hegel and Marx not only "refuse[d]" but also "transformed and reintroduced . . . the use and guarantee of the categories of Origin and Subject," yet he does not observe, in their reformation of Kant's "issuing bank," a money of the mind like the one that informs his own purportedly "self-critical" thinking and that his own financial troping—philosophical "circulation," for example—helps to indicate.

6 / *"What Is Truth?"*

LESSING'S NUMISMATICS
AND HEIDEGGER'S ALCHEMY

A COIN is both a proposition and a thing. It is an inscription and a thing on which the inscription is stamped, to which it refers, and together with which it becomes legal tender. A coin, then, is an epigram that, as Lessing notes in *On the Epigram*, cannot be thought of apart from that into which it is inscribed.[1] A coin is a numismatic epigram in which the inscription and the inscribed are one.

Truth, as Heidegger notes in *Being and Time*, is traditionally associated with the adequation of a proposition and a thing.[2] Many writings about truth, as it happens, rely on propositions about coins in order to exemplify the possibility or impossibility of such adequation. When the propositional character of coins themselves is ignored or misunderstood, however, such reliance leads to a systematic distortion of the concept of truth.

In this chapter we shall study the internalization of a unique monetary form, the numismatic epigram, in literary and philosophical discourse. Lessing's play *Nathan the Wise*[3] and Heidegger's essay "On the

1. G. E. Lessing, *Zerstreute Anmerkungen über das Epigramm* [On the Epigram], in *Lessings Werke*, Vollständige Ausgabe, eds. J. Petersen, W. v. Olhausen, et al., 25 vols. (Berlin, [1925]), 14:118–208. Cf. Johann Gottfried Herder, *Anmerkungen über das griechische Epigramm*, in *Herders Sämmtliche Werke*, ed. Bernhard Suphan (Berlin, 1888), 15:337–92.

2. Martin Heidegger, *Sein und Zeit* (Halle, 1929), pp. 214–26; hereafter abbreviated as *SZ*. Translations from Heidegger, *Being and Time*, trans. J. Macquarrie and E. Robinson (New York, 1962).

3. G. E. Lessing, *Nathan der Weise*, in *Lessings Werke*, vol. 2; translation adapted from Lessing, *Nathan the Wise*, trans. G. Reinhardt (New York, 1959).

Essence of Truth"[4] both posit (as an initial hypothesis) that truth concerns the relationship between proposition and thing, and offer as examples of this relationship propositions about coins. As we shall see, the example of coinage is necessary to and symptomatic of the thought of these two radically different thinkers. The discourse about truth, which began in Greece at about the same time and in about the same place as the development of coinage, appears in their thought as a numismatic "epigrammatology"[5] or logic of the relationship between the inscription and the inscribed thing.

Nathan the Wise

In the middle scene of the middle act of Lessing's *Nathan the Wise*, Nathan, the Jewish descendant of Solomon the Wise, is asked by Saladin, the Muslim ruler, which of the three religions of the book (Judaism, Christianity, and Islam) is genuine. Nathan expected to be asked for money. He is asked instead a question like that of Pilate to Jesus: "What is truth?"[6] Alone on stage, the puzzled Nathan considers how to answer Saladin's question. He compares truth, about which Saladin actually asked him, with coin, for which be believed Saladin would ask him and which, as the spectator knows, Saladin still hopes to receive from him by tricking him into either abandoning Judaism or criticizing Islam.

> I am prepared for a demand for money [*Geld*], and he wants—
> truth. Truth! And wants it like that—so bare [*bar*], so blank—as
> though truth were coin [*Münze*]! Indeed, as though it were an-
> cient coin [*uralte Münze*] that was being weighed! That could
> still pass! However, such modern coin [*neue Münze*] that is only
> made by stamp, that one only needs to count unto the counting

4. Martin Heidegger, *Vom Wesen der Wahrheit* (Frankfurt, 1967); hereafter abbreviated as WW. Translation adapted from Heidegger, "On the Essence of Truth," trans. R. F. C. Hull and Alan Crick, in Heidegger, *Existence and Being*, introd. Werner Brook (Chicago, 1949).

5. For "epigrammatology," see Geoffrey Hartman, "Monsieur Texte: On Jacques Derrida, His *Glas*," *The Georgia Review* (Winter, 1975): 761; Jacques Derrida, *De la grammatologie* (Paris, 1967); and Eugenio Donato, "'Here, Now'/'Always Already': Incidental Remarks on Some Recent Characterizations of the Text," *Diacritics* (Fall 1976): 25.

6. John 18:38.

board—that is not what truth is by any means. Like money into the bag, one should be able to sweep truth into the head?

In most of Lessing's writings, money is an example of something different from truth.[7] In this monologue, however, the wisdom of Nathan the merchant and moneylender compares truth with ancient or primordial (*uralte*) coin and distinguishes it from modern or new (*neue*) coin. "Ancient coin" is exchanged by virtue of its material weight (and implicitly its purity), just as are all commodities in a barter economy;[8] "modern coin" acts as a medium of exchange (at least in part) by virtue of the stamped inscription (or type) impressed into the face of metal ingots in a money economy. Nathan suggests that the identification of truth with "ancient coin" could "pass" because such coin is as creditable as "hard cash." In eighteenth-century Germany the phrase "Ich nehme es nicht für baare Münze" meant, one contemporary dictionary says, "Non habeo pro certo."[9] "Sound common sense" accepts as true only "hard cash." (See figure 45.) Like small shopkeepers and philosophical empiricists, men with such sense refuse to take things at their face value. They seem to heed John Locke's warning (in "Error") that truth should never be accepted "in the lump" (i.e., wholesale, or without first testing it with a balance and a touchstone).[10] "Ancient coin" must always be so tested. "Modern coin," on the other hand, has a stamp or inscription by which the trader, no longer armed with a

7. See Helmut Göbel, *Bild und Sprache bei Lessing* (Munich, 1971), esp. pp. 177–93.

8. One other passage in which Lessing compares truth favorably to gold or to coin is his *Briefe antiquarischen* [Antiquarian Letters], no. 52 (*Werke*, 17:246): "I unwind the spun yarns of the silkworm, not in order to learn to spin like the silkworm, but rather in order to make from the silk a purse for myself and for those like me; a purse, to pursue the simile, in which I can collect the small coins [*Münze*] of particular feelings until I can change [*umsetzen*] these coins into good weighty goldpieces [*Goldstücke*] of general observations, and then beat [*schlagen*] these goldpieces into the capital of self-remembered [*selbstgedachter*] truth." Cf. the common German phrase "die Zinsen zum Kapital schlagen." The purse in which Lessing would "collect" truth is a topos similar to the bag of which Nathan speaks in his monologue.

9. Georg Thomas Serz, *Deutsche Idiotismen* (Nuremberg, 1797), p. 102b.

10. In "Error" (1672) Locke writes that "he that takes up the opinions of any church in the lump, without examining them, has truly neither searched after nor found the truth, but has only found those that he thinks have found the truth, and so receives what they say with an implicit faith, and so pays them the homage that is due only to God" (John Locke, "Error," in Lord King, *The Life of John Locke with Extracts from His Correspondence, Journals, and Common-place Books*, 2 vols. [London, 1830], 2:75–76).

balance and a touchstone, can be misled through the habit of counting empty symbols.

Those who trust only "ancient coin" do not merit the praise that Nathan seems to give them. We and he know that coinage is necessarily not only commodity (which can be tested with a balance and a touchstone) but also medium of exchange (which cannot be so tested, since it is not material), and that its status as medium of exchange is equal or superior to its status as commodity. Those who with "sound common sense" pay no heed to the inscriptions on coins or who refuse to take things at their face value distrust the very things, such as banknotes and the credit economy, by which Nathan earns his livelihood. Many empiricists of the eighteenth century did dislike the concept of a credit economy, of which banknotes or paper money (the extreme form of "modern coin") are typical. Lessing, however, who greatly influenced the idealists, suggests that the empiricists mistake the nature of money and truth. They mistake weight and purity for the authority of the state. They do not understand the role of counterfeit things in a money economy, and so cannot distinguish the true from either the merely counterfeit or the blatantly fake.

In a barter economy, one (large) metallic ingot is weighed in the balance against many (small) ingots, and the touchstone is applied to it. The development of metal ingots identical in weight and homogeneous in purity does away with the need for the balance and the touchstone only if the weight and purity of the ingots are guaranteed (however misleadingly) by the author of the coins and if that author is the political authority. A coin is an ingot on which are inscribed (among other things) propositions about purity, weight, and issuing authority. Whether a coin as money ("modern coin") is true or counterfeit, however, does not depend on the agreement or disagreement of the ingot's purity and weight with propositions about its purity and weight. For Archimedes, the determination of the relationship between the purity and the weight of a piece of metal, such as a crown (the royal circlet) or an ingot (ancient coin), was important. His discovery (*heureka!*) of the subjection to numerical government of specific gravity supported the Platonic claim that the universe is governed by number. The importance of determining purity, weight, and the relationship between them, however, applies to coins only as pieces of metal, not as money. The relationship of propositions about the material properties of a coin to its actual material properties does not affect its status as money. During the development of coinage in Greece, indeed, the actual weight and purity of individual coins did not matter for purposes of exchange (within the polis).[11] A lack of correspondence between the actual and the stated material properties was both typical and immaterial.

What does matter in considering whether a coin is genuine or counterfeit is the issuing authority. A coin as money is counterfeit when the stated place of origin does not correspond to the actual place of origin. A counterfeit coin may claim to have and may actually have the same weight and purity as the legitimate coin of which it is the counterfeit. It is, however, treason for a private citizen to mint coins. The political issue is crucial. Archimedes, after all, did not confuse his study of the relationship between the purity and weight of the metal of a crown with the study of the political authority of which the crown is the symbol.

Whether a coin is counterfeit, then, may be determined by discovering its issuing authority, or its origin. In *Nathan the Wise*, however, the principal task seems to be to discover the authority not of a coin but of a religion. To this end the spectator of *Nathan the Wise* would interpret its plot, Saladin would interpret the tale of the rings that Nathan tells in order to answer or to avoid answering the question of which religion is genuine, and everyone (including Nathan himself) would determine by some sort of evaluation which of the three religions, if any, is genuine. In this play, truth is supposed to be attainable by evaluation. In his consideration of *Nathan the Wise* in the *Phenomenology of Mind*, however, Hegel argues that "truth is not stamped [*ausgeprägte*] coin that is issued ready from the mint and so can be taken up and used."[12] What, then, does literary and philosophical evaluation demand?

We are, I suppose, predisposed to look for truth in artful tales and philosophy. That art is "counterfeit" (stamped, imitative) does not mean that it is "untrue."[13] As collectors and investors know, however,

---

11. Many Greek cities had two kinds of coins: those for trade within, and those for trade without, the polis. The former were like "modern coin," the latter, "ancient coin."

12. G. W. F. Hegel, *Phänomenologie des Geistes* in *Werke*, 20 vols. (Frankfurt, 1970), 3:40; translation adapted from Hegel, *The Phenomenology of Mind*, trans. J. B. Baillie (New York, 1967), p. 98.

13. The "truth" of art may be discoverable in homogeneity and difference (e.g., between original and copy or between whole and part) rather than in disagreement and falsehood. Art may be supposed to be different from but homogeneous with the truth. Even Plato explained the artful lies of the Socratic dialogues as counterfeit in this sense

there are fake counterfeits, or copies of works of art. The artful fable of the three rings that Nathan tells to Saladin describes and may itself be one of such fakes. Each of the three rings that the father bequeaths to his three sons stands for one of the religions of the book about which Saladin has asked. But which is the original, or the genuine, ring? Or are none—or somehow all—genuine? Archimedes was able to determine the genuineness of the metal of the crown that the king presented to him. From the fable alone, however, we are unable to determine which ring(s), if any, is (are) true.[14] Nathan's fabulous answer to Saladin is as prudent, or "economic,"[15] as Jesus' answer to those who ask Him to whom belongs a coin on which is stamped the likeness of Caesar.[16]

Nathan's fable of the rings can be compared to the artful but fake Paduan coins that Lessing describes in *On the Epigram*; these coins mislead the observer, as do poor epigrams, by disappointing his expectation (*Erwartung*) with a deceptive or unsatisfactory resolution (*Aufschluß*).[17] Nathan's monologue comparing truth and coin, however, is concerned with coins not merely as works of art (a category that includes epigrams as well as rings, fables, and fake Paduan coins) but also as money (i.e., "modern coin," which we have identified as a unique

---

of "truthful" disagreement or falsehood. (See the discussion of *arithmos eidētikos* in Jakob Klein, *Greek Mathematical Thought and the Origin of Algebra* [Cambridge, Mass., 1958]. pp. 77–99.)

14. The tale of the three rings that Nathan tells does not settle the problem of which religion is true. The audience will discover an adequate solution to this problem or perhaps the inadequacy of the position of the problem by observing what happens to the Christian child he has adopted and raised as his daughter. Shakespeare's *Merchant of Venice* is another play in which the relationship between father and daughter is the dramatic vehicle.

15. On *economy* as "prudent esotericism," see Marc Shell, *The Economy of Literature* (Baltimore, 1978), pp. 105–7. Like Melchizedek, who tells a similar tale in Boccaccio's *Decameron*, Nathan "escapes the snares set at his feet" (*Decameron*, First Day, Third Story). At the end of Nathan's tale, as at the end of the tale in Boccaccio, "the question [as to which of the three rings or religions is genuine] still pendeth."

16. Jesus says "Render therefore unto Caesar the things which are Caesar's; and unto God the things that are God's" (Matt. 22:21, also Mark 12:17, Luke 20:25), without stating openly whether the metal, from which the coin was minted, is owned by Caesar or by God. Jesus does not ignore the political authority to which he, like Nathan, would render what is its.

17. Peter Heller ("Paduan Coins, Concerning Lessing's Parable of the Three Rings," *Lessing Yearbook*, 1973) discusses this relationship between the Paduan coins and the coin in Nathan's monologue.

epigrammatic form). With what kind of *money* is truth properly comparable? Or is truth itself counterfeit and all works of art fake? Lessing's play recognizes but deftly sidesteps the problem of what truth is, just as the fable sidesteps the problem of which religion is true. In the end, as Hegel and Lukács suggest, the brilliant play, *Nathan the Wise*, appears to be merely an "enlightened" work of pseudophilosophy.

Lessing compares truth with coin (as commodity, as money, and as art). Were Lessing's enlightening attempt to understand the relationship between truth and coin but a single instance in the history of philosophy, we might set it aside as an unnecessary metaphor. The metaphor, however, recurs throughout the history of literature, the metaphysics of number, and philosophy itself. Lessing's particular interpretation of the economics of truth was a compendium of previous consideration of the problem, and a powerful influence on such thinkers as Kant, Schelling, Hegel, Nietzsche, Husserl, and Heidegger.

On the Essence of Truth

> The question, famed of old, by which logicians
> were supposed to be driven into a cor-
> ner, . . . is the question: What is Truth?
> KANT, *Critique of Pure Reason*

In *Being and Time* Heidegger distinguishes between the traditional and the ancient or primordial (*uralte*) conceptions of truth (SZ, 212–30). The traditional conception of truth associates it with the Aristotelian and Thomistic agreement or adequation (*homoiōsis, adequatio*) of *intellectus* with *res* (SZ, 214); or, as Kant puts it, truth is "the agreement (*Übereinstimmung*) of knowledge with its object."[18] Kant argues that only the mistaken dialecticians, or "artists of illusion," believe that the traditional laws of logic can confirm absolutely the knowledge of objects, and he claims that analytic logic, though a kind of touchstone, is unable to confirm any account of the truth of things. Heidegger, however, supports an untraditional and supposedly primordial conception of truth, which he discovers in an etymology of the

18. Immanuel Kant, *Kritik der reinen Vernunft*, A 57–8 = B 82; translated as *Immanuel Kant's Critique of Pure Reason*, trans. Norman Kemp Smith (London, 1933), p. 97. For references to the *Kritik der reinen Vernunft*, numbers preceded by A refer to pages of the first edition (Riga, 1781), and numbers preceded by B refer to pages of the second edition (Riga, 1787).

Greek word for truth, *alētheia*, as "the unconcealed."[19] He argues that the phenomenon of truth as unconcealment is prior to that of truth as adequation. In his later works, Heidegger modified his position about the historical validity, at least, of his argument that the concept of truth as unconcealment is "older" than the traditional concept as agreement (*orthotēs*).[20] The distinction between traditional truth and primordial truth, however, informs works from all stages of his career, including the crucial and carefully revised essay of his middle period, "On the Essence of Truth."[21] In this essay, which marks a turning point in his philosophical development, Heidegger revises the realm of projection, or the manifest character of Being of what-is.

"On the Essence of Truth" begins with a subtle association of the traditional concept of truth with "economic calculation [*wirtschaftliche Berechnung*]," or "'sound' common sense ['*gesunde*' *Menschenverstand*]." Common sense, says Heidegger, merely "harps on the claims of what is palpably useful and inveighs against all knowledge of the nature of what-is—that essential knowledge which has long been called 'Philosophy'" (WW, 5). Heidegger's initial critique of "sound common sense" is like that of the German idealist, Schelling. In one of his essays on academic studies, Schelling at once admires and condemns the attitude of those men who demand the coin of their truth in "hard cash." He writes:

> That understanding which nonphilosophy calls common sense merely because it is common to all, actually demands the coin of its truth in hard cash [*die baare und klingende Münze*], and it

19. See, for example, Heidegger, SZ, 33, 219–23, and Heidegger, *Platons Lehre von der Wahrheit* [Plato's Doctrine of Truth] (Bern, 1947). Plato's ironic Socrates offers a different etymology of *alētheia* as "divine wandering" (*alē theia*) (*Cratylus* 421b).

20. In *Zur Sache des Denkens*, for example, Heidegger doubts that the traditional conception of truth as propositional correctness, or *orthotēs*, is historically derived from the conception of truth as *alētheia*. The use of *alētheia* in Homer to mean propositional correctness—at a time before the beginning of Western philosophy—causes Heidegger to reconsider his first position. He acknowledges that *alētheia*, unconcealment, in the sense of the opening of presence, was "originally" experienced only as *orthotēs*, as the correctness of representations and statements (Martin Heidegger, *Zur Sache des Denkens* [Tübingen, 1969], p. 78). Heidegger avoids contradicting his earlier work by arguing that *originally* (which is a historical term) is not the same as *primordially* (which is an ontological term).

21. In the 1920s Heidegger offered a series of seminars on truth; in the early 1930s he delivered a lecture on truth; after many revisions, "On the Essence of Truth" was published in the early 1940s.

seeks to obtain it without regard to the insufficiency of its means. When transplanted into philosophy, this understanding creates the monster of a crude, dogmatic philosophy, which attempts to measure the unlimited by the limited, and to extend the finite into the infinite.[22]

Schelling suggests that common sense is not wisdom because wisdom requires the ability to hypothesize, or to take something on credit. In this way he attacks the antiphilosophical empiricism of John Locke and Francis Bacon and perhaps even the dogmatism of Gottfried Wilhelm von Leibniz and Christian Wolff. Schelling maintains an important and subtle distinction between their antiphilosophical attitude and the unphilosophical attitude that is suitable for measuring the limited and making finite extensions, and from which philosophy can arise if it is properly nourished or "drawn out" by an adept teacher. Nonphilosophy, then, can be either antiphilosophy or unphilosophy. Only from the latter can philosophy arise.

After the introductory section of "On the Essence of Truth," Heidegger proceeds to try to draw out from common sense the essence of truth. Unlike Schelling, and certainly unlike the careful midwife of truth, Socrates, Heidegger finds that the attempt to draw the essence of truth from the traditional conception of truth is finally unfruitful.

In the first section of "On the Essence of Truth," entitled "The Current [*geläufige*] Concept of Truth," Heidegger presents to us a hypothetical conversation between himself and a persona of "'sound' common sense." While Lessing and Schelling begin their consideration of truth with the example of hard cash (*baare Münze*, a kind of bare ingot), Heidegger's Common Sense is supposed to think of truth nonphilosophically, merely as gold:

> The true is the real [*das Wirkliche*]. In the same way we speak of true gold as distinct from false. False gold is not really [*wirklich*] what it seems [*erscheint*]. It is only a "seeming" [*Schein*] and therefore unreal. The unreal stands for [*gilt*] the opposite of the real.   (WW, 7)

Heidegger suggests that Common Sense is mistaken to believe that the validity (*Geltung*, compare *gilt*) of the unreal is the opposite of the validity of the real. He argues:

22. F. W. J. von Schelling, *Vorlesungen über das akademische Studium* (1802), in *Werke*, ed. Manfred Schöter, 6 vols. (Munich, 1927–28), 3:290.

> But counterfeit gold [*Scheingold*] is something real. Hence we say
> more precisely: real gold is genuine [*echte*] gold.   (WW, 7)

Common Sense, however, is not allowed to rest easy with the association of reality with genuineness that Heidegger encourages it to make. The philosopher disassociates them by arguing that

> Both are "real," the current [*umlaufende*] ingenuine gold in circulation no less than the genuine. Therefore the truth [*das Wahre*] of the genuine gold cannot be verified [*bewährt sein*] by its reality. (WW, 7)

The discussions of verification (*Bewährung*) and validity (*Geltung*) seem to merge into a discussion of currency or circulation (*Umlauf*) in general. That which is accepted or which circulates is sometimes assumed to be true. Heidegger, however, argues that mere circulation cannot confer truth.

At this point in the first section of "On the Essence of Truth," Heidegger might be expected to attend to the sovereign, who grants to some entities (even words) their currency. As little here as elsewhere, however, does Heidegger consider this aspect of what he calls the inauthentic (*uneigentlich*) they-world of politics. Instead he supplies us with another version of the quandary with which Common Sense began, and which he believes to inform the entire Western tradition:

> The question returns: What do genuine and true [*wahr*] mean here? Genuine gold is that real thing whose reality agrees with [*in der Übereinstimmung steht mit*] what we always and in advance "authentically" [*eigentlich*] mean by gold. Conversely, where we suspect false gold we say "There is something not quite right here" [*Hier stimmt etwas nicht*]. On the other hand, we say of something that it is "as it should be": "It's right" [*es stimmt*]. (WW, 7)

We are told that Common Sense rests or tries to rest with the simple position that "the true, then, be it a true thing or a true proposition, is that which is right, which corresponds [*das Stimmende*]."

In section 2 of "On the Essence of Truth," entitled "The Inner Possibility of Agreement [*Übereinstimmung*]," Heidegger tries to convince Common Sense to abandon its position by demonstrating to it the logical problems of assuming two kinds of agreement: that between one thing and another, and that between a thing and a proposition about it. At the same time Heidegger subtly transforms gold, in terms of which he discusses truth in section 1, first into coin as thing and then into coin as money.[23] In his attempt to demonstrate the logical problems of assuming the possibility of correspondence between one thing and another, for example, he presents to us the opinion of Common Sense about two similar coins:

> We say, for example, seeing two five-mark pieces [*Fünfmark-stücke*] on the table, that they agree with one another, are like one another [*stimmen miteinander überein*]. (WW, 10)

Heidegger seems to have made a transition from a barter economy (where *Gold* is traded as a material commodity like any other) to a monetary economy (where *Geltung* alone is what matters). This transition, however, is not yet significant to the direction of the essay. Common Sense does not compare the five-mark pieces in terms of their monetary validity; it focuses only on their material qualities (such as weight, purity, shape, and so on), which they share with other things.[24] (Common Sense might as well have used the example of pieces of metal instead of coined money.) On the basis of apparent correspondences between material properties, Heidegger argues, no two things can be said to agree fully with each other. There can never be identity or equation between things. Differences, such as that of space, always remain. Heidegger thus finds lacking the definition of truth as correspondence between one thing and another.

The second kind of correspondence Heidegger considers is that between a thing and statements (*Aussagen*) about it. Heidegger returns to the numismatic example, and discusses the relationship between a coin and three propositions about it:

23. Heidegger's discussion of the reality of gold in section 1 led us to consider validity (*Geltung*) and circulation, but this does not justify the translators and interpreters who treat Heidegger's *Gold* ("gold") as if it were *Münze* ("coin") or *Geld* ("money"). This error obscures the general direction of Heidegger's essay, which, as we shall see, is from *Gold* to *Geld* ("money"). (For *Gold* translated as "coin," see "On the Essence of Truth," trans. Hull and Crick, pp. 292–94; for *Gold* misinterpreted as *monnaie* ["money"], see Reuben Guilead, *Être et liberté: une étude sur le dernier Heidegger* [Paris, 1965], p. 59).

24. Compare William Stanley Jevons (*The Principles of Science: A Treatise on Logic and Scientific Method* [London, 1920]), who, in his discussion of "the propagating power of similarity" (p. 20), discusses likeness in terms of resemblances between a coin and the die from which it was minted and also between two coins that were minted from the same die. For a five-mark piece of the kind Heidegger discusses in "On the Essence of Truth," see figure 46.

The coin [*Geldstück*] is round.   (WW, 10)
The coin is of metal.   (WW, 10)
With the coin one can buy something.   (WW, 11)

The first two propositions about the coin concern its material properties—shape and composition.[25] In his discussion of the impossibility of
agreement between one thing and another, Heidegger had shown that
two things could never be identical to each other. Similarly, he shows
that the first two propositions about the coin do not agree with the coin
because, unlike the coin, they are not material (*dinghaft* [WW, 11],
compare *stofflich*). According to the current (*geläufigen*) idea of truth,
this agreement is supposed to be a kind of adequation (*Angleichung*;
WW, 11). But something completely unlike the coin—i.e., a statement—can hardly approximate to it.

> How can something completely unlike the coin [*Ungleiche*]—the
> statement—approximate to [*angleichen*] the coin? It would have
> to *become* the coin, and present itself entirely in that form. No
> statement can do that.   (WW, 11)

Heidegger's consideration of the first two propositions about the coin
supports this contention that a statement cannot become a thing, or an
intellectus a *res*, so that the definition of truth as correspondence between a thing and a statement about it is unsatisfactory. As we shall
see, however, the example of the third statement tends to undermine
Heidegger's contention that a statement cannot become a thing.

Heidegger tries to show, in his discussion of the relationship between
the third proposition and the thing, that any agreement between them
cannot become one of complete homogeneity. For the third proposition, which states that one can buy something with the coin, Heidegger again supposes an essential heterogeneity between statement and
thing.

> With the coin you can buy something; but the statement about it
> can never be legal tender [*Zahlungsmittel*].   (WW, 11)

The coin and the statement are supposed to heterogeneous because
only with the former, which is an instrument of exchange (*Zahlungs-*

25. In his consideration of truth, Jevons discusses the relationship between a coin
and statements about its physical properties: "If I declare that 'this coin is made of
gold,' I must base the judgement upon the exact *likeness* of the substance in several
qualities to other pieces of substance which are undoubtedly gold" (Jevons, *Principles
of Science*, p. 37; italics mine).

mittel), can one purchase something. If we were to allow this disassociation of statement from thing to stand, we might accept Heidegger's way of surpassing the traditional concept of truth, and his related position that the truth of one or two coins—lying on a table, round, metal, and monetary—resides in a primordial (*uralte*) unconcealment.

The third proposition, however, is not about the material properties of the coin (which all kind of things, or *Stücke*, have); it is rather about its monetary properties (which only *Geldstücke* have, and which confer on them legitimate currency [*Umlauf*]). Heidegger fails to remark on this difference between the third statement (which concerns our understanding of money) and the first two statements (which concern our understanding of all [other] material things). (The only sign that he may have noticed the difference is the verbal transition from *Fünfmarkstücke*, which he used in his discussion of the correspondence of one thing with another, to *Geldstücke*, which he uses in his discussion of the correspondence of a thing with a proposition about it.) The failure to distinguish between discussing the validity (*Geltung*) of statements about the material properties of things and discussing the validity of statements about the validity of money (*Geld*) involves a revealing error in Heidegger's consideration of adequation. Heidegger's claim, that a statement cannot become a thing (coin), or that a thing (coin) is never a statement, is inaccurate and uniquely problematical.

The case of paper money helps to specify the inaccuracy. Paper money is a statement unattached by financial necessity to a material thing. (It is printed on paper, which is a material thing, and it is often convertible to material things, but these attachments are not necessary to its role as money.) What confers validity (*Geltung*) on paper money (*Geldscheine*) is not any material property of the paper but rather the authorized statement that appears on it, for example, "With this you can buy something." False gold (*Scheingold*), with the discussion of which Heidegger begins his consideration of the correspondence theory of truth, is sometimes counterfeit in the way that Heidegger suggests (WW, 7); the inflated paper money (*Scheingeld*) that circulated in Germany while Heidegger was writing *Being and Time* was often close to worthless (see figures 25–39 and 44); paper money, however, is essentially both a statement and a valid instrument of exchange.

Coined money, like paper money, is a statement. An ingot of gold becomes money when a statement (*Aussage*), such as "five-mark piece," is inscribed in, or becomes part of, the ingot. A coin is composed of both the thing and the statement; as participants in the same whole, the thing and the statement are homogeneous. Heidegger's contention, that a thing and a statement are always heterogeneous, thus becomes erroneous when he ceases to discuss the currency of gold (*Gold*) and begins to discuss the validity (*Geltung*) of money (*Geld*).

Heidegger's arguments about the lack of correspondence between two things and between a thing and statements about its material properties do not, of course, depend on the numismatic examples that he brings to bear.[26] However, his more important argument about the validity of statements themselves *is* affected, even informed, by his conception of coin as money. A numismatic epigraph, such as "This is a five-mark piece with which you can buy something," can transform into coin an ingot in which it is impressed and to which it refers; an epigraph can make for its own validity as statement. Such a statement has a relationship to the ingot (together with which it composes a coin) like the relationship between statement and thing (coin) that Heidegger discusses in "On the Essence of Truth." Heidegger's consideration of the validity of a statement about the validity of a coin thus signals the role of monetary relationships in his thinking about the validity of

26. The use of a numismatic example or metaphor in a philosophical argument is not in itself a "necessary sign" (*tekmērion* [Aristotle, *Rhetoric* 1.2.16–17]) that the logic of the argument is affected by monetary exchange or representation. Coins are often examples merely because denominational and material differences between one coin and another are easy to specify. Thus Gottlob Frege considers the remark of Jevons that "three coins are three coins, whether we count them successively or regard them all simultaneously. In many cases neither time nor space is the ground difference, but pure quality alone enters. We can discriminate, for instance, the weight, inertia, and hardness of gold as these qualities, though none of these is before or after the other, either in space or time" (Jevons, *The Principles of Science* [London, 1879], p. 157; quoted in Frege, *The Foundations of Arithmetic/Die Grundlagen der Arithmetik*, trans. J. Austin [Oxford, 1974], p. 52ᵉ). Frege goes on to consider the observation of Spinoza that "a thing is called one or single with respect to its existence, and not with respect to its essence; for we only think of things in terms of number after they have first been reduced to a common genus. For example, a man who holds in his hand a sesterce and a dollar will not think of the number two unless he can cover his sesterce and his dollar with one and the same name, viz., pieces of silver, or coin; then, he can affirm that he has two pieces of silver, or two coins; since he designates by the name piece of silver or coin not only the sesterce but also the dollar. From this it is clear, therefore, that nothing is called one or single except when some other thing has first been conceived which, as has been said, matches it" (Baruch Spinoza, *Epistolae doctorum quorundam virorum*, no. 50, *ad* J. Jelles; quoted in Frege, *Foundations*, p. 62ᵉ). In such cases, other examples (eggs, for instance, or apples and oranges as fruit) would do as well.

statements. Even if Heidegger had deleted the example of the third statement (which he did not do, probably because he wished to point out an unresolved question involving intellectual currency or, less likely, because he failed to notice the difference between the third statement and the two other statements), the alethiological and political problems of which the "five-mark" piece is a symptom would continue to inform his general argument about truth as adequation.

On the Epigram

> What, then, does the being of values or their "validity" [*Geltung*], which Lotze took as a mode of "affirmation," really amount to ontologically?
>
> HEIDEGGER, *Being and Time* (SZ, 99)

In his discussion of truth as adequation, Immanuel Kant distinguishes between analytic logic, which holds that the truth of objects can never be known absolutely, and dialectic, which holds that the formal laws of general logic can somehow apply to the objects of the world. The dialectician Hegel prefaces his *Phenomenology* with attacks on Kantian formalism and on Kant's adoption of a premature limit to human knowledge and implicit argument that the Substance (to adopt Hegelian terminology) is not the Subject. The crucial connection between known things and knower, or between objects and propositions about them, is the principal subject of epigraphy, or the study of the relationship of things to statements written on their surfaces or impressed into them.

In *On the Epigram*, Lessing notes that a single epigram has two inseparable parts: the "anticipation," such as a metal ingot, and the "resolution," such as an inscription impressed into the anticipation and explaining it or making it what it is.[27] The epigram should not be thought of apart from that whereon it is inscribed. In Lessing's *Nathan the Wise* we encounter an example of a numismatic epigram: modern coin. Modern coin is necessarily epigrammatic. It cannot be thought of apart from its inscription. The inscribed weight and purity (of which the statement speaks) usually differs from the actual weight and purity,

27. Lessing, *Zerstreute Anmerkungen über das Epigramm* [On the Epigram], pt. 1, sec. 4, in *Lessings Werke*, 14:143–47.

but even if it did not, the inscription alone is what makes the ingot (or mere commodity) into a legal coin. Modern coin is in this sense as much proposition as thing. Like paper money, modern coin derives its status as instrument of exchange (*Zahlungsmittel*) from the inscribed proposition. As an epigram, modern coin is as much an "intellectual" number or tale (*Zahl*) as it is a "material" thing that is tolled (*Anzahl*).

The English word *number* refers both to a group, or number (*Anzahl*), of things and to a numeral, or number (*Zahl*)—both to things disposed and to what is supposed to dispose them. The etymology of *number* includes the Latin *nummus* and the Greek *nomismos*, which mean "coined money" or "coin."[28] The etymology is explicable when we consider that a coin, like a number, concerns both things and symbols. As an ingot of metal, it has material properties (e.g., weight) like those of the members of a group or number of things; and as a monetary unit it has numerical, or symbolic, properties. The etymology of *number* suggests how number theory often elucidates problems that arise in monetary theory and how monetary theory often elucidates the truth of things.[29]

The analysis of a coin as both commodity (inscribed thing) and symbol (inscription), and the consideration of the relationship between coin and number, suggest why epigraphy, philosophy, and number theory changed with the historical development of modern coin, the first widely circulating "publications" in human history, in the sixth and seventh centuries B.C. Naive writers, for example, declared a unity of measurement and measured things: "You, O God, disposed all things by measure, number, and weight" ("Omnia in mensura et numero et pondere disposuisti"). The author of this sentence from The Wisdom of Solomon (11:20) adapts to Judaism the pseudo-Platonic argument that the economy (*dispositio*) of the universe is governed by

28. The Latin *numerus* ("number"), like the English *number*, signifies both "group" and "numeral." Some scholars associate *numerus*, the direct etymon of *number*, with cognates meaning "money" (*Geld*); others associate *numerus* with *nummus* ("coin"), which is a Sicilian-dialect version of the Greek *nomismos* ("coin"). For bibliographical information, see Marc Shell, *The Economy of Literature*, p. 66n. Compare the apparent etymological connections both of *nummus* and of *nomismos* with the Latin *numen* ("name").

29. Compare Oswald Spengler's argument that "abstract number corresponds exactly to abstract money" (*The Decline of the West*, trans. C. A. Atkinson, 2 vols. [New York, 1926–28], 2:481–82; and vol. 1, chap. 2).

number,[30] or that there is a necessary correspondence between the truth of the things of the universe and that of numerality.[31]

In his discussion of the changing relationship between thing and symbol during the pre-Socratic period, Hegel attaches great importance to the epigram because through it the changing relationship of proposition to thing is made explicit. In the epigram, says Hegel, "we have the thing itself in a double way: (a) the external existent and (b) then its meaning and explanation; these are pressed together as an epigram with the most salient and most apposite touches."[32] The epigram is thus the aesthetic form that makes the transition, during the pre-Socratic period, from symbolic to classical art; through the epigram the thing "comes forward" to us, as does the answer to the riddle of the Sphinx. In Hegel's *Aesthetics*, the relationship betweeen "external shape" and "inner meaning," between subject and predicate, or between Subject and Substance, makes the epigram both a quintessential transitional form and a critical example of art in its symbolic, classical, and romantic stages.[33]

Heidegger, like Hegel, looks to the pre-Socratic period as the beginning of Western philosophy, but, unlike Hegel, he does not focus on developments in epigraphy; instead, he considers the development of a new kind of "economic calculation," which he allies with "'sound'

30. The sentence from the Apocrypha appears to be a naive adaptation of Plato, *Republic* 602 c-d, etc.

31. Belief in such correspondence is crucial to much Western thinking. In literature, for example, this sentence from the Apocrypha inspired a tradition of compositions in which number dominated both form and content. (See Hermann Krings, *Ordo: Philosophisch-historische Grundlegung einer abendländischen Idee* [Halle, 1941]). In science, the Platonic position gave rise to a tradition that includes Archimedes and other "marvellous assayers of nature" (Francesco Bonaventura Cavalieri, referring to the Platonic Galileo; quoted by Alexander Koyré, *Metaphysics and Measurement: Essays in the Scientific Revolution* [London, 1968], p. 14.)

32. Hegel, *Vorlesungen über die Ästhetik*, in *Werke*, 13:545; translated as *Aesthetics: Lectures on Fine Art*, trans. T. M. Knox, 2 vols. (Oxford, 1975), 1:425.

33. In his study of the end of romantic art and hence of the transition from art to philosophy, Hegel remarks that "just as in the advance from symbolic to classical art we considered the . . . epigram . . . , so here in romantic art we have to make mention of a similar transitional form. . . . In this connection we may contrast such final blossomings of art with the old Greek epigram in which this form appeared first and simplest. The form here meant displays itself only when talk of the object is not just to name it. . . . What is especially at stake is that the heart . . . make out of the object something new" (*Ästhetik*, *Werke*, 14:239–40; trans. Knox, 1:608–10). Not all epi-

common sense" (WW, 5). "At the moment when philosophy came to birth," writes Heidegger, "there also began, and not before, the express [*ausgeprägte*] domination of sound common sense (Sophism)" (WW, 26). Fearing that during the pre-Socratic period "all Western languages [were permanently] minted [*geprägt*] with an exclusive metaphysics," Heidegger dismisses most attempts to "recast those languages into the coin of a new terminology [*die Sprache umzumünzen*]."[34] His own work, with its emphasis on a concept of philosophical validity (*Geltung*) adapted from and set against Hermann Lotze,[35] is an attempt to explore and overcome the Sophists' money of the mind, but his position, that the problem in the language of Western metaphysics is "nearly irresolvable," keeps him from further study of the conceptual connection between money and philosophy. For example, Heidegger avoids the interrelationship between economic and intellectual form in Heraclitus. Although he calls Heraclitus' Fragment 1 the oldest fragment of philosophical doctrine and cites it as a confirmation of his theory of truth as unconcealment (*alētheia*) (SZ, 33), he ignores fragments of Heraclitus which ally the essential substance of the universe

---

grams unite symbol and thing. During the epoch of the epic, for example, "an inscription is as it were a spiritual hand pointing to something, because its words explain something existent apart from them. . . . In this case the epigraph simply says what *this* thing is" (*Ästhetik, Werke*, 15:325; trans. Knox, 2:1040). In some lyric and much ancient poetry, however, the "original essence of the epigram [*ursprünglich Wesen des Epigramms*]" is fully revealed.

For the connection with riddles, see Hegel's discussion of allegory as a symbolic comparison that starts from the meaning and his consideration of inscriptions like "Know thyself" (at the temple of Apollo at Delphi) as archetypes of the classical art form (*Ästhetik, Werke*, 13:510–11 and 14:50–52; trans. Knox, 1:398 and 1:456–58).

34. Heidegger, *Identität und Differenz*; translated as *Identity and Difference*, trans. Joan Stammbaugh (New York, 1974), pp. 73–74, and 141–42).

35. For Heidegger on *Geltung* in Lotze, see Heidegger, SZ, 99, and Heidegger, *Logik (Die Frage nach der Wahrheit)*, WS 1925/26, in *Gesamtausgabe* (Frankfurt, 1975), esp. 21:62–88. For Lotze on *Geltung*, see Hermann Lotze, *Logik* (Leipzig, 1880), esp. par. 320, and the discussion of validity and reality (*Wirklichkeit*) in par. 318; and Felix Maria Gatz, *Die Begriffe der Geltung bei Lotze* (Stuttgart, 1928). For the concept *Geltung* in Germany during the period before the publication of *Being and Time*, see Leo Ssalagoff, *Vom Begriff des Geltens in der modernen Logik* (Leipzig, 1910); Arthur Liebert, *Das Problem der Geltung* (Berlin, 1914); Arthur Liebert, *Der Geltungswert der Metaphysik* (Berlin, 1915); and Emil Lask, *Zum System der Logik*, in *Gesammelte Schriften*, ed. Eugen Herrigel (Tübingen, 1924), 3:57–170. For the further use of *gelten* in "On the Essence of Truth" see WW, 9, 12, 14, 17, 18, 22.

with monetary transaction. Heraclitus' Fragment 90, for instance, states that "there is an exchange of fire for all things and all things for fire, as there is of gold [*chrusos*] for wares and wares for gold." [36] Through metaphorical exchanges of meaning, Heraclitus explores the transition from an economy of barter exchange, in which wares are traded for wares, to an economy of monetary exchange, in which there is a simultaneous exchange of money for wares (purchase) and wares for money (sale), and he hints at a disturbing relationship between metaphysical substance (fire) and the new monetary form. Heidegger sidesteps this critical metaphysics of the Ephesian market place, a metaphysics that suggests an informing tension between purchase/sale and philosophical statement. [37]

Heidegger tries to attain in thought, at least, a barter or premonetary (pre-Heraclitean) economy of words as well as wares. In doing so he hypothesizes a period when ingots were merely commodities (Lessing's "ancient [*uralte*] coin") and words were really words—a period whose status as historical or nonhistorical (Heidegger sometimes calls it "Homeric," sometimes "primordial" [*uralte*]) he leaves unclear in the same way that he leaves unclear the status of the period when *alētheia* meant "unconcealed." [38] For Heidegger, "words are usually thrown around on the cheap, and in the process are worn out;" [39] in place of these "paper money words," he says, we should resurrect the "old, worthy words [*alten, ehrwürdigen Worten*]." [40] His poem, "Language," asks "When

36. Heraclitus, Fragment 90, in H. Diels, *Fragmente der Vorsokratiker*, 5th ed. (Berlin, 1934). For an analysis of the monetary form of this fragment, see Marc Shell, *The Economy of Literature*, pp. 49–62.

37. During Heidegger's absence from a session on Fragment 90, Eugen Fink adopted Oswald Spengler's interpretation of *chrusos* ("gold") as "the golden color of the sun" (Martin Heidegger and Eugen Fink, *Heraklit: Seminar Wintersemester 1966/ 1967* [Frankfurt, 1970], esp. pp. 170–71). (For Spengler, see his *Metaphysische Grundgedanke der Heraklitischen Philosophie* [Halle, 1904]). Although Heidegger elsewhere criticizes Spengler's thought as the mere "'expression' of 'culture' ['Ausdruck' der 'Kultur']" (WW, 27), he did not take up Fink's discussion when he returned to the seminar. The same avoidance of Fragment 90 occurs in Heidegger, *Der Anfang des abendländischen Denkens (Heraklits)*, SS 1943, and Heidegger, *Logik (Heraklits Lehre vom Logos)*, SS 1944 (in *Gesamtausgabe*, vols. 55 and 56).

38. See note 20.

39. Heidegger, *Was Heisst Denken?* [What Is Called Thinking?] (Tübingen, 1945), p. 87.

40. Heidegger, *Über "Die Linie,"* in *The Question of Being*, trans. Jean T. Wilde and William Kluback (New Haven, Conn., 1958), p. 108. Heidegger approves Goethe's observation that "if anyone regards words and expressions as sacred testi-

will words / Again be word?" and refers the reader to a linguistic "place /
of primordial owning [*uralter Eignis*]."[41]

In attempting to disassociate truth from money, Heidegger adopts
Edmund Husserl's claim that the trader's truth and the scientist's truth
are basically heterogeneous,[42] and he adapts Nietzsche's position that
truth is associable with indecipherable monetary impressions.

> What is truth? A mobile army of metaphors, metonyms and an-
> thropomorphisms—in short, a sum of human relations which
> have been enhanced, transposed, and embellished poetically and
> rhetorically, and which, after long use, seem firm and canonical:
> truths are illusions about which one has forgotten that this is what
> they are; metaphors which are worn out and without sensuous
> power; coins which have lost their pictures and now matter only
> as metal, no longer as coins.[43]

Nietzsche takes into his account of "truth," which he conflates with
"truths," the difference between coin, which acts as money only by vir-

---

monials and does not put them, like currency [*Scheidemünze*] and paper money
[*Papiergeld*], into quick, immediate circulation, but wants to see them exchanged in
the intellectual trade and barter [*geistigen Handel und Wandel*] as true equivalents,
then one cannot blame him if he draws attention to the fact that traditional expressions, at which one no longer takes offense, nevertheless exert a damaging influence,
confuse opinions, distort understanding and give entire fields of subject-matter a false
direction" (ibid., loc. cit.).

41. Heidegger, "Sprache," in *Philosophy Today* 20 (Winter, 1976): 291. "Wann
werden Wörter / Wieder Wort?"

42. Husserl writes that "the trader in the market has his market-truth. In the relationship in which it stands, is his truth not a good one, and the best that a trader can
use? Is it a pseudotruth [*Scheinwahrheit*], merely because the scientist, involved in a
different relativity and judging with other aims and ideas, looks for other truths—with
which a great many more things can be done, but not the one thing that has to be done
in the market?" (Edmund Husserl, *Formale und Transzendentale Logik* [The Hague,
1974], p. 284; translated as *Formal and Transcendental Logic*, trans. Dorion Cairns
[The Hague, 1969], p. 278). On Husserl's definition of truth, see SZ, 218, note. In
"On the Essence of Truth," Heidegger makes a similar distinction between sound common sense and philosophy: "What philosophy is in the estimation [*Schätzung*] of
sound common sense, which is perfectly justified in its own domain, does not affect its
essence, which is determined solely by its relation with the original truth of what-is-as-
such in totality" (WW, 26).

43. Friedrich Nietzsche, *Werke*, ed. Karl Schlechta, 3 vols. (Munich, 1955–66),
3:314; translated as "On Truth and Lie in an Extra-Moral Sense," in *The Portable
Nietzsche*, ed. and trans. Walter Kaufmann (New York, 1954). Cf. Jacques Derrida,
"La Mythologie blanche," in *Marges de la philosophie* (Paris, 1972), esp. pp. 249–
273.

tue of the impression in it, and bare ingots. Nietzsche, of course, does not hanker after the primordial images that he pretends might explain the illusions that are truths. For him the truth is, to use Lessing's terminology, an "anticipation" of which the "resolution" is forever necessarily lost.

Nietzsche's consideration of truth occurs in an essay, entitled "On Truth and Lie in an Extra-Moral Sense," which brings an apolitical or even nihilistic dimension to the study of being and verification. Nietzsche, however, knew that his metaphor explains, not the essence of truth, but only the illusive truth of some things. The prejudice implied in the metaphors of Heidegger's Common Sense is that truth must somehow be comparable to the material properties of "hard cash" or ingots without impressions. Heidegger takes such a prejudice as the false position from which to develop an argument about validity, but he is trapped by the implications of his own example of the validity of a statement about monetary validity. He ignores or is ignorant of the political authority recognized by Nathan the Jew.[44] In *Being and Time* the political world is associated explicitly with the "inauthentic" they-world. It is the they-world that makes coins and some statements "authentic," yet Heidegger's understanding of authentic (*eigentlich*) untruth derives from a strictly apolitical theory of the counterfeit or of ungenuineness (*Unechtheit*).[45]

Heidegger's elenchus of Sound Common Sense goads us to question our hypotheses of logical and historical origins (including the origins of coinage and philosophy). The challenge, however, becomes a philosophical and political monster when it refuses, as do the final sections

---

44. That authority is recognized in the same way by Jesus of Nazareth, who bears witness to the truth about which Pilate asks. When presented with a coin bearing the impression of Caesar, Jesus tells his auditors to render unto Caesar the things that are Caesar's.

45. In their English translation of *Being and Time* (p. 24n), Macquarrie and Robinson try to make a clear distinction between an "informal" use of *eigentlich* (to mean "on its part") and a "stronger" use (to mean "genuinely"). In both cases, however, Heidegger relies on the connection of *eigentlich* with *eigen* ("own"). Compare *echt* and *genuin* in Heidegger's consideration of coins and statements about coins (WW, 7); and see his discussion of the relationships between *uneigentlich, nicht-eigentlich*, and *eigentlich nicht* (SZ, 176), his comments on "untruth as dissimulation" (WW, 21–23), and his explanation of how false gold may be real (WW, 7). "*Da-sein*, insofar as it ex-sists, reaffirms [*verwahrt*] the first and most extreme non-revelation of all: authentic untruth [*eigentliche Un-wahrheit*]. The authentic 'dis-essence' of truth [*Wahrheit*]—that is the mystery" (WW, 21).

of "On the Essence of Truth", to account for the transition from *Gold* to *Geld* or for the epigraphic relationship between inscription and inscribed thing. The truthseeker with his question differs from the money changer with his balance and the minter with his stamp, but adequation in alethiology is no easier to transcend than equation and inscription in political economy. Lessing's sound considerations of coinage and of the relationship between things and propositions about things do not pretend to give access to the alkahestic revelation of which Heidegger writes. At the same time, however, they do not bar us prematurely from the Platonic or the Hegelian ways of transcending the theory of truth as adequation. Heidegger wants to return to a barter economy of wares and words; Lessing teaches us not to ignore the numismatic and epigraphic character of truth.

Conclusion

MUCH LITERARY theory concerns "idols of the Exchange" like the *idola fori* that Francis Bacon believes to "have crept into the understanding through the alliances of words and names."[1] Bacon has it that these fictions can be expelled through the advancement of learning; idols, for him, are merely temporary hindrances to our eventual enlightenment. Other thinkers argue that transcending an ideology is possible only through practical elevation (*Aufhebung*). In "On the Essence of Money," for example, Moses Hess writes that "we can always emancipate ourselves in theory from the inverted conscience of the world, but so long as we do not exit in practice from the inverted world itself, we must howl, as the proverb says, with the wolves."[2] Bacon's protestant enlightenment and Hess's messianic vision keep them from suspecting, as does John Wheeler, how it may be that "all that a man . . . discourseth in his spirit is nothing but merchandise"[3]—all discourse, including the kind that would, like many a new organon, eradicate the idols of the exchange.

1. Bacon discusses the four idols, including the *idola fori*, in the *Novum Organon* (in *The Works of Francis Bacon*, ed. J. Spedding, R. L. Ellis, and D. D. Heath, 15 vols. [Boston, 1860–64], 1:252, 261–62; English translation, 8:78, 86–87). Cf. Roger Bacon's discussion of the "four hindrances . . . whereby men are kept back from the attainment of true knowledge" (Roger Bacon, *Opus majus*, ed. John Henry Bridges, 3 vols. [Oxford, 1897–1900; rpr. Frankfurt, 1964], 1:2–3 and 3:2–3).

2. Moses Hess, "Über das Geldwesen," in *Philosophischen und sozialistischen Schriften: 1837–1850*, ed. Auguste Cornu and Wolfgang Mönke (Berlin, 1961), p. 335.

3. John Wheeler, A *Treatise of Commerce* [1601], ed. G. B. Hotchkiss (New York, 1931), p. 317.

In this book I have attempted to introduce the thesis that monetary exchange and symbolization, as well as associated processes of production, pervade literature and philosophy, providing thought with form and with a discomforting, but motivating, resistance. The iconoclasts called money the quintessential "graven image" of the spirit.[4] Bacon, like Lessing, would use learning as a hammer with which to drive out the "idols which beset men's minds," but Nietzsche, who knows the cunning of idols, teaches us to sound them out instead with a tuning fork.[5]

Recognizing money of the mind involves locating monetary form in linguistic exchange. "Money," writes Georg Simmel, "is similar to the forms of logic, which lend themselves equally to any particular content, regardless of that content's development or combination."[6] That money and language are complementary or competing systems of tropic production and exchange suggests that money not only is one theme, metaphoric content, or "root metaphor"[7] in some works of language, but also participates actively in all. My argument is not that money is talked about in particular works of literature and philosophy (which is certainly the case), but that money talks in and through discourse in general. The monetary information of thought, unlike its content, cannot be eradicated from discourse without changing thought

4. For the association of "graven images" (Exodus 20:4) with both material coin and nonmaterial money, see the interpretation of Isaiah 40:18–19 which John, called Hylilas, is reported to have delivered to the iconoclast (image breaker) Emperor Leo V, called the Armenian; reported by the Continuators of Theophanes, in *Patrologiae cursus completus* [Series Graeca], ed. Jacques-Paul Migne (Paris, 1857–66), vol. 1, 45c, and by Joseph Genesios, ibid., vol. 109, 1009c. During the examination of the iconodule (image server) Stephen by the iconoclast Emperor Constantine V, Stephen tried to demonstrate the correctness of his attitude to images by trampling on a coin bearing the emperor's effigy (*Vitae Stephani*, in *Patrologiae* [Graeca], vol. 100, 1160a; cf. Edward Martin, *A History of the Iconoclastic Controversy* [New York, 1930], p. 58).

5. Friedrich Nietzsche, *Götzen-Dämmerung, oder Wie man mit dem Hammer philosophiert* [Twilight of the Idols, or How One Philosophizes with a Hammer], in Nietzsche, *Werke*, ed. Karl Schlechta, 3 vols. (Munich, 1955–66), 2:941–42, 1033. Nietzsche, too, considers "four great errors [*Irrtümer*]" (2:971–78).

6. Georg Simmel, *The Philosophy of Money*, trans. Tom Bottomore and David Frisby (London, 1978), p. 441 (adapted). Cf. Simmel, "The Metropolis and Mental Life," in *The Sociology of Georg Simmel*, trans., ed., and introd. Kurt H. Wolf (New York, 1950), esp. pp. 411–15.

7. On "root metaphors" see Colin Murray Turbayne, *The Myth of Metaphor* (Columbia, S.C., 1971) and Stephen C. Pepper, *World Hypotheses* (Berkeley and Los Angeles, 1970).

itself, within whose tropes and processes the language of wares (*Warensprache*) is an ineradicable participant.[8] The principal foci in the preceding studies—dispensation, usury, hypothesizing, adequation, and dialectic itself—are telling intellectual procedures through which economic form expresses itself in language.

Philosophical dialectic is intellectual procession toward truth, a procession that works through division and generation. Division concerns the relationships of parts to other parts and of parts to wholes, and generation concerns how some parts are partial to the whole and how they generate or tend toward it. Division is departmental and universal: it holds in one vision the indivisible part and the whole, the atom and the universe. Its scope is every time and all time, every space and all space. The dialectician proceeds along the way of division by theorizing about the articulative homogeneity and heterogeneity of things and concepts. Like the poet and the rhetorician, he must be a master of metaphor, but unlike them he must try to account systematically for one trope and for all. Dialectical division is a tropology that would not only participate in, but also wholly oversee, the ordinary organization of thought and language.

The representative types of monetary and linguistic symbolization and production I have studied are related in a historical sequence that suggests crucial quandaries in dialectical reasoning.[9] The topos of the

---

8. This is not to argue that disagreements and misunderstandings about production and distribution are fundamentally problems of semantics and definition (as L. M. Fraser argues in *Economic Thought and Language* [London, 1937]). Nor is it to claim that the terms of classical economic theory, such as *supply and demand*, are "ceremonial forms" without important content, and that the value of labor is merely a "figurative expression" or "fiction" (as Pierre Joseph Proudhon suggests in *Système des contradictions économiques, ou philosophie de la misère* [Paris, 1846], 1:49–50 and 61). "Labor-commodity," says Karl Marx, "is not nothing but a grammatical ellipse" (Marx, *Das Elend der Philosophie*, in Marx and Engels, *Werke*, ed. Institut für Marxismus-Leninismus beim ZK der SED [Berlin, 1956–68], 4:88; translated as *Poverty of Philosophy*, trans. Emile Burns, in Marx and Engels, *Collected Works* [New York, 1975–], 6:129; hereafter this edition of Marx and Engels, *Werke*, will be referred to as MEW). For the association of such terms as *value of labor* with poetic license, see Marx, *Das Kapital*, MEW, 23:559–60n; translated as Marx, *Capital*, trans. S. Moore and E. Aveling (New York, 1967), 1:537n. On the *Warensprache*, see Marc Shell, "The Forked Tongue: Bilingual Advertisement in Quebec," *Semiotica* 4 (1978): 259–69.

9. Karl Marx argues that "in order to examine the connection between spiritual and material production it is necessary to grasp the latter itself not as a general category

cornucopia, for example, appears to solve the dialectical problem of the relationship of the whole to its parts because it is one source or producer of many things and so seems to represent them all. This apparent solution necessarily skirts crucial problems. In the grail tales, whether the all-producing cornucopia produces itself is left unclear. Similarly, the supposition of a cornucopia sidesteps two problems of labor (of which speech is an instrument): the division of labor and the relationship between the linguistic worker and his product.[10]

The cornucopia is both a representative common denominator of many (perhaps all) things and their generator, just as an etymon is both a common denominator and generator of a whole group of words. Of such conflations of representation with generation, none has been more crucial to the elementary articulation of dialectic than the one that informs the logic of taxonomy. Natural taxonomy, for example, is concerned with relationships among species and genera. In *The Merchant of Venice* this divisional categorization involves white and black *homines sapientes*, Christians and Jews, Venetians and aliens, and monetary use and animal ewes. Such taxonomy divides or parts all things into their natural generic divisions or partitions, but at the same time it begs the question of the ontological or original status of nature.

Genetics, a natural science related to taxonomy, is concerned with the imparting of genomes, or the reproduction of special traits in individuals of the same family.[11] The conflation of taxonomy with genetics is often logically inevitable; the special archetype (in taxonomy) and

---

but in definite historical form" (Marx, *Theorien über den Mehrwert*, MEW, 26.1: 256–57; translated as *Theories of Surplus Value*, trans. Emile Burns [Moscow, 1975], 1:285). Max Weber argues that in Simmel "the money economy and capitalism are too closely identified to the detriment of [Simmel's] concrete analysis" (Weber, *The Protestant Ethic and the Spirit of Capitalism*, trans. T. Parsons [London, 1930], p. 185). Yet Simmel argues that "the understanding of the essence of money is not only facilitated by its interaction with intellectuality, which gives money and intellectuality a formal similarity, but perhaps also by an underlying principle that is manifested in the similarity of their historical development" (*Philosophy of Money*, p. 440).

10. On these problems in the study of material and nonmaterial (especially linguistic) production, see G. W. F. Hegel, *Jenaer Realphilosophie*, ed. Hoffmeister (Leipzig, 1931), esp. 1:197, 211, and 2:183; and chapter 5, section entitled "Putting Hegel Down."

11. The reproduction of genotypes in minting is the principal analogue for taxonomy; the numismatic type imparts to all the coins in which it appears a characteristic mark (Greek *charaktēr*, German *Merkmal*) that homogenizes them into heterogeneous classes or denominations.

the familial generant (in genetics) become indistinguishable. For example, Adam in Genesis is the archetype of the species *homo*, the "common name to all men,"[12] and Adam is also the progenitor of all men, including his other part, Eve. (Ultimately the progenitor is God, of whom Adam is a metonymic likeness.) Adam, then, is the genotype of the species *homo*, which the members of the family of men share in common, or as partners in a joint-stock company.

Neither taxonomy nor genetics can tell whether Jessica is a crossbreed or a genuine offspring of Shylock and Leah. She is his flesh and blood, but flesh and blood have no part in the manners of man, which, she hopes, constitute the essence of human being. In *The Merchant of Venice* this problem in the relationship between division and generation includes the critical division of one species (Adam's Man) into two sexes. (The ewe Leah even more than the Iew Shylock is the progenitor of Jessica.) The bipartite division of one species' labor or reproduction into two parts (female and male) seems different from the other divisions in taxonomy because the two parts are in apparently polar opposition to each other. From this division of the Platonic One (the resourceful agency of generation) into two parts homogeneous with the One but heterogeneous with each other—both are two but each is one—is generated the potential for production.

Sexual reproduction is associated with financial and intellectual development. Plato suggests in his early dialogues that a divinity has deposited with Socrates the seminal Idea of the Good, just as a creditor deposits a hypothecal principal with a banker. Socrates dispenses to his interlocutor an offspring of this Good, which is homogeneous with the Good, just as a child (*tokos*) is a likeness of its parent and as monetary interest (*tokos*) is homogeneous with its principal.[13] After inseminating his interlocutor with part of the good, Socrates oversees its geniture. Attending to the labor of those who are of like sex (homosexual) with him, his midwifery leads to a series of abortions and rebirths of *tokoi* partial of and partial to the whole that is the Good. The series is sublationary rather than inflationary: the "tokens" become better and better, just as the hypotheses figured on Socrates' divided line approach more and more closely the Idea of the Good. Plato's irony is that Soc-

12. Shakespeare, 1 *Henry IV*, ed. A. R. Humphreys, (London, 1966), 2. 1. 93. The Hebrew *adam* means "man."
13. Plato, *Republic* 509 and 534.

rates draws out the Idea from hypotheses just as a banker draws out interest, which may be compounded indefinitely (if not absolutely), from hypothecs.

Hypothesizing in Hegel's *Phenomenology* involves a similar generation of parts (theses and antitheses) and wholes (syntheses). It involves one cancellation of two partial hypotheses in polar opposition to each other, and their incorporation and transcendence by a third hypothesis. The last of the three movements of dialectical sublation (*Aufhebung*) in Hegel, transcendence, is the "cashing in" of a canceled bond or exhausted hypothec. In Hegelian dialectic, partial hypotheses are continuously sublated or compounded until, as Lessing and Goethe put it, the whole of wealth lies before us, yet that wealth is not the One (as in Plato), but rather nothing at all.

Dialectical generation is associated with imitation (the production of likenesses) and with plotting (the production of action). Sublation, the principal movement of dialectical generation, involves differentiation, hence sameness (identity) and imitation. Similarly, intellectual hypothesizing is connected with literary plots (*hupothēsēs*). The counterpart in rhetoric to intellectual hypothesizing and financial hypothecation is the intriguing generation of action from verbal position (Faust's Act from Luther's Word). Beginnings of literary narratives and dramas are like contractual hypotheses or hypothecs from which middles and endings are drawn. Thus "The Gold-Bug," *The Merchant of Venice*, and *Faust* begin with hypothetical letters of hypothecation. In *The Merchant of Venice* and "The Gold-Bug," the largest literary trope (the plot) is the supplement to or interest on this hypothecation, and the smallest tropes (the puns on *use* and *gold*) generate useful meanings. In *Faust*, Mephistopheles, bound both to God and to Faust, plays out the part of the prompter (*hupothētēs*) of the plot, a role like that of the linguistic alienation of meaning in translation and the monetary alienation of property in purchase and sale.

Both the modern critique of the traditional notion of truth as the adequation between two ontologically dissimilar things (*intellectus* and *res*) and, implicitly, the outstanding symbolic debt (*reus*) that arises from some philosophical systems[14] suggest a liberating epigrammatology. My treatment of epigrams—Captain Kidd's cryptic note in "The Gold-Bug," the inscribed swords in the grail tales, the metal caskets

14. Cf. Jacques Lacan, "La Chose freudienne," *Ecrits* (Paris, 1966), esp. p. 434.

and Nerissa's ring in *The Merchant of Venice*, the contracts and paper moneys in *Faust*, and the five-mark piece in "On the Essence of Truth"—moves towards an analysis of monetary tokens as ideological links between thought and matter, or between shadowy symbols and substantial things, a link with important consequences for philosophical thinking. According to Hegel, for whom the epigram defines both the historically changing relationship between symbol and thing symbolized and the formal dialectic of Subject and Substance, what is unique about genuinely philosophical discourse—what distinguishes it from literature and from Plato's philosophical dialogues—is that through it the material aspect of language becomes absolutely immaterial (inaudible and invisible) and no longer matters.[15] Philosophy is all inscription, so to speak, and not at all ingot. The Absolute of Hegelian dialectic is not coin (*solidus*), nor is it sensible like the solid ingot of which coin is partly composed. Moderns, such as Heidegger, attempt to erase the *intellectus* from the conceptual *res*, or, as Nietzsche says, the graven numismatic inscription from the coin or inscribed ingot, but they do not nullify dialectic.

The old Nietzschean mole mines below the mines of those ancients who first broke ground and established philosophy by a diligent distinction between the rhetoric of Sophists, who teach the art of persuasion for money, and the logic of dialecticians, who would help to reveal the truth for free. Can we now properly undermine and hence get over the pervasive involvement of monetary symbolization in thought? Iconoclasts like Rameau's nephew—the other part of *Moi* ("myself") in Diderot's duologue—have claimed to do so,[16] and so have other think-

---

15. This argument by Hegel has been overlooked in recent studies, including Rosalind Coward and John Ellis, *Language and Materialism: Developments in Semiology and the Theory of the Subject* (London, 1977).

16. "The alien god [*dieu étranger*] takes his place unobtrusively on the altar beside the idol of the country; little by little he strengthens his position, and one fine day he gives his comrade a shove with his elbow and wallop! [*patatras!*] down goes the idol" (Denis Diderot, *Le Neveu de Rameau*, ed. Jean Fabre [Paris, 1950], p. 82). Rameau's nephew (*Lui*), however, is dominated by his idol-like "uncle of stone" and by the alien power of royal money (the *louis* issued by King Louis and bearing his impression); he cannot displace the idol without simultaneously replacing it (ibid., pp. 92, 99). Cf. Hegel's discussion of *Rameau's Nephew* and the struggle between enlightenment and superstition (*Phänomenologie des Geistes*, in Hegel, *Werke*, 20 vols. [Frankfurt, 1970], 3 : 403; translated as *The Phenomenology of Mind*, trans. J. B. Baillie [New York, 1967], pp. 564–65).

ers who lived before and after the historical purview of this book. For example, medieval students of chrysography (writing with gold ink)—a practice that began among the peoples of the Book at the same time as the introduction of coinage (writing impressed in gold ingots) and ended in the twelfth and thirteenth centuries, at the same time as the introduction of paper money (writing on paper that is exchangeable for gold)—offered solutions to the theological problems posed by the participation of moneyed discourse in sacred writing. Similarly, modern cultural institutions, such as econometrics and psychoanalysis, make telling promises of social and individual liberation.[17] The representative studies in this book suggest the pitfalls besetting such discourses, which, as I plan to demonstrate elsewhere, are willy-nilly participants in the countinghouse of language rather than successful escapees from it.

Hillel, the first rabbi to formulate definite hermeneutic principles, says that "whoever deals much in merchantry cannot become wise," and Rabbi Meir enjoined his fellows, "Busy yourself little with merchantry, busy yourself rather with learning." "No Christian ought to be a merchant," echo the church fathers. Yet the teachers came to confront exchange, not only as a material necessity, but also as an inevitable, if disquieting, component within the art of attaining wisdom. "Is it not said: Rabban Jochanan ben Sakkaj was a merchant for forty years, a scholar for forty years, and a teacher for forty years."[18] Concealing or attempting to avoid the internalization of monetary form in thought and language turns it, as Plato suggested long ago, into an even more dangerous intellectual disease by hiding its symptoms; it anaesthetizes the potentially motivating sting of economic processes. On the other hand, revealing or attempting to deal with monetary form within thought often drives thought to become philosophy, as Plato has it, or to overcome philosophy, as some modern thinkers have it. From the age of ancient electrum to that of contemporary electricity, men have

17. See Appendices.
18. Hillel is quoted from Mishnah Aboth 4. 10, and Meir from Mishnah Aboth 2. 5 (*Mishnah*, trans. Herbert Danby [Oxford, 1938]). The statement about Jochanan, repeated with variations in several books of the Talmud, is here quoted from *Rosh Hashana* 31b (trans. Maurice Simon [1938], in *The Babylonian Talmud*, ed. I. Epstein [London, 1935–48]). See Arye Ben-David, *Talmudische Ökonomie* (Hildesheim, 1974). The church fathers write, "Nullus Christianus debet esse mercator, aut, si voluerit esse, projiacator de ecclesia Dei" (*Decretum Gratiani*, in *Patrologiae cursus completus* [Series Latina], ed. Jacques-Paul Migne [Paris, 1844–64], 187:419).

been trying to expel money from the mind or to transform money of the mind into an agent of liberation. Time and again the same quandary returns, albeit in different guises. Insofar as the thoughtful confrontation with the interiorization of economic form in thought is necessary to thought, literature and philosophy are inadequate to the task they are driven to set themselves.

Appendices

APPENDIX I

BEYOND CHRYSOGRAPHY

IN CHRISTENDOM, from the first to the twelfth centuries, a few writers approached the problem of the internalization of economic form in language and in thought in general. Instead of writing about "moneyed words," as did the Greeks, they wrote about the practice of writing words in ink of gold (*chrusos*). (See figure 8b.)

Chrysography (golden inscriptions on paper) became a widespread practice among Jews, Christians, and Muslims at the same time as did minting coins (inscriptions on golden ingots), and it began to decline as a serious art in the twelfth and thirteenth centuries, at the same time as the first issuing of negotiable paper (inscriptions on paper exchangeable for gold). Chrysography provided the three peoples of the Book with a topical center for discussing the general relationship between language and money. (*Chrusos* means "money" as well as "gold.")[1] And it provided a visible enemy for attacking *Gellt*, or gold qua money, as the "language of the devil."[2]

Among the Jews in the first century, chrysography was already a controversial topic. The *Tractate for Scribes*, for example, explored the intellectual and spiritual implications of writing in gold, as had been done when the Pentateuch was translated into Greek in the third century B.C., and it prohibited chrysographic scrolls for synagogal pur-

1. For *chrusos* as "coin" see Constantinus VII Porphyrogenetus in the tenth century (*De cerimoniis aulae Byzantinae* [Bonn, 1829–40], 379, 20) and Sophronius in the seventh century (in *Patrologiae cursus completus* [Series Graeca], ed. Jacques-Paul Migne [Paris, 1857–66], 87:3597b).

2. For *Gellt* as *verbum diaboli*, see Martin Luther, *Tischreden*, 6 vols. (Weimar, 1912–21), vol. 1, no. 391.

poses.[3] There were practical reasons for such a prohibition,[4] but the Talmudists and the church fathers who copied them had spiritual ones as well. In chrysography, letters, which are the sensible (visible) substance of the written medium of linguistic exchange, are penned in ink of gold, the economically valuable substance of monetary exchange. The rabbis and fathers argued that the monetary value of the written letter should not conflict with spiritual value: the aura of gold should not compete with the aureole of God. (*Aurum* means "gold.") Chrysographic letters draw attention to themselves rather than to the Law, not only because they are beautiful (calligraphic), but also because they are made of the substance of money. Jerome called chrysographic manuscripts "burdens rather than books," and John argued that in chrysography the commodity value of the gold ink can appear to override the spiritual value of the words. Others suggested that the value of ink as commodity can infect the spiritual value of words, and feared that words written in gold would be identical to the gilded words of Dion Chrysostomos ("golden-mouthed").[5]

Chrysography thus provided one of the only traditional foci for discussion of linguistic and monetary values. The discourse about chrys-

---

3. *Tractate for Scribes* 1. 8, in *The Minor Tractates of the Talmud*, ed. A. Cohen (London, 1966). See also Sabbath 103b, in *The Babylonian Talmud*, ed. I. Epstein (London, 1935–48). The first extant reference to a chrysographic text occurs in Aristeas (*Aristeas Judaeus*, ed. P. Wendland [Leipzig, 1900], par. 176). When Ptolemy Philadelphus requested that the Pentateuch be translated into the Greek tongue, says Aristeas, the high priest of Jerusalem sent him a scroll of the Torah written in letters of gold. It is said that all of the seventy-two elders whom Ptolemy individually set to the task of translating the Hebrew book produced identical Greek translations of the sacred text.

4. "One of the main purposes of luxurious book production in the Byzantine Empire was to preserve copies of the Holy Scripture" (David Diringer, *The Illuminated Book* [London, 1958], p. 84). Chrysographic books, however, were often stolen and destroyed for the gold with which they were written.

5. For eight hundred years there has been no serious study of the aesthetic and theological aspects of chrysography, nor even a philological study of the word. For Latin texts see Jerome (Eusebius Hieronymous Sophronius [A.D. 342–420]), especially the preface to his translation of the Hebrew Book of Job into Latin, and his *Letterae familiares* (no. 18). Jerome knew little Hebrew and felt the burden of the past—the golden words that the high priest sent Ptolemy after translating the Pentateuch into Greek. See too Trebellius Pollio (fourth century), *Claudius* 14.5, in *Scriptores historiae Augustae*, ed. and trans. D. Magie (Cambridge, Mass., 1953). On John Chrysostom see Photius, *Bibliotheca*, codex 277: John Chrysostom, in *Patrologiae* (Graeca), 104:280.

ography helped to connect figuratively the ideology of writing impressed in electrum or gold ingots with the ideology of writing printed on paper that is exchangeable for gold (and, perhaps, with the ideology of money whose only material is electric circuits printed in gold). The visible ink in which letters are written is not a necessary sign of the invisible money of the mind, however, and the theological critiques of chrysography were ultimately distractions from the general problem of the participation of economic form in discourse.

For Greek references to *chrusographia* in the Byzantine period and among the church fathers, see the second- or third-century papyrus printed in *Graeci musei antiquarii publici Lugdani—Batavi*, ed. C. Leemans, 2 vols. (Leiden, 1843 and 1885), 10; John Chrysostom (A.D. 344–407); Dionysius Aeropagites (pseudo.) at the close of the fifth century (*Patrologiae* [Graeca], 232:13), esp. "Christon chrusographia" ("writing Christ in gold"); Theodorus Studia (A.D. 749–826), esp. his *Refutatio Poëmatum Iconomachorum* (*Patrologiae* [Graeca], 99:436b); Georgius Syncellus in the ninth century (*Georgius Syncellus et Nicephorus*, ed. Wilhelm Dindorf and Jacques Goar [Bonn, 1829], 517. 8; in *Corpus scriptorum historiae Byzantinae*, 50 vols. [Bonn, 1828–97], vols. 41–42); Meletius Monachus in the ninth century, especially his *De natura hominis* (*Patrologiae* [Graeca], 64:1309); and Georgius Cedrenus in the eleventh century (*Georgius Cedrenus [et] Ioannis Scylitzae*, ed. Immanuel Bekker [Bonn, 1838–39], I, 787. 22; in *Corpus scriptorum historiae Byzantinae*, vols. 25–27). On Dion Chrysostomos, see Menander of Laodicea, *Peri epideiktikōn* (in *Rhetores Graeci*, ed. Leonhard von Spengel [Leipzig, 1853–56], 3:390S).

APPENDIX II

LIKENESS AND LIKELIHOOD

HEGEL ignored or deplored the development of calculus by thinkers, such as Leibniz and Newton, who tried to deal with the physics and mathematics of infinity and zero. Yet calculus is motivated in part by dialectical problems involving infinite plenitude and the production of likenesses that approach ever more closely the qualities of the things of which they are likenesses, including their spatial and temporal characteristics.[1] During the period that included the publication of Kant's essay on negative quantities and Hegel's *Logic*, calculus made possible a new understanding of probability that bears on the connections between the economic and metaphysical problems we have considered. Many scientists even argued that there was a logical link between their studies of likelihood or probability (with which problems of likeness and adequation or agreement are associated) and their "moral arithmetic of belief" or "econometrics of marginal evaluation." This link was signalled by the similarity between the item *tossed in* the games of chance that they analyzed using the new calculus (often a coin as material object with two distinguishable but like and equally weighted sides) and the item *tossed for* in the gambling and merchant ventures that they analyzed using psychology and theology (often coin as measure).[2] However, the distinction between coin as material object and as

1. Eighteenth-century expositions of calculus often begin with the problem, frequently posed in Platonic dialogues, of when an imitation becomes so like the original that it becomes the original itself. Cf. Aristotle's discussion of probability and imitation in the *Rhetoric*.

2. Most examples arise from attempts to solve the St. Petersburg Paradox. See Paul Samuelson, "St. Petersburg Paradoxes: Defanged, Dissected, and Historically De-

measure suggests the logical as well as ideological difficulties inherent in such an argument. Moreover, the resort to calculus already foreshadowed the fusion of mathematics with political as well as natural economy that predominates in our time and that Hegelian theory is unable to take into its anachronistic purview.

---

scribed," *The Journal of Economic Literature* 15 (March 1977): 24–55. The paradox is extended beyond gambling and econometrics by Pascal, who discusses, in terms of *croix et pile* ("heads or tails"), whether it is worthwhile to believe in, or gamble on, the existence of God (Blaise Pascal, *Pensées*, pt. 2, sec. 2, no. 3: "Infini-rien: le pari," in Pascal, *Oeuvres complètes*, ed. Jacques Chevalier [Paris, 1954], p. 1213). See William Stanley Jevons, *The Principles of Science: A Treatise on Logic and Scientific Method* (London, 1920), p. 214; cf. chapter 5. For discussion of the many writers who have discussed probability in terms of heads or tails, see John Maynard Keynes, *A Treatise on Probability* (London, 1929).

APPENDIX III

THE MONEY COMPLEX
OF PSYCHOANALYSIS

"ALL AESTHETICS has its root in repressed anal erotism," says the psychoanalyst,[1] but he fails to link his fundamental thesis about money, that lucre is filthy, with his own collection of patient's funds. Psychoanalysis not only treats patients who have a "money complex," but also presents itself as a unique money complex.[2] The clearest symptoms of this complex are, first, that psychoanalysis treats money only as

1. S. Ferenczi, "On the Ontogenesis of the Interest in Money," in *Sex in Psychoanalysis*, trans. E. Jones (New York, 1950), p. 325.
2. For the phrase "gold complex" see Sigmund Freud, "Character and Anal Eroticism," in *Collected Papers*, ed. J. Riviere and J. Strachey, 5 vols. (London, 1949–50), 2:45–50. The psychoanalytic link between feces and money has been the common theme of M. Wulff, "Zur Neurosensymbolik: Kot-Geld," *Zentralblatt für Psychoanalyse und Psychotherapie*, Jahr 1, p. 337; Richard M. Griffith, "Dreams of Finding Money," *American Journal of Psychotherapy* 5 (1951): 521–30; Sandor Feldman, "Interpretation of a Typical Dream: Finding Money," *Psychiatric Quarterly* 17 (1943): 423–25; Feldman, "Contributions to the Interpretation of a Typical Dream: Finding Money," *Psychiatric Quarterly* 26 (1952): 663–67; Otto Fenichel, *The Psychoanalytic Theory of Neurosis* (New York, 1945), esp. pp. 487–88; Theodor Reik, "Geld und Kot," *Zeitschrift für Psychoanalyse* 3 (1915): 183; J. Harnik, "Kulturgeschichtliches zum Thema: Geldkomplex und Analerotik," *Zeitschrift für angewandte Psychologie und Charakterkunde* 5 (1919): 121–22; Marie Bonaparte, *The Life and Works of Edgar Allan Poe: A Psycho-Analytic Interpretation* (London, 1949); Robert Fliess, *Erogeneity and Libido* (New York, 1957); and Ernest Jones, "Anal-Erotic Character Traits," in *Papers on Psychoanalysis* (Boston, 1961), pp. 413–37. See too Melanie Klein, "The Development of a Child," in *Love, Guilt and Reparation and Other Works 1921–45* (New York, 1977), esp. p. 12n; Hans Göppert, *Das Ich: Grundlagen der psychoanalytischen Ich-lehre* (Munich, 1968), esp. pp. 93–99; Ernest Borneman, *Psychoanalyse des Geldes: Eine kritische Untersuchung psychoanalytischer Geldtheorien* (Frankfurt, 1973); and, for a political interpretation of money, Gilles Deleuze and

196

a material thing (a shiny ingot of gold or silver) or as that thing's supposed counterpart (feces), not as an economic token or sign,[3] and, second, that psychoanalysis tries to disengage concern with money from
the politics of the Oedipal struggle[4] and thus shares Queen Gertrude's
blind belief that the paternal ghost crown prince Hamlet sees is merely
the "coinage of [his] brain."[5] Karl Abraham's unusual attempt to associate money with the Oedipus complex proves interesting for what it
observes and what it neglects. Abraham tells a story (a case history)
about a patient who,

> as a boy, did not play at battles with lead soldiers like other chil-
> dren, but with pieces of money. He got people to give him copper
> coins, and these represented ordinary soldiers. Nickel ones were
> non-commissioned officers of various ranks, and silver ones were
> officers. A silver five-mark piece was the field marshall. This of-
> ficer was secured from all attack in a special building "behind the
> front." One side took "prisoners" from the other in the battle and
> added them to its own army. In this manner one side increased
> possession of money until the other had nothing left.[6]

Abraham diagnoses the patient as having "a pronounced anal character." Noting that the struggle in the patient's unconscious was against
his rich father, Abraham observes that in the patient's mind "money
[had] entirely replaced human beings" so that "he took no personal interest in people whatever; only the possession of money and money

Félix Guattari, *Capitalisme et schizophrénie: l'anti-Oedipe* (Paris, 1972). On the psychological significance of monetary transactions between patient and psychoanalyst,
see G. Angelo DiBella, "Mastering Money Issues that Complicate Treatment: The
Last Taboo," *American Journal of Psychotherapy* 34 (1980): 510–22; and K. R. Eissler,
"On Some Theoretical and Technical Problems Regarding the Payment of Fees for
Psychoanalytic Treatment," *International Review of Psycho-analysis* 1 (1974): 73–
101.

3. Carl Gustav Jung (*Psychology and Alchemy* [Princeton, N.J., 1968], pp. 80–
81), claiming to base his position in Nietzsche's philosophy, goes so far as to argue
against treating dream coins as money and for treating them only as mandala-like
symbols.

4. Cf. Géza Roheim, "Heiliges Geld in Melanesien," *Internationale Zeitschrift für
Psychoanalyse* 9 (1923): 384–401.

5. Shakespeare, *Hamlet*, 3. 4. 38.

6. Karl Abraham, "The Anal Character," in *Selected Papers of Karl Abraham*,
introd. Ernest Jones, trans. Douglas Bryan and Alex Strachey (London, 1948), pp.
387–88.

values attracted him." Yet Abraham neglects to distinguish pieces of money (coins), with which his patient used to play, from money itself, which Abraham claims his patient confused with people. There is one tradition of associating men with coins. (Simmel notes that "one finds [in the twelfth century] the statement that the knight, baron and earl are related to each other as shilling, mark and pound, since these are the proportions of their escheat.")[7] There is a different tradition of associating men with possessions, to which large category coins as commodities belong. Abraham conflates the confusion of people with (coins as) money and the confusion of people with (coins as) commodities. Not surprisingly, he fails to recognize how his patient's manipulation of coins recalls the way German accountants (perhaps the rich father was one) figured their profits and losses by manipulating counters that had neither monetary nor commodity value.

Psychoanalysis usually makes this symptomatic failure to distinguish the material aspect of coins from their denominational, economic role in exchange and accounting, and thus treats coin and paper money as the same kind of symbol. It promises liberation from money of the mind, but the result, as we have observed, is an entrapment of its own: an ideological inability to distinguish conceptually between coin and paper money (which is not shiny) and between coin and money in general, even when embarking on politically ambitious examinations of discontented civilizations.[8] Norman O. Brown defines certain limits of psychoanalysis, and of most other "liberating movements" of our time, when he says, with some despair, that "if we can imagine an unrepressed man—a man strong enough to live and therefore strong enough

7. Georg Simmel, *The Philosophy of Money*, trans. Tom Bottomore and David Frisby (London, 1978), p. 355.

8. The "economy of the libido" in Freudian psychoanalysis is grounded in frequently unexamined ideas about expenditure in the political economy, ideas that resemble conceptions of restrictive input and output like those supposed to obtain in the "closed economy" of Fichte's almost medieval "closed commercial state." Sigmund Freud sometimes seems to overcome this limitation (see *Civilization and Its Discontents* [New York, 1960], esp. pp. 43–47, 60), yet he, too, thinks of economy as a closed system ("The Economic Problem of Masochism," in *Collected Papers*, 2:255–68). In Freud's "economy of wit" and his interpretation of masochism, moreover, the psychology of pleasure is a simple analogue to the notion of scarcity in Adam Smith's political economy (David Reisman, "The Themes of Work and Play in the Structure of Freud's Thought," *Psychiatry* 13 [1950]: 116), but without Smith's understanding of the role of credit money in the expansion of a capitalist economy.

to die, and therefore what no man has ever been, an individual—such a man, having overcome guilt and anxiety, could have no money complex."[9]

9. Norman O. Brown, *Life Against Death* (New York, 1959), p. 291. Cf. Freud's remark that "money questions will be treated by cultured people in the same manner as sexual matters, with the same inconsistency, prudishness and hypocrisy" ("On Beginning the Treatment" ["Further Recommendations in the Technique of Psychoanalysis: I"], in *Collected Papers*, 2:351).

Illustrations

Fig. 1. Cartoon, "A Shadow Is Not a Substance." By M. A. Woolf. United States, nineteenth century. From David A. Wells, *Robinson Crusoe's Money; or, The Remarkable Financial Fortunes and Misfortunes of a Remote Island Community*, with illus. by Thomas Nast (New York, 1876).

Fig. 2. Cartoon, "Milk-Tickets for Babies, in Place of Milk." By Thomas Nast. United States, nineteenth century. From David A. Wells, *Robinson Crusoe's Money; or, The Remarkable Financial Fortunes and Misfortunes of a Remote Island Community*, with illus. by Thomas Nast (New York, 1876).

Fig. 3.   Cartoon, "Ideal Money." By Thomas Nast. United States, nineteenth century. From *Harper's Weekly* 48 (January 19, 1878). (Library of Congress)

Fig. 4. Caricature of a shinplaster, "Great Locofoco Juggernaut." Drawn by D. C. Johnston, United States, 1837. During the depression of 1837–40 the suspension of specie payments by the banks led to the issuing by corporations, cities, and individuals of small change notes, which were often called "shinplasters." In Johnston's caricature, Martin Van Buren appears at top center as a cat sitting on a bag marked DEPOSITS. To the left Van Buren as a monkey waits for an issuance from Andrew Jackson, who appears as a jackass. In the center Jackson or Thomas Hart Benton (senator from Missouri and a long-time anti-Bank leader) appears as a bug that sets the "ball" in motion. In the verse inscription, BENT-ON may be interpreted as Benton, WOULD-BURY as Levi Woodbury (secretary of the Treasury), KENN'D ALL as Amos Kendall (member of Jackson's "Kitchen Cabinet"), WIT-KNEE as Reuben Whitney (who assisted Kendall in setting up the deposit system for the "pet" state banks), VAN as Van Buren, HICKORY as Jackson, and BEN TON (the signature) as Benton. (American Antiquarian Society)

Fig. 5. Caricature of a shinplaster, "Treasury Note." By Napoleon Sarony. United States, 1837. At the right Van Buren collects funds from Jackson, the jackass carrying the bag marked MINT DROPS (compare the phrase "Benton mint drops"). At bottom Van Buren (?) appears as a dung beetle (?) rolling the "ball." (American Antiquarian Society)

Fig. 6. Caricature of a shinplaster, "Gold Humbug." Issued by H. R. Robinson. United States, 1837. At the right Jackson chases the "Gold Humbug." (American Antiquarian Society)

Fig. 7.   Cartoon, "The Bubbler's-Kingdom in the Aireal World." England, 1720. This satire of the South Sea Bubble includes an ape that evacuates "All Wind" into the mouth of a fallen man, near whose figure is written, "Catch at all and hold Nothing." A donkey expels wind, inscribed, "Nothing but Stench." A man fires a mortar, which sends forth labels marked "Golden Mines in Jamaica," and so on. Below him is "The Gold is Melted & nothing but Bubbles it produces." From *Het Groote Tafereel der Dwaasheid* (Amsterdam, 1720). (British Museum)

Fig. 8a. Portrait of Matthew and chrysographic initial page, facing pages of the Ebo Gospel of Matthew. France, Carolingian, between 816 and 835. The illumination shows Matthew inscribing the Gospel in a book. He is inspired by an abundant store (*copia*) of material, apparently from the flowing scroll that the winged angel holds over his inkhorn (*cornu*).

Fig. 8b. *Incipit* and first verse, the Ebo Gospel of Matthew. Perhaps it is these words that the painter has the fervent evangelist write down with his feather. (Bibliothèque municipale, Épernay; photograph by Ann Münchow)

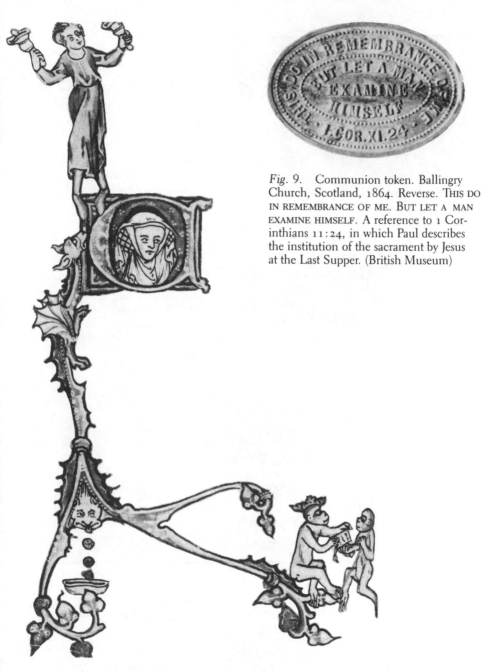

Fig. 9. Communion token. Ballingry Church, Scotland, 1864. Reverse. THIS DO IN REMEMBRANCE OF ME. BUT LET A MAN EXAMINE HIMSELF. A reference to 1 Corinthians 11:24, in which Paul describes the institution of the sacrament by Jesus at the Last Supper. (British Museum)

Fig. 10. Illuminated Manuscript. Flanders, ca. 1325. A monster head vomits gold coins into a golden bowl. (Bodleian Library)

Fig. 11. Gold octadrachm of Ptolemy III. 246–221 B.C. Cornucopia bound with diadem and surmounted by radiate crown. (Hirmer Verlag)

Fig. 12. Illumination from *Lancelot du Lac*. Painted by Master of Berry's Cleres Femmes and associates, France, early fifteenth century; repainted later fifteenth century. Arthur's Round Table is realistically represented with a white tablecloth and a circular opening in the middle. Within this opening is a surface that, in contrast to the tesselated floor, recalls the checkerboard (*échiquier*) used by treasurers (*eschequiers*) in feudal times (see *Livre des Rois*, ca. 1190). From the grail, as from a divine presence, radiates effulgence, indicated by lines of gold. Through the open door a vista shows Galahad pulling out the sword. (Bibliothèque nationale)

Fig. 13. Cartoon, "A Monument Dedicated to Posterity in commemoration of y^c incredible Folly transacted in the Year 1720." Engraved by B. Picart. From *Het Groote Tafereel der Dwaasheid* (Amsterdam, 1720). (British Museum)

Fig. 14. Bronze coin of Vetranio. Ca. A.D. 350. Inscribed HOC SIGNO VICTOR ERIS (You will be victor through this sign). (British Museum)

Fig. 15. Medal commemorating John Law and the Mississippi System. France, 1720. Obverse. In field, a windmill; on the post by which it is supported and on which it revolves, MERCURE (Mercury, the god of merchants); on the base or floor, MONOYE (money); and on the side to right, reading downward, BANCO (bank). Into two of the arms (or sails) winged coins, jewelry, and art objects are entering; the other two are industriously showering forth slips of paper labeled ACTIEN (shares) and BILLETS (bank bills). A head at the right, in cocked hat and wig, supplies the wind, labeled LOVIS-DORS, by which the sails are made to revolve. Legend: LES RICHESSES DE FRANCE (The Riches of France). In exergue: 1720. (American Numismatic Society)

Fig. 16a. Medal commemorating John Law and the Mississippi System. Germany, 1720. Obverse. A man, cloaked, walks toward the right and operates a bellows, from the nozzle of which is discharged a quantity of shares or bills, while from his mouth issue the words WER KAVFT ACTIEN (Who buys shares?). Legend: WER SICH DVRCH DIESEN WIND DEN GELDGEITZ LAESSET FVHREN (He who [deceived] by this wind allows himself to be led by covetousness). In exergue: SEY KLYG·V·WIZIG·IN / VERKEHREN (Be wise and keen-witted in traffic).

Fig. 16b. Reverse. A dog on a bridge, crossing a stream and carrying in his mouth a piece of meat, sees the reflection in the water, snaps at the imaginary meat, and in so doing loses what he has; the whole is an illustration of Aesop's well-known fable. Legend, continued from the obverse: DER KAN VERWIRRVUNGS VOLL / SEIN HAAB·V·GVTH·VERLIEREN (that man will be full of trouble and lose his possessions and goods). In exergue: SOLL DICH ESOPI HVND / NICHT LEHREN· / 1720 (Shall not Aesop's dog teach thee?). (American Numismatic Socicty)

Fig. 17a. Medal commemorating John Law and the Mississippi System. France and Germany, 1720. Obverse. In the field, an empty hat, wig, and coat, in position, seen from behind; on the waist (or belt) of the coat, MDCCI. Legend: BANQVERODT ist A LA MODE· (Bankruptcy is all the fashion). In the field, to left, reading upward, VISIBILIS (visible), and to the right, reading downward, INVISIBILIS (invisible; or "Now you see it and now you don't").

Fig. 17b. Reverse. A man lies face down on the ground, his head toward the left; his right hand grasps the caduceus of Mercury, the god of merchants, and his left, a package on which is WEXEL / BRIEFE (bill of exchange). Legend: CREDIT ist mausse-todt (Credit is dead as a mouse). (American Numismatic Society)

Fig. 18. Medal commemorating John Law and the Mississippi System. Germany, 1720. Obverse. A man in cocked hat and court dress stands facing left; he holds in his right hand a magnifying glass, marked 100, through which he is looking at a quantity of bills or shares of different denominations (1000, 200, 100); his left hand, extended behind him, points toward an open chest full of coined money. Legend, a rhymed couplet, in three curved lines above: VERGRÖSRVUNGS GLAS THVTS HIER VND AN SO VIELEN ENDEN / DAS SICH DIE KLVGSTEN AVCH DIE GELDSVCHT LASSEN / BLEN DEN (The magnifying glass here serves so many ends, that even the knowing ones allow themselves to be blinded by the lust for money). In exergue: DER ACTIEN BETRVG / VND LIST (The shares are a trick and a fraud). (American Numismatic Society)

Fig. 19. Cartoon, "Law, als een tweede Don-Quichot, op Sanches Graauwtje zit ten Spot" (Law, like another Don Quixote, sits on Sancho's Ass, being everyone's fool). Netherlands, 1720. The engraving shows John Law riding on an ass. On the flag is, "Ik koom. Ik koom Dulcinia" (I come, I come, Dulcinea). A coffer, filled with bags of money, is inscribed, "Bombarioos Geld kist 1720" (Bombario's [i.e., Humbug's] money box, 1720). Behind Law is a devil, the "Henry" of the text; he holds up the tail of the ass. The ass voids papers inscribed 1000, o, oo, and so on. From *Het Groote Tafereel der Dwaasheid* (Amsterdam, 1720). (Buffalo and Erie County Library)

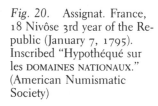

Fig. 20. Assignat. France, 18 Nivôse 3rd year of the Republic (January 7, 1795). Inscribed "Hypothéqué sur les DOMAINES NATIONAUX." (American Numismatic Society)

Fig. 21. Cartoon, "De Verslagen ACTIONIST in de STOEL met RINKELS, overreeden geweest van 't geLAUwerd Pard van TROJE" (The defeated Stock-jobber seated in the Chair with Jingles, having been defeated by the LAUreated Horse of TROY). Netherlands, 1720. The illustration shows part of this engraved satire on the South Sea Company. A man flies a kite, which is about to fall. The inscription may be translated as "My kite loses its tail, I will drown myself in the South Sea." From *Het Groote Tafereel der Dwaasheid* (Amsterdam, 1720). (Buffalo and Erie County Library)

Fig. 22. Cartoon, "The Blessings of Paper Money." By George Cruikshank. From *Scourge and Satirist; or Literary, Theatrical and Miscellaneous Magazine* (London) 2 (August 1, 1811): 87. (Johns Hopkins University Library)

Fig. 23. Tetradrachm. Abdera, ca. 473/70–449/8 B.C. Obverse. Griffin seated with fore-paw raised. (Hirmer Verlag)

Fig. 24. Bank note. Bayerische Hypotheken- und Wechsel-Bank, Germany, 1836. (Sammlung Albert Pick [Hypobank, Munich])

Fig. 25. Emergency money. Vohwinkel. Shows a fantastic face value of 50 billion marks, with a quotation from *Faust* 1994–99. Emergency money (*Notgeld*) was issued by most German states during the great inflation of the early 1920s, when conventional banknotes had become virtually worthless. The paper money inflation of the 1920s, like that of the 1720s (John Law's system), influenced even the most serious philosophy of the time. The aesthetic interpretation of monetary inflation—insinuated by Mephistopheles in the study of the small world and in the court of the large one—was adapted by Fascist "philosophers" and ideologues in their attempt to aestheticize politics. Like a number of issues of emergency money, those represented in figs. 25–39, dating between 1920 and 1923, depict and quote scenes and passages from Goethe's *Faust*. (Figs. 25–39: Sammlung Albert Pick [Hypobank, Munich], Museum des Deutschen Bundesbank, and American Numismatic Society)

Fig. 26. Emergency money. Vohwinkel. *Faust* 2540–53. Shows a face value of 50 million marks while at the same time quoting the multiplication table or arithmetical hocus-pocus in Witch's Kitchen.

Fig. 27. Emergency money. Vohwinkel. *Faust* 2802–4.

Fig. 28. Emergency money.
Hasloh (Schleswig-Holstein).
Faust 2802–4.

Fig. 29. Emergency money.
Schierke am Harz (Sachsen).
Faust 4127.

Fig. 30. Emergency money.
Roda. Faust riding on a flying
horse (Mephistopheles).

Fig. 31. Emergency money.
Vohwinkel. *Faust* 4778–86 and
4799–802.

Fig. 32. Emergency money. Vohwinkel. *Faust* 4839–42 and 4847–51.

Fig. 33. Emergency money. Hasloh (Schleswig-Holstein). *Faust* 4852–54.

Fig. 34. Emergency money. Hasloh (Schleswig-Holstein). *Faust* 4889–92.

Fig. 35. Emergency money. Staufen. *Faust* 6057–58 (adapted).

Fig. 36. Emergency money.
Schleswig-Holstein. *Faust*
6119–20.

Fig. 37. Emergency money.
Roda. Faust's courting of Helen.

Fig. 38. Emergency money.
Hasloh (Schleswig-Holstein).
Faust 9229–32 (adapted).

Fig. 39. Emergency money.
Hasloh (Schleswig-Holstein).
Faust 9275 (adapted).

Fig. 40. Illumination, the Court of the Exchequer. England, ca. 1450. An usher stands on the table, apparently speaking; in the foreground is a square cage, grated and barred, behind which are two prisoners; there are two large, iron-bound chests, suggestive of treasure. From G. R. Corner, "King's Bench, Common Pleas, and Exchequer, at Westminster," *Archaeologia; or, Miscellaneous Tracts Relating to Antiquity*, vol. 39 (1868).

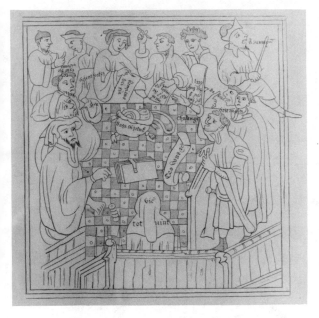

Fig. 41. Pen and ink sketch, the Court of the Exchequer. Drawn during the reign of Henry IV (1367–1413). At center is the square checkerboard. In the Red Book in the Chief Remembrancers Office, Four Courts, Dublin. From James F. Ferguson, "A Calendar of the Contents of the Red Book of the Irish Exchequer," *Proceedings and Transactions of the Kilkenny and South-East of Ireland Archeological Society*, vol. 3: 1854–55 (Dublin, 1856).

Figs. 42a and 42b. Counter. Nuremberg, early seventeenth century. (British Museum)

Fig. 43. Vignette, the old and new arithmetic. A comparison of calculation by the counting-board and by Arabic numerals. From Gregor Reisch, *Margarita Philosophica* (Freiburg, 1503). (George Arents Research Library, Syracuse University)

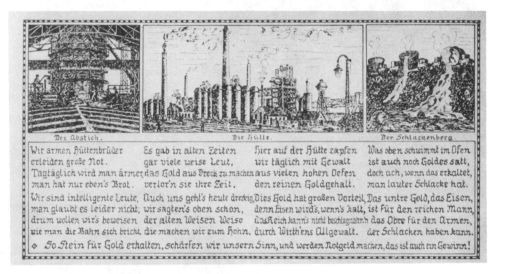

Figs. 44a and 44b. Emergency money. Rheinhausen, 1921. The inscription in the bottom border reads: HEB' MICH GUT AUF UND LÖS' MICH NIEMALS EIN!! (Preserve me and never redeem me!!). Not an official issue, but a private one (*Scherzschein*, or "joke note") issued by a *Kollegenschaft* ("group of colleagues") in Rheinhausen. (Museum des Deutschen Bundesbank)

THE SURVIVAL OF THE FITTEST.

Fig. 45. Cartoon, "The Survival of the Fittest." By Thomas Nast. United States, nineteenth century. From David A. Wells, *Robinson Crusoe's Money; or, The Remarkable Financial Fortunes and Misfortunes of a Remote Island Community*, with illus. by Thomas Nast (New York, 1876).

Fig. 46. Five-mark piece. Germany, Nazi regime, 1936. (Staatliche Museen zu Berlin)

Index

50–51, 56; Portia as fertile, 59; and wasteland, 25, 27, 29, 32, 43. *See also* Castration; Usury

Feudalism, 34, 91, 92, 96, 111, 117; grail as ideal response to waning of, 37

Fichte, Johann Gottlieb, 137, 138, 145–46. WORKS: *Closed Commercial State*, 144n, 198n; *Foundations of Natural Right According to the Principles of the Science of Knowledge*, 144n; *On the Ground of Our Belief in the Divine Government of the World*, 91n; *Presentation of the Science of Knowledge*, 146n; "Theory of the Right of Exchange," 144; *Vocation of Man*, 138

Fiction: of convert's death, 61, 62; of marriage, 63; of injured free man's slavery, 65; of value of labor, 181n

Filthy lucre, 12, 38, 62n, 112, 196–99. *See also* Psychoanalysis

Fink, Eugen, 174n

Five-mark piece, 166, *fig. 46*

Flattery, 35, 49, 97

Fliess, Robert, 69n

Flying money, 99, 101, 110, 116; "kite," 101, *fig. 21*

Food, 27, 28; cannibalism, 55, 69n; Eucharist, 27, 40–43, 45, 69n; exchange of words for food, 28, 29, 35, 43; and expectoration of coins, 43; Jacob's exchange for birthright, 52; Jewish dietary laws, 54–55; loaves and fishes, 29; manna, 29, 79; and origin of money, 42–43; spiritual nourishment, 27, 29, 35, 41–42

Fool, 31, 102, 130

Fores, Samuel William, 113n

Form: analytic logic confined to form, 136, 137; and content, 3–4, 180; and content of literary plots, 9, 13, 126; as demand and supply, 181–82n; and epigram, 172; and Helen, 118; as hypothesizing, 126; money form, 107, 144, 151; of purchase and sale, 2, 32, 103, 174; in Spengler, 123n. *See also* Idea

Formalism, 137–39, 170

Formula, marriage, 63

Fortunatus, 44

France, 5n, 19n, 100. *See also* Law, John

Francke, Kuno, 94n

Fraser, L. M., 181n

Frederick Barbarossa, 38, 39

Freedom: in aesthetic play, 93; in commercial contracting, 67, 68; and grace, 24–25; and liberal free-market economy, 135; manumission from slavery, 20, 66; from resistance, 95; and work, 124. *See also* Gratis

Frege, Gottlob, 169n

Freud, Sigmund, 58–59n, 113n, 196n, 198n, 199n

Fuller, Lon L., 63n

Fust, Johann, 98n

Galbraith, John Kenneth, 24n

Galileo, 172

Gandz, A., 143n

Garrick, David, 127n

Gatz, Felix Maria, 173n

Geld. See Money

Geldscheine (paper money), 97, 113–14, 168

Gellius, Aulus, 67n

Geltung (validity), 110, 164–66, 168–70, 173; in Lotze, 170–73nn

Genealogy and succession, 37–39, 49–52, 82n

Generation (production), 81, 131, 132–33, 181; and grail, 47; of land, 118, 119, 121; material and spiritual, 152, 181–82n; from nothing, 14, 15, 21–22; as theme of *Merchant*, 48, 81n. *See also* Origin; Poetry; Sexual and non-sexual generation

Genetics, 182–83

Genuineness. *See* Authenticity and genuineness

Genus and species, 129; their articulation as the work of dialectic, 132, 181; of cornucopia, God, grail, and money, 40–43; species, specie, specimen, 10–14. *See also* Man (human being) and animal

George III (of England), 113n

Georgius Cedrenus, 193n

Georgius Syncellus, 193n

Gertrude (in *Hamlet*), 197

losophy, 102, 104, 154–55n. See also
Hypothec
Guattari, Félix, 197n
Guilead, Reuben, 166n
Günther von Schwarzburg, 119n
Gutenberg, Johann, 98n

Hagar, 52
Halakah (law), 127n
Hamlet, 197
Harnik, J., 196
Harris, William T., 133n
Hartman, Geoffrey, 157n
Hassel, J. Woodrow, Jr., 18n
Hawthorne, Nathaniel, 15, 22n
Heaven and hell, 107; in Divine Com-
edy, 36; in Faust, 124, 128; heaven as
theorized merchant world, 153
Hebung (mining, elevation), 97, 103,
129
Hegel, Georg Wilhelm Friedrich,
67–68n, 126, 130, 131–55, 162, 177,
185. WORKS: Aphorisms from Hegel's
Wastebook, 145n; Confidential Letters
(trans. by. Hegel), 145n; Difference Be-
tween Fichte's and Schelling's System
of Philosophy, 144, 145n; Encyclopedia of the Philosophical Sciences,
117n, 118n, 139n; Faith and Knowledge, 138; First Philosophy of Spirit
(Jena), 154; Instruction in Right,
Duty, and Religion, 151n; Lectures on
Aesthetics, 172; Lectures on the History of Philosophy, 138, 148; Lectures
on the Philosophy of Religion, 145n;
Jena Logic, 139n; Jena Realphiloso-
phie, 182n; On the English Reform
Bill, 144–45n; Phenomenology of
Mind, 82n, 117n, 128, 129, 137–38,
141n, 147–50, 160, 170, 184, 185n;
Philosophy of Mind (Encyclopedia,
III), 117n, 118n; Philosophy of Right,
128, 142n, 151, 154; "Religion is
One . . . ," 148–49; Science of Logic,
139, 140, 147, 150n, 194; System of
Ethical Life, 154
Heidegger, Martin: WORKS: Being and
Time, 156, 162, 163n, 170, 173n,
175n, 176; The Beginning of Western
Thought (Heraclitus), 174n; Her-

aclitus, 174n; Identity and Difference,
173; "Language," 174–75; Logic (Her-
aclitus), 174n; Logic (The Question
After Truth), 173n; "On the Essence
of Truth," 156–57, 162–70, 173n,
175n; On "The Line," 174n; On the
Matter of Thinking, 163n; Plato's Doc-
trine of Truth, 163n; What Is Called
Thinking?, 174n
Heine, Heinrich, 66n
Heinzelman, Kurt, 3n
Helen (in Faust), 111–17
Helena (mother of Constantine), 98
Hélinand, 26
Heller, Peter, 161n
Henry VII (of England), 72
Henry VIII (of England), 72
Heraclitus: WORKS: Frag. 22, 22, 85;
Frag. 67, 149n; Frag. 90, 3, 174
Herder, Johann Gottfried von, 27n,
105–6n, 156n
Herford, Charles H., 44n
Hermes Trismegistus, 41n
Hermetic tradition, 41
Hess, Moses, 152–53, 179
Hill, G. F., 43n
Hillel (Rabbi), 186
History: historical and primordial past,
26, 158, 162–63, 174, 175; and ideol-
ogy, 151–52, 181–82n; in Kant, 135;
and myth, 37; ruse of, 135; union of
ideal and real in, 38. See also Ideology
Hoard: hoarding and capitalism, 38;
Nibelung Hoard, 36–40; Shylock as
miser of words, 49
Hobbes, Thomas, 24n, 68n, 110n
Holmes, Urban T., 44n
Homer, 163n, 174
Homicide, 55, 61–63, 65n, 122
Homosexuality, and sodomy, 73n, 183
Homunculus (in Faust), 116, 118, 119
Horne, Richard Hengist, 69n, 70n
Hufeland, Gottlieb, 144
Hughes, Thomas Patrick, 49n
Hull, R. F. C., 166n
"Humbug," 5, 10, 12, 13, 14, fig. 6
Hume, David, 110, 152
Hupothētēs (prompter), 81n, 87, 127,
184; in Faust, 92, 114–15; and Trieb-
feder, 87, 127

Husserl, Edmund, 162, 175
Hypothec (*hupothēkē*), 103, 142n, 146,
183, 184; Antonio and Shylock as, 74;
and *asmakhta*, 127n; and conditional
contracts, 54, 70, 73–74, 84; as content of *Faust*, 126; and Faust's soul,
87, 125, 126, 129; hypothecal hypotheses in plot of *Merchant*, 81n; hypothecal paper money, *figs. 20, 24*; as
subterranean treasure, 127. See also
Sumbolon
Hypothesis (*hupothēsis*)
—as literary plot, 81–82, 87, 126, 127,
184; detective, 22; *deus ex machina,
dea in machina*, 69, 76, 125, 130; dis-
continuities in, 16–17; two plots in
Merchant, 48–49, 82–83
—in philosophizing, 181; in Aristotle,
141n; and *asmakhta*, 127n; and credit,
164; and *Faust*, 87, 126–30; of free,
large gift, 24–27; in Hegel, 103–29,
132–33, 146–47, 181, 184; in Kant,
141; in Newton, 141n; in Plato, 2, 81,
132, 147, 181, 183; as "put-down,"
153n; and thesis, antithesis, synthesis,
83, 184
Hyppolite, Jean, 151n

Ibn Khaldûn, 50n
Ibsen, Henrik, 123n
Iconoclasm, 180–81, 185
Idea: *arithmos eidētikos*, 161; and commodity, 84; as exchange value, 108;
Platonic One, 2, 132, 135–36, 146,
147, 150, 183, 184. See also Form
Ideal: Hellenic, 111–17; "Ideal Money,"
fig. 3; money, 16n, 104n; and poetry,
35, 39; and real estate, 34–39, 103
Idealism, 8, 152, 159; criticized by
Marx, 19, 106; in exchange theory,
144; and the grail, 37–39; and paper
money, 102, 104; and utopian theory
of money and commodity, 109. See
also Formalism; Nominalism
Ideology, 1, 10, 150–52, 193; and development of paper money, 7, 8,
14, 98–99, 108; kinds of analyses,
150–52; largesse, charity, and merchantry, 34; material conditions for
spiritual production, 143, 150–52,

181–82n; monetary tokens as link between thought and matter, 108–9,
185; nihilism, 176; and semantics, 1n;
sub- and superstructure, 38
Idol, 179, 180, 185n
Image (*Bild*) in *Faust*, 97n, 111, 113,
115, 124
India, 134
Ineffability, 29; of feeling, 91
Infinite, 150n, 194; endless determinations, 145; infinite economy, 35; infinitely large gift, 24–25; topos of
inexhaustible purse, 44. See also
Plenitude
Inflation, 7, 99–102, 116, 168, 183, *fig.
25* (legend)
Inheritance, 86, 143; and calculation,
151
Inscription, 184–85; anticipation or expectation (*Erwartung*) in, 161, 170,
176; changing relationship between
inscription and inscribed, 172; coin
as, 1, 19, 56, 105, 156, 158–59, 170–
71; Hegel on, 172, 173n, 184–85; indecipherable or worn out, 15, 174,
175; Lessing on, 105, 156–57, 170–
71; as literature, 15; paper money as,
97, 105, 110, 129; resolution (*Aufschluß*) in, 161, 170
Inscriptions: caskets in *Merchant*, 56,
58, 70; Kidd's cartograph, 14, 16, 17;
"Know thyself," 173n; list of major,
184–85; posy in Nerissa's ring, 77;
sword in *Quest*, 33
Inscriptions on coins and paper money:
DEUS CHARITAS EST, 36; GRATIA DEI
OMNE DONUM, 43; HEB' MICH GUT UND
LÖS' MICH NIEMALS EIN!!, 145, *fig. 44*;
HOC SIGNO VICTOR ERIS, 98–99n;
"With the coin you can buy some-
thing," 167
Insurance, 47, 54, 82
Intellectus and *res*, 40, 135, 137, 147,
162, 184, 185. See also Adequation
Interest. See Usury
Interpretation, 160–61; of caskets in
Merchant, 56–58; as charity, 36; and
detection, 22; of law in *Merchant*,
69–70; of masque in *Faust*, 93; as
mining meaning, 84–85, 91–97,

Designer: Eric Jungerman
Compositor: G & S Typesetters, Inc.
Text: VIP Electra
Display: Phototypositor Bank Script and VIP Electra
Printer: Edwards Brothers, Inc.
Binder: Edwards Brothers, Inc.